HOW TO THINK ABOUT MEANING

Philosophical Studies Series

VOLUME 109

The titles published in this series are listed at the end of this volume.

HOW TO THINK ABOUT MEANING

PAUL SAKA
University of Houston, TX, USA

A C.I.P. Catalogue record for this book is available from the Library of Congress.

ISBN 978-1-4020-5856-1 (HB)
ISBN 978-1-4020-5857-8 (e-book)

Published by Springer,
P.O. Box 17, 3300 AA Dordrecht, The Netherlands.

www.springer.com

Printed on acid-free paper

060408-X12

I think that the notion of meaning is always more or less psychological, and that it is not possible to get a pure logical theory of meaning or of the symbol. I think that it is the essence of the explanation of what you mean by a symbol to take account of such things as knowing, of cognitive relations, and probably also of association.

– Bertrand Russell, 1918: 45

CONTENTS

PART II: CASE STUDIES

PREFACE

I first started thinking about referential semantics in grammar school. A noun stands for a person, place, or thing, I was taught, while a verb stands for a state or action. But I never believed it, for reasons I can now articulate. Depending on one's construal of "thing", for instance, either states and actions would count as things, in which case verbs would be nouns, or justice, energy, and vacuum would not be things, in which case not all nouns would be nouns. (It is sometimes added that nouns cover ideas too, and that ideas are things, but if "justice" referred to an idea, "justice exists" would be trivially true.)

I first started thinking about truth-conditional semantics when I entered graduate school at the University of Arizona, in 1985. To know the meaning of a sentence, I was taught, is to know what conditions would make the sentence true. But I didn't believe it, partly for the reasons pressed in my 1991 and 1998 doctoral dissertations. Segments of these dissertations went to hundreds of philosophers during my time on the job market, and I would like to think that they helped spur the subsequent research booms on quotation and on pejoratives.

My dark thoughts about truth-conditionalism continue in the present work. Chapters 2 and 8 were supported, in part, by a grant from the City University of New York PSC-CUNY Research Award Program, for which I am grateful. A version of Chapter 3.3 first appeared as "Spurning Charity" in *Axiomathes* (2006), a version of Chapter 7.1 first appeared as "Demonstrative and Identity Theories of Quotation" in the *Journal of Philosophy* (2006), and a version of Chapter 7.2 first appeared as "Quotational Construction" in the *Belgian Journal of Linguistics* (2005). I would like to thank the publishers of all three journals for permission to reprint.

It is with enormous pleasure that I acknowledge suggestions, corrections, and encouragement from Jonathan Adler, Philippe de Brabanter, Ben Caplan, Rob Cummins, Jim Garson, Christopher Gauker, Patrick Grim, Susan Haack, Ray Jackendoff, Julia Jorgensen, Chris Kennedy, Terry Langendoen, Adrienne Lehrer, Keith Lehrer, Justin Leiber, Bill Lycan, Tim McCarthy, Vann McGee, Arthur Melnick, Doug Patterson, Dave Phillips, David Robb,

Fred Schmitt, Rob Stainton, Steve Todd, Steve Wagner, Roger Wertheimer, Seiichiro Yasuda, and anonymous reviewers, plus colloquium audiences at Berkeley, CSU Bakersfield, CUNY Brooklyn, Delaware, Houston, Rice, Texas A&M, Urbana-Champaign, and conference audiences in Chicago, Istanbul, New York, Pasadena, Portland, San Francisco, and Vancouver. I would also like to thank Mike Anderson and his collaborators for computationally implementing some of my work on quotation.

Finally, I wish to thank my parents, Mark and Joyce. I am grateful for their remarkable fortitude in the face of extraordinary hardships. For instance, my father lost his youth in an American prison camp – neither charged nor tried nor convicted – guilty for having Japanese grandparents. (The point is worth making because of its renewed relevance today, as the rule of law disintegrates.) My parents heroically raised me to see through humbug, and to them I lovingly dedicate this work.

NOTATIONAL CONVENTIONS

I use "TC" to stand for *truth-conditions* or *truth-conditional*, depending on grammatical context. I use " $\equiv$ " and "iff" as short for the English biconditional "if and only if". The English "if and only if", note, is not always material or truth-functional. Depending on context, its import may variously be analytic, nomological, inferential, or unspecified.

I use "S" schematically to stand for a language-using subject – a speaker, hearer, or overhearer. I use "P" schematically to stand, neutrally, for a sentence or statement or proposition. I also sometimes use it to stand for a *term that denotes* a sentence, statement, or proposition, when context makes it clear. When context is insufficient, or when I wish to heighten the difference between a sentence and its name, for the latter I use "Φ".

As a rule I use ordinary quotation marks for metalinguistic citation and reportive quotation; I use apostrophes or italics for quotation inside of quotation and also for glosses; and I use small capitals for paragraph headings, concepts, and names of theses and arguments to which I later refer. In using quotation marks I follow the sensible style of punctuation that often appears in the linguistics literature [see Pullum (1991)].

I generally assign my examples Arabic numerals, adding a prime or double-prime when I entertain one or two different analyses of a given example; I use capital letters mnemonically chosen for especially important display items; I use small letters for premises in arguments; and I use roman numerals to distinguish points made in the text. In this, as in all else, consistency is occasionally sacrificed for clarity or grace.

PART I THEORETICAL ISSUES

Chapter 1

INTRODUCTION

The present work puts forth a new theory of linguistic meaning, one that takes seriously the connection between meaning and the propositional attitudes. ATTITUDINAL SEMANTICS, as I call it, advocates a naturalistic kind of mentalism, which is to say that it is a brand of psychologistic or cognitive semantics.

Section 1 previews the book and Section 2 spells out some standards for what would count as theoretical success. A theory is successful to the extent that it comes to grip with its subject matter, and does so at least as convincingly as other available theories. The leading theories of meaning now available are catalogued in Section 3. They do not solve problems as well as attitudinal semantics, or so I ultimately shall argue.

1. Semantics with Attitude

It is, I trust, no big deal to claim that (1) is true, where S is a proficient speaker of English:

(1) If S thinks "vacation will last a fortnight" then S thinks that vacation will last two weeks.

Likewise, I trust it is no big deal to claim that (2), charitably construed, is true:

(2) If S thinks that vacation will last two weeks then S thinks "vacation will last a fortnight".

If S thinks that vacation will last two weeks then, given that S is a proficient anglophone, S surely bears some thought-like cognitive relation, at least implicitly and dispositionally, to the sentence "vacation will last a fortnight". Taken together, then, we get an "if-and-only-if" equivalence:

(3) S thinks "vacation will last a fortnight" $\equiv$ S thinks that vacation will last two weeks.

Now for the contentious part. I propose not only that (3) is true, but that it serves as a semantic analysis for the sentence "vacation will last a fortnight". More precisely, it serves as a partial explanation of the meaning of that portion of the explanandum that does not appear in the explanans, namely the phrase "a fortnight".

In order to appreciate the force of my proposal, one needs to understand how it differs from prevailing views. According to almost every theory of meaning found in philosophy, and most found in linguistics, anthropology, psychology, and computer science, meaning is specified at least partly in terms of reference, truth, or both. More particularly, the meaning of a sentence is given by specifying the conditions under which that sentence would be true. The result is TRUTH-CONDITIONAL SEMANTICS – TC semantics or truth-conditionalism, as I shall call it – with analyses like:

(4) "Vacation will last a fortnight" is true $\equiv$ vacation will last two weeks.

In general, TC semantics holds that the proper analysis of meaning takes the following form:

(TC) Φ is true $\equiv$ P.

The influence of the TC formula goes beyond semantics. In the tradition of Socrates, many epistemologists, metaphysicians, and moral philosophers today conceive of their enterprise as the giving of necessary and sufficient conditions – in effect, finding instances of (TC).

Following the stipulation of Morris (1938), some philosophers regard truth-conditionalism as definitionally constitutive of semantics. Lewis (1970: 169), for instance, writes that "semantics with no treatment of truth-conditions is not semantics". Such decrees do a great disservice to inquiry into the nature of language, however, for they use a word that looks like it applies to a *subject area* in actual reference to a *theory*. To say that semantics is the study of linguistic meaning – which follows the usage of most linguists, most cognitive psychologists, some philosophers, and the present work – is to make a vague pretheoretical claim; to say that semantics is the study of word-world relations is to imply, given the precedent use of "semantics", that meaning is to be explicated in terms of word-world relations. The latter assertion does not identify a field of inquiry, it stakes a highly theoretical and tendentious claim.

The approach to semantics taken here explicates meaning in terms of *attitude-conditions* – those conditions under which an expression is entertained or otherwise held under some propositional attitude. Attitude-conditional, or attitudinal, semantics issues analyses of the following form:

(A) S thinks $\Phi \equiv$ S thinks that P.

When I say that (A) serves as a general formula for semantic analysis, I mean two things. First, I mean that *(A) is necessary* because no other available format will do the required work. My reason for saying this is developed at length in Part Two: whereas TC semantics is incapable of analyzing connotation, ambiguity, the use-mention distinction, and the truth predicate, attitudinal semantics does the trick for each. Second, I mean that *(TC) is unnecessary or worse*; it fails to shed light on the topics just mentioned, and indeed it contradicts both common sense (Chap. 2) and the laws of logic (Chap. 8). My thesis, then, is that *truth-conditional semantics ought to be abandoned in favor of attitude-conditional semantics*; that semantic analyses ought to yield the form of not (TC) but (A).

My project thus aims to provide philosophical and linguistic aid and comfort to mentalist as opposed to mind-independent, reference-based, truth-conditional semantics. Such semantics, fueled both by spectacular achievements in logic and by the positivism of the early twentieth century, remains dominant. As it undergoes its own internal challenges from contextualism (§3.6), speech-act theory (§3.7), and two-factor conceptual role semantics (§3.9), it is also beginning to meet more opposition from mentalist semantics. Mentalism is congenial to the methodological solipsism of cognitive science, which has just this past generation prevailed over behaviorism, and it characterizes the growing movement of cognitive linguistics. Cognitive linguists, unlike traditional generative linguists, emphasize meaning as a product of human agency embodied in particular biological and cultural matrices. The first step to capturing this agency and embodiment, I suggest, can be taken by explicitly incorporating into our analysis of a language the subjects who speak, hear, and otherwise use it, as in (A).

After wrapping up preliminaries in Chapter 1, in Chapter 2 I show the need for an alternative to the truth-conditional theory of meaning. Even if it does not convince you, I hope that, by shifting the burden of proof in some measure, it helps to level the playing field for subsequent chapters. Chapter 3 presents a top-down argument for attitudinal semantics, and there I also discuss its analytic framework in greater detail. Chapter 4 counters both arguments for truth-conditionalism and objections against attitudinal semantics. In the end, though, theories are to be judged by their fruit, and so the rest of the book turns toward applying attitudinal semantics to phenomena that are poorly understood by existing theory.

Part Two, aside from serving as a series of bottom-up arguments against truth-conditionalism and in favor of attitudinal semantics, consists of studies in select topics that should be of interest in their own right. Chapter 5 addresses the emotive content of slurs and pejoratives (e.g. "Polack"), and connotation generally, arguing that it cannot be accounted for by truth-based semantics. In comparison, the meaning of a pejorative is easily captured by the attitudinal framework, which can appeal to both cognitive and affective attitudes. To anticipate: against the various analyses given under (5), I propose (6).

(5) "Nietzsche was a kraut" is true $\equiv$ Nietzsche was a kraut.
"Nietzsche was a kraut" is true $\equiv$ Nietzsche was German.
"Nietzsche was a kraut" is true $\equiv$ Nietzsche was German and Germans are despicable.
"Nietzsche was a kraut" is true $\equiv$ Nietzsche exemplifies the negative stereotype of Germans.

(6) S thinks "Nietzsche was a kraut" $\equiv$ S thinks Nietzsche was German and S disdains Germans.

The importance of mentalism cannot be overemphasized if, as I believe, all natural language is suffused with connotation.

Chapter 6 points out difficulties for various truth-conditional representations of ambiguity, including (7), (8), and (9), to which the attitudinal account (10) is immune.

(7) "x is a bank" is true $\equiv$ x is a [kind of] financial institution or
"x is a bank" is true $\equiv$ x is a [kind of] slope.
(8) "x is a bank" is true $\equiv$ x is a financial institution or x is a slope.
(9) "x is a bank$_1$" is true $\equiv$ x is a financial institution and
"x is a bank$_2$" is true $\equiv$ x is a slope.
(10) S thinks "x is a bank" $\equiv$
S thinks x is a financial institution or S thinks x is a slope.

Like the previous chapter, this one on ambiguity, whether it goes in the right direction or no, at the very minimum dramatizes the need for contemporary theorizing to get up and go.

Chapter 7 is a contribution to the burgeoning area of quotation studies. The distinction between plain language and quotation, subserving that of use and mention, grounds the discipline of linguistics by delimiting its subject matter. It also poses persistent problems pertaining to such foundational matters as opacity and compositionality, the nature and very existence of logical form, convention and intention, and the comparative roles of semantics and pragmatics. According to the semantic Demonstrative Theory, (11) is equivalent to a sequence of sentences, each having its own truth-conditions:

> (11) Bush said that he'd "cut taxes".
> (11′) $\exists$u(SAIDb, u & SAME-SAIDu, x & SAME-TOKENEDu, y). He'd cut taxes.
> [where x points to the whole of the second sentence, y to just "cut taxes"]

According to one version of the more pragmatic Identity Theory, (11) is equivalent to (11″):

> (11″) Bush said that he'd cut taxes.

According to the attitudinal view put forth here, (11) is not regarded as necessarily-and-sufficiently equivalent to (11′), (11″), or anything else. Rather, (11) is analytically inseparable from (12), which in turn is regarded as equivalent to (12′).

> (12) S thinks "Bush said that he'd "cut taxes"".
> (12′) S thinks "Bush said that he'd cut taxes" and S thinks of "cut taxes".

This equivalence is an idealization of the following defeasible equivalences.

> (13) S utters "Bush said that he'd "cut taxes"" $\equiv$
> (a) S *uses* "Bush said that he'd cut taxes" and (b) S *mentions* "cut taxes" $\equiv$
> (a′) S intends to draw attention to the proposition that Bush said that he'd cut taxes and
> (b′) S intends to draw special attention, for some unspecified reason, to the sequence of words [cut] [taxes].

One reason for drawing special attention to a given expression, especially in the context of "said that", is to indicate that those very words have been used, but there are other reasons as well.

Chapter 8 argues that TC semantics is invalidated by the existence of the liar paradox. The naive T-schema (T) is incoherent and its Tarskian cousin (T$_i$), which invokes a hierarchy of distinct languages, is useless for the purposes of natural-language semantics. Thus the very foundations of TC semantics fail.

(T) Φ is true ≡ P.

(T$_i$) Φ is true$_i$ ≡ P$_j$, for i < j.

Attitudinal semantics, on the other hand, does not rely on any notion of truth at all. It can, however, consistently describe our use of the predicate "true" by means of (T$_\psi$).

(T$_\psi$) S thinks "Φ is true" ≡ S thinks that P.

To summarize, Part One motivates, spells out, and defends the attitudinal framework, while Part Two applies it to neglected and otherwise unsolved problems. Before proceeding, however, I set forth some comparatively uncontroversial premises. The next section identifies the aims and scope of the theory of meaning, which I take to be ostensively defined by those working in the field. This follows as one corollary of my methodology, which is empirical and anti-foundationalist. In particular, I emphasize the fallibility of inquiry and thus make no claims for the correctness of my theory, only for its superiority to alternative accounts that are now prominently available. My approach therefore requires a prior understanding of what the alternative accounts are and what they claim, which are set forth in the last section of this chapter.

2.   Ends and Means

In the following chapters I articulate, apply, and defend *a theory of linguistic meaning*. Before I do that, however, I want to clarify my aims by explaining just what I mean by this phrase.

First, what I propose is a *theory*. I make no claim about completeness or formal rigor, for my work is avowedly programmatic. It is for all of that a theory – a set of interlocking claims that purports to explain something.[1] Second, I advocate a theory of *linguistic* meaning – word meaning, sentence

---

[1]   Katz & Fodor (1963: 170), Davidson (1973a: 68), and Devitt (1996: 4) characterize their own works as meta-theories or programs rather than as theories proper. But I question their distinctions in regard to both principle and practice. In practice, for instance, Davidson's own work rests on a plain theoretical component insofar as it invokes the success of the

meaning, utterance meaning, discourse meaning [the "non-natural" meaning of Grice (1957)]; I am not interested here in the meaning of evidence left behind at the scene of a crime, or in the meaning of dark clouds and distant thunder. Third, my interest is in *natural* language. If we arrive at a semantic theory adequate for formal calculi, but inapplicable to English, Swahili, Navaho, or any other natural language whatsoever, then our project will be worse than incomplete; it will be a non-starter.

The notion of a natural language raises neglected philosophical issues, for instance the problem of individuation. When you and I understand artificial languages like propositional logic, do we know them in addition to English, or do we know them as one fraction of our logicians' dialect of English? And is English one language that extends from the Middle Ages and into the future, from England to America, Australia, and India? My own take on the matter is atomistic: the complicated facts of dialect, sociolect, isogloss, etc. are just results of aggregate individual behavior. Though individual behavior is undoubtedly regulated by conceptions of the social norm, these conceptions operate in the individual (Chomsky 2000). I shall not argue these points, as my work does not rely on them, but I do register them as issues that merit more attention.

Finally, what is meaning? Unfortunately, a clean characterization cannot come until after its study matures (imagine Aristotle trying to define the boundaries of physics). Instead I will spend a few pages listing, in no particular order, some research areas that occupy the attention of those who regard their work as inquiries into meaning. Figuring out what meaning is and how it works involves figuring out what the following are and how they work.

- *Translation.* Texts – arrangements of one or more words in a context – translate across languages. Although multiple distinct translations are typically possible, and though none is necessarily perfect, translation exists insofar as it seems that at least one translation satisfies for any given purpose. For entry to the literature on translation, see Mauranen (2004), Hatim & Munday (2005), *The Translator*.
- *Intentionality.* Expressions usually appear to be *about* various objects, properties, actions, events, and states. Consider, for instance, the

---

Tarskian treatment of quantification; and I shall myself propose analyses of specific kinds of construction. Specific analyses are impossible without a general analytic framework, while the analytic framework cannot be supported without specific analyses. Partly for this reason, theory and meta-theory – linguistics and the philosophy of language, if you will – are interdependent if not inseparable.

sentence "Jay wants to kiss Kay": "Jay" is about Jay, "wants" is about presently wanting, "kiss" is about kissing, "Kay" is about Kay, and "Jay wants to kiss Kay" is about Jay presently wanting to kiss Kay. ("To", however, is not about anything.) Intentionality is implicated in denotation, designation, reference, representation, and topicality (the topic, what the sentence is "mainly about", tends to get expressed by the grammatical subject). Moreover, the notion of intentionality is used in our understanding of information and truth. For more on intentionality, see Kripke (1980), Fodor (1987), Stich & Warfield (1994), Clapin (2002); for more on topicality and focus, see Lambrecht (1994), Erteschik-Shir (1997).

- *Information and truth.* Language is used to convey information: declarative sentences are informative of the speaker's beliefs (if sincere) and of the world (if true), imperatives are informative of the speaker's desires (if serious) and of some subsequent state of the world (if obeyed), and interrogatives may be informative of the speaker's ignorance and desire to acquire belief. The notion of information is sometimes understood in terms of reference and truth. For more on information, see Harris (1991); for more on truth-conditions, see §3 below.

- *Inference.* Truth in turn is sometimes used to define inference (though assertability is sometimes used for this purpose). Every declarative sentence entails a host of other sentences. For instance, "Jay kissed his (own) sister" entails:

   > Jay kissed someone; Someone kissed Jay's sister; Someone kissed his own sister; Jay did something to his sister; Jay kissed his female sibling; Jay kissed a relative; Jay's lips touched his sister; Jay touched his sister.

   In addition, non-declarative sentences may be said to have entailments too: the satisfaction of "Jay, kiss your sister!" entails the satisfaction of "Jay, kiss your sibling!" See §3.7.

- *Intensionality.* In some contexts, the substitution of co-referential terms preserves overall truth-value; in others, it does not. For example, "Oedipus wanted to marry Jocaste" does not entail "Oedipus wanted to marry his mother". Thus, "Jocaste" and "Oedipus's mother", though extensionally identical, are intensionally distinct (Chaps. 3.2.2, 5.9xiv).

- *Productivity, systematicity, compositionality.* Speakers can produce novel sentences and listeners can comprehend them. In part this is because language is systematic, perhaps even compositional, in which case the meaning of a complex expression would be a function strictly of the component meanings and their mode of combination. Just as important to productivity is the fact that natural-language lexicons are open-ended, allowing for neologisms due to imaginative coining, extending, stipulating, and so forth. The standard view accepts the principle of compositionality, and challenges to it can be found in Schiffer (1987: Chap. 8), Gaifman (1992: §iii), Cummins (1996), Pelletier (1994), Seuren (1998: 400), Jennings (2007); see also §3.6 below.

- *Thematic roles.* Grammar contributes meaning to sentences, as we've seen in the cases of topicality and compositionality. Grammar is sometimes held to assign agency to the subject and patience to the object: in "the lion ate the tiger", the lion is the doer and the tiger is the did-to. For the classic work on thematic roles, also known as "theta roles" or "abstract case", see Fillmore (1968), Jackendoff (1987), Wilkins (1988).

- *Illocutionary force.* A sentence may be uttered as an assertion, a question, a command, a request, etc. To distinguish these, Frege (1892) introduces the term "force", Austin (1962) recognizes its importance, and Sadock & Zwicky (1985) report on how force is grammaticized across languages. See too Searle (1969), Bach & Harnish (1979), Davidson (1979a), Vanderveken (1990, 2004), Tsohatzidis (1994), Alston (2000).

- *Lexical relations.* Words are related to each other by synonymy; hyponymy ("dog" is a hyponym of "animal"); meronymy ("paw" is a meronym of "dog"); various forms of opposition including antonymy, converseness, and reversion; and so forth (Cruse 1986, Fellbaum 1998). Such lexical relations may involve semantic fields (Lehrer 1974b, Lehrer & Kittay 1992) and may involve componential analysis (Katz & Fodor 1963, Tyler 1969, Nida 1975a, International Linguistics Department 1999).

- *Presupposition.* Proposition P semantically presupposes proposition Q iff the affirmation of P and the negation of P each entails the truth of Q. An example is "Kay kissed Jay", which presupposes that Kay exists insofar as "Kay kissed Jay" and "Kay did not kiss Jay" each entails that Kay exists. For more on presupposition, see Levinson (1983: Chap. 4), Beaver (2001).

- *Conversational implicature and impliciture.* When a letter of recommendation says only that so-and-so has beautiful handwriting, the letter *indicates* without actually *saying* that so-and-so's relevant qualifications are best left unmentioned. This follows from the Principle of Cooperation as described by Grice (1967). See also Bach (1994), Davis (1998), Levinson (2000), Carston (2002), Atlas (2005).

- *Indexicality.* Indexicals, named by C.S. Peirce, are also known as deictics (the Stoics), egocentric particulars (Russell), token reflexives (Reichenbach), and shifters (Jakobson). They are expressions whose reference is context-dependent, e.g. pronouns, demonstrative articles, and tense inflections. In English, *every* sentence is indexical, since every sentence refers to either the past, present, or future, as specified relative to the time of the sentence's utterance. For more on indexicals, see Fillmore (1997), Nunberg (1993), Diessel (1999), Simon & Wiese (2002) in linguistics, Clark (1992) in psychology, and Yourgrau (1990), Cresswell (1996), Perry (1979), Gross (2001), Corazza (2004) in philosophy.
- *Vagueness.* Words are rarely if ever fully determinate in their applicability. Scalar terms like "bald" are vague, in part because they do not in themselves specify a standard of comparison. Even "Larry is balder than Moe, but not bald in comparison to Curly", though determinate insofar as it may specify enough for us to judge the sentence true in the actual world, is indeterminate insofar as it still is questionable in some possible worlds. This is not only because "is" remains vague as to how long the present moment is understood as enduring, and "Larry" is vague too, but because vagueness is multi-dimensional. The applicability of "bald", for instance, depends not only on the number of hairs and their length, but also on the distribution of hair and the nature of the hair. For instance, if a man's pate is covered by synthetic fibers sewn into the scalp, should we call him bald or not? The answer, I think, is indeterminate; "bald" is vague in this regard, and its applicability depends on the context. For more on vagueness, see Ballmer & Pinkal (1983), Channell (1993), Williamson (1994), Keefe & Smith (1997), Keefe (2000), Saka (1998a: Chap. 5.3.1), Sorensen (2002), Beall (2003).
- *Ambiguity.* Any expression can be understood in multifarious and incompatible ways. Distinct readings may be generated by structural (syntactic) ambiguity, lexical ambiguity, polysemy, and pragmatic ambiguity stemming from, e.g., indexicals, implicature, and illocutionary intention (was a given expression used or mentioned? was it meant as a warning or a threat?) (Chap. 6).
- *Anomaly.* There is something funny about sentences like "Round colorless green ideas sleep furiously". According to some philosophers [e.g. Ryle (1938)], they commit category mistakes and are meaningless; according to some linguists [e.g. Chomsky (1965)], they violate selection restrictions and are ungrammatical; according to some, the ungrammatical amounts to the meaningless [Davidson

(1967: 21), (1970: 60)]; according to yet others, anomalous sentences are neither ungrammatical nor unsemantical but rather manifestly false and therefore, in typical contexts, unpragmatical [Saka (1998a: Chap. 3.2); cf. Erwin (1970)].

- *Prototypicality.* Many of our concepts seem to center on exemplars and ideal models independent of necessary-and-sufficient conditions. For instance, we associate "tiger" with stripedness, even though the possession of stripes is neither necessary nor sufficient for something to count as a tiger. Prototypes affect language use, language structure, and non-verbal cognition. See Austin (1940), Wittgenstein (1953) in philosophy, Lakoff (1987), Taylor (1995), Geeraerts (1997) in linguistics, and the interdisciplinary Tsohatzidis (1990).

- *Perspective.* The differential use of indexicals in direct and indirect discourse ("She said, 'I am happy' " vs. "She said that she was happy") reflects a difference in perspective (Clark 1974). Perspectival effects also appear with topicalization, with focus, and with contrastive stress ["The man in the monkey suit stole the bananas" vs. "It was the man in the monkey suit who stole the bananas"; Boer (1979), Stein & Wright (1995); in opaque vs. transparent ascriptions of belief (Fauconnier 1994); in negation asymmetry ("x is as tall as y" entails that the height of x = the height of y, whereas "x is not as tall as y" entails that the height of x < the height of y); in the difference between "the glass is half full" and "the glass is half empty"; in categorization judgments (Taylor & MacLaury 1995); and elsewhere (in St Petersburg, freezing point is called "melting point")].

- *Register.* Different social contexts call for different levels of linguistic style (e.g. "father" vs. "dad", "kiss" vs. "osculate"). Operative factors include politeness, occupation, intimacy, and genre. For sociolinguistic studies, see Hymes (1972), Brown & Levinson (1987), Chambers et al. (2001), Holmes & Meyerhoff (2003).

- *Figurative speech.* Metaphor and other figures of speech have been recognized as important in rhetoric and literary studies for many centuries, and in the current generation they have caught the attention of cognitive scientists. The importance of metaphor for cognitive science is argued in the groundbreaking Lakoff & Johnson (1980). See Kittay & Lehrer (1981) in linguistics, Gibbs (1994) and Jorgensen (1996) in psychology, Johnson (1981), MacCormac (1985) and Kittay (1987) in philosophy, and above all the interdisciplinary reader Ortony (1993).

- *Connotation.* Conversational implicature, register, and figurative meaning all contribute to what rhetoricians call connotation. [By this

    I do not mean what the idiosyncratic J.S. Mill does, but what Frege (1892) means by "fragrance", "coloring", and "tone".] Another kind of connotation is pejoration, discussed in Chapter 5.

- *Diachrony.* Lexical meaning changes over time, e.g. "bowl", "bull", "ball", and "phallus" all derive from Proto-Indo-European "bhel", 'to blow or swell'. Furthermore, language is fundamentally neologistic: it is always possible to invent new terms and to stipulate new meanings for them. See Sweetser (1990), Geeraerts (1997), Traugott & Dasher (2002) in linguistics and Jennings (2004) in philosophy.

I have just listed some of the going concerns of meaning theorists. This is not to say that they must all be addressed by the correct and final theory of meaning. That would be impossible anyhow, since contradictory things have been said about each item on this list. The purported linguistic phenomena, it must be emphasized, are not indisputable. They reflect judgments informed by theory, judgments that might turn out to be in error. Some of the items on my list may easily be chimeras, to be disregarded in the end. Indeed, I regard intentionality as such. Other items are undoubtedly missing from the list, and will need to be added as research progresses. The items now on the list may easily belong to two or more independent theories – semantics proper and pragmatics, say, a distinction that is difficult and theory-laden (Turner 1999, Bianchi 2004, Szabo 2004). No, the significance of the list is that the items on it constitute the "empirical" point of departure for current theorizing.

    Repeatedly now I have assumed post-positivist empiricism, and in the remainder of this section I will make this commitment of mine more explicit because it affects the course of my research. To me, state-of-the-art empiricism entails a number of more or less related views. To begin with, it deserves credit for recognizing and emphasizing:

    (14) THEORY-LADENNESS. Every observation and intuition is modulated by background mental state (auxiliary beliefs and even desires and actions).[2]

This theory-ladenness is holistic in character:

    (15) HOLISM. Any observation or principle taken from one intellectual domain may have epistemic bearing on another.

---

[2] Theory-laden (top-down) effects on the speed, accuracy, and content of both perception and judgment are abundantly established in the psychological literature, e.g. Warren & Warren (1970).

Holism allows me to follow the lead of Chomsky in supposing that empirical linguistic facts (performance) can best be explained as interaction effects of competence on the one hand and general psychology and biology and history and so forth on the other.

Holism also yields a criterion for deciding between rival theories. If theories θ_1 and θ_2 equally explain phenomenon Φ, and if it turns out that θ_1 also helps to explain something beyond Φ while θ_1 does not, then θ_1 is preferable to θ_2, all else being equal. Most notably, it is a virtue to explain, on top of Φ, why rival theorists believe as they do:

> (16) CRITERION OF SECOND-ORDER PREFERENCE. If θ_1 and θ_2 equally explain a given phenomenon, and if θ_1 also helps to explain why some theorists subscribe to θ_2, but not vice versa, then θ_1 is preferable to θ_2.

This criterion, implicit e.g. in Neale (1999: 56), forges one connection I see between philosophy and cognitive science, namely that for every philosophical theory θ there must be a socio-psychological account of θ's fortunes.

Theory-ladenness and holism pave one path to:

> (17) NON-FOUNDATIONALISM. We are all passengers on Neurath's Peircean ship. We must begin with our current conceptual resources and proceed from there.

In other words, we must reject the Plato-Cartesian project of starting from nowhere or of forging for ourselves a God's-eye point of view. Just as we cannot establish the existence of knowledge from first principles, we cannot, from first principles, discover the nature of meaning. This is one reason why I reject the aprioristic claim that semantics is the study of word-world relations, and instead emphasize the many features of language listed above that do not evidently have anything to do with intentionality or truth. Another reason for the rejection of a priori dogma stems from the intellectual modesty implied by (14, 15, 17) epitomized here:

> (18) FALLIBILISM. Few if any beliefs are unrevisable.

In particular I shall reject the sheer dogma that the identification of meaning with truth-conditions is somehow beyond possible doubt.

Non-foundationalism, by reference to our currently situated understanding of reality, leads to:

(19) NATURALISM. Reality is a natural, causal order that is to be under-
     stood by the sciences.

By "the sciences", I hasten to add, I include both the natural and the
human sciences, thus counting the physical, biological, behavioral, and
social sciences, and some work in the humanities as well. Naturalism is
not the same as reductive scientism but, rather, stands in contrast to the
supernaturalism that is held by the bulk of the population. Wagner (1993)
observes that such a notion of naturalism is uncontroversial and therefore
uninteresting. Applied to philosophers, this observation is partly correct. But
in general, wishful thinking, "the will to believe", and appeals to authority,
tradition, and divination are all powerful determinants of deep and popular
convictions. To deny their legitimacy is no trivial matter.

   In addition, naturalism as I understand it precludes platonism and modal
realism, and furthermore it lends support to:

(20) METHODOLOGICAL SOLIPSISM. Scientific psychology operates
     without reference to anything outside the causal powers of
     individual and subpersonal agents. Therefore meaning, insofar as it
     makes any difference to human beings, must be understood solip-
     sistically.

The questions of modal irrealism and methodological solipsism are controversial [e.g. Fodor (1980), Stich (1986), Devitt (1996), Wilson (2004)].
I mention them not because I shall be making official use of them, but to
acknowledge their role in some of my actual motivations.

   Empiricist strictures entail neither behaviorism nor eliminativism. As a
cognitive scientist and as a non-foundationalist who assumes current posits,
I hold the hypothesis that the familiar mental idioms are acceptable – though
as a fallibilist, I also emphasize that they are provisional:

(21) COGNITIVISM. Talk about beliefs and desires and other internal states
     is legitimate, if not as objective realities then at least as instrumental
     posits and at least for the time being.

Thesis (21) underwrites the competence/performance distinction, which is
also supported by holism.

   Naturalism, meaning scientific philosophy, is not only opposed to
platonism, tolerant of cognitivism, and committed to the methodological
solipsism that is implicit in the view that causality is local, it also prescribes
rules of intellectual engagement. This is so because science is fundamentally
a social institution premised on fallibilism and the proposition that two heads

are better than one. One's idea is more likely to be valuable if it takes into account the ideas of others; progress is made when old ideas are confirmed, jettisoned, or revised, *not* when old ideas are flat ignored. Granted, attending to all conceivable ideas is impossible, and it is usually wise to neglect the following: theories that are prima facie unrelated to the phenomena under study; theories that are relevant, but so implausible as to have no known proponents; theories that are relevant and seriously propounded, but only by cranks and crackpots (those outside the social institution of science, for whom lack of training and credentials, lack of research facilities, and lack of network contacts all give reason-based grounds for a priori suspicion); relevant, expertly championed theories that have been outmoded by new and uncontroversial developments; and relevant, expert, state-of-the-art theories that are privately or guardedly held against free discussion and honest criticism. Unless a condition such as the above holds, however, then if you are aware of a theory θ that purports to explain the phenomena under your study, you are obliged to address θ, whether to dispute errors, salvage half-truths, honor insight, or at least to flag a precedent. Again, this is true because science is a conversation, and it's a conversation because open dialog is our surest path toward the truth:

(22) SCIENCE AS DIALOG. Scientific reasoners, including genuinely naturalistic philosophers, attend to and respect the voices of others (at least within the limits sketched).

This point is worth emphasizing because my chapter on hate speech has repeatedly been criticized for addressing "dated" theories, namely those from 1981 by Grim, Stenner, and Taylor. The objection is not that these works have clearly been contradicted by subsequent research, for they have not. Rather the idea seems to be that, aside from a restricted number of canonical works, only the "hot" publications of the past few years matter; that indeed unreviewed and selectively distributed mimeographs merit more attention, if they are recent, than refereed and publicly available thinking that happens to be older. This attitude, though understandable inasmuch as human beings, including scholars, are moved by fad and fashion, is unreasonable. Grim's work may have appeared prior to the advent of, say, two-dimensional semantics; but unless two-dimensional semantics clearly solves Grim's problem, which it does not, then Grim's proposed solution remains in the running and deserves a hearing, other things being equal.

To repeat, intellectual virtue on the part of scholar S demands that S respect the judgments of others (not that S must think highly of others, but S must give others a conversational turn). As a corollary, scholars must respect the judgments of others even when they believe that said judgments are worthless; any other policy is a kind of egocentricity, antithetical to the intersubjective ambitions of science. To criticize my honoring Donald Davidson and Brendan Gillon (Chaps. 5.1, 6.3), on the grounds that their positions are "obvious non-starters", is intellectually vicious.

Alongside my central commitment to naturalism, with its fallibilism and openness to competing ideas regardless of their date, I hold:

> (23) EMPIRICISM. Theories are to be evaluated by their empirical adequacy.

As indicated, empiricism must be qualified by the recognition of theory-ladenness. This is why non-foundationalism is important, and why we must seek broad reflective equilibrium. That said, theories are best measured by their success. Because success is largely a comparative notion, *my primary objective is to develop a theory that works better than all rivals* in the sort of research areas listed. In order to set the stage for my project, therefore, I shall briefly review the major theories of meaning now available, and say a bit about their strengths and weaknesses.

3.   The State of Play

In this section I shall conduct another quick tour of the theory of meaning, but this time instead of identifying question areas I will report on some of the leading approaches taken to providing answers. I do this for multiple reasons. First, my methodology, which justifies a given theory on the basis of how it fares in comparison to other available theories, demands an understanding of the prominent options on the market. Second, any given idea is better understood when set in contrast to others; hence the study of attitudinal semantics and the study of its rivals complement each other. Third, I wish to bring up, casually, a few problems for truth-conditionalism before commencing my sustained and more rigorous assault in Chapter 2.

Approaches to the theory of meaning mostly fall under the umbrella of truth-conditional semantics. Because TC semantics offers a powerful approach to meaning, giving accounts of compositionality and entailment that admit of formal rigor, it is widely assumed in cognitive science, and in philosophy it is the reigning paradigm. It has been called "obvious" (Davidson 1967: 24), "truistic...the merest platitude" (McDowell 1998: 319), "not merely theoretical" (Lycan 1984: 18), and true by definition (Lewis 1970, Cresswell 1985: 145); it is "received wisdom" (Dummett 1978: xxi), "the mainstream view" (Bezuidenhout 2002: 105), "the standard view"

(Recanati 2002: 301), and "uncontroversial" (Schiffer 1987: 1, 3), enjoying "practical unanimity" (Szabo 1999: 3), "virtual unanimity" (Baker & Hacker 1984: 121), and "the status of indisputable orthodoxy" (Glock 2003: 151). It is common to realists and verificationists (Dummett 1978: xxi), it is "implicitly acknowledged among communication theorists" such as Austin, Searle, and Grice (Strawson 1970: 114), and its mate, referential semantics, "now enjoys something of a hegemony in linguistics and philosophy" (Katz 1996: 615). It is even said to be "accepted as literally true even by its critics" (Platts 1997: 62)!!

The chorus does not sing in exact harmony, however, for truth-conditionalism encompasses a diverse range of ideas. I will now survey both this range and the range of alternatives to truth-conditionalism.

3.1 Truth Theory and Model Theory

TC semantics is implicit in Plato's dialogs, which effectively treat definitions as statements of objectively necessary and sufficient conditions. It is first made explicit and vigorously advocated at the very beginning of our own philosophical era, by Frege (1892). For Frege, meaning consists of two important aspects, reference and sense. The reference of a sentence is its truth-value; sense is that which, in combination with the facts of the world, determines reference. Thus, the sense of a sentence is its truth-condition.

The Fregean legacy has given rise to two semantic paradigms, the truth-theoretic or Davidsonian and the model-theoretic or Montagovian. The former, probably *the* leading theory of meaning in philosophy, is propounded by Davidson (1984), Evans & McDowell (1976), Lycan (1984), Larson & Segal (1995), Platts (1997):

> (24) TRUTH-THEORETIC SEMANTICS. Meaning is explicated by truth-conditions, and truth-conditions are explicated by a theory of truth.

According to truth-theoretic semantics, the correct theory of meaning for a language L is a theory of truth that generates, for every sentence in L, a *T-sentence*, an analytic biconditional that instantiates truth-schema (T):

> (T) Φ is true (in L) $\equiv$ P (where Φ denotes sentence P).

For Davidsonians, the operative theory of truth is a Tarskian, extensional one. In addition Davidsonians sometimes advocate DISQUOTATIONALISM, where Φ is a quotation of P, which makes for homophonic T-sentences.

In contrast to disquotational and non-disquotational truth-theories, MODEL-THEORETIC SEMANTICS gives the meaning of a sentence by translating it into a formula of intensional logic that is then interpreted by some model using POSSIBLE-WORLDS or abstract SITUATIONS. The leading theory of meaning in linguistics, and quite popular in philosophy too, it is propounded by Montague (1974), Lewis (1970), Partee (1976), Barwise & Perry (1983), and Cresswell (1985–1996), in the textbooks of Dowty et al. (1981), Gamut (1991), Cann (1993), and Chierchia & McConnell-Ginet (2000), and by most work published in the journal *Linguistics & Philosophy*. Note that model-theory deals not with truth simpliciter but with the solecism "truth-in-a-model". This concept attains clarity, however, when we assume a theory modeled on the actual world, thus effectively reducing the relativistic notion of truth in a model to the familiar absolute notion of truth.

Possible-world semanticists identify a proposition P, that is the meaning of a sentence, as a set of possible worlds, namely the worlds in which P is true. They identity tautologies with the universal set and contradictions with the null set; and presumably they would identify both the liar sentence "This statement is false" and its negation "That sentence was not false" with the null set – all of which is perfectly coherent. Such identity claims that link meaning and possible worlds, however, are invariably accompanied by one truth-related equivalence claim or another, for example by the model-theoretic T-schema (T′).

(T′) Φ is true in M ≡ the denotations in M of the various constituents of Φ stand in the appropriate relations to each other. [E.g. "Fa" is true in M ≡ denotation ("a") in M ∈ denotation ("F") in M.]

Although model-theoretic and truth-theoretic semantics remain very different in their technical apparatus and in their manner of representing meaning [see Davidson (1973a: 68, 75)], the celebrated ontological difference between the two thus recedes to insignificance from my point of view. They both end up giving absolute truth-conditions, and they both presuppose REFERENTIALISM, the thesis that reference to the external world plays a role in the explanation of linguistic meaning [e.g. Field (1972), Davidson (1993)].

Reference, broadly construed, is any word-world relation such as the following: designation, the correspondence between singular term and individual object; application, the correspondence between predicate and set; truth, the correspondence between a whole sentence or statement and fact, situation, or state of affairs; denotation, any standing correspondence between term and referent; and speaker-reference, any nonce correspondence between a term in use and a referent. Because reference includes truth, every truth-conditional semantics is committed to referentialism, strictly speaking. I shall sometimes speak more narrowly, however, according to which reference encompasses just those denotative relations other than truth.

Even when thus limited, referentialism and truth-conditionalism have a tendency to go together. If you are a TC semanticist, and you think that a sentence is about a state of affairs or about a range of possible worlds, then in order to get at a compositional semantics it would be natural to think that a singular term denotes an individual and that a predicate denotes a property. Conversely, if you are a referentialist, and you think that a singular term denotes an individual and that a predicate denotes a property, then it's hardly a stretch to think that combining the two yields a description of the world that is either true or false.

3.2   Direct Reference and Mediated Reference

According to our grammar-school theory of language, a noun *stands for*, or denotes, a person, place, or thing; a verb denotes a state or action; an adjective denotes a quality; and so forth. To go one step further, and identify the denotation of a word with its *meaning*, yields what I shall call NAIVE REFERENTIALISM.

Naive referentialism falls to the fact that co-referential terms are not always synonymous. For example, why don't "centaur" and "satyr" mean the same given that they denote the same? Why don't "Adolf Hitler" and "Adolf Schicklgruber" mean the same? The resulting so-called puzzles of empty names, informative identity statements, and opaque belief reports together constitute the PROBLEM OF INTENSIONALITY.

One solution, the analytic, maintains the referentialist intuition by refiguring the unit of reference (either by breaking it down or by repositioning it as a syncategorematic element in a larger unit). The basic idea is that even though the words "centaur" and "satyr" do not themselves denote, they abbreviate phrases – "half human, half horse" and "half human, half goat", respectively – and these phrases ultimately contain elements that either denote directly or enter into denotation syncategorematically. A sophisticated development of this analytic approach, one version of the theory known as DIRECT REFERENCE, is due to Bertrand Russell. For Russell (1905, 1940), "Adolf Hitler" and "Adolf Schicklgruber" might translate into "the Nazi dictator" and "the bastard son of Herr Schicklgruber and Frau Hitler", respectively. "The Nazi dictator died in 1945", in turn, translates into $\exists x \ (Nx \ \& \ \forall y \ [Ny \rightarrow x = y] \ \& \ Dx)$ – 'there is exactly one Nazi dictator, x, and x died in 1945'. The analyses continue until we achieve a formula where every non-logical symbol denotes some actual existent entity. [Recent direct-reference theorists include Kripke (1980), Salmon (1986), Almog et al. (1989), and Soames (2002, 2005)].

Alternatively reference may be taken as mediated by SENSE, where sense is whatever determines reference. For Frege (1892), "centaur" and "satyr" both yield empty reference in the actual world, but they possess distinct senses because they would yield distinct referents were the world different. Thus the direct-reference identity thesis that reference *is* meaning is dropped in favor of the functional thesis that the reference of an expression is *determined* by its meaning. Note that reference continues to fill center stage, being both the telos of sense and essential to defining sense. (A naturalistic variant, due to Devitt (1981), takes sense to be a causal network grounded in some referent.)

Frege's theory of sense maintains the referentialist intuition also by positing a reality that is larger than life. Specifically, according to Montague semantics, "centaur" and "satyr" co-refer in the actual world but diverge in denotation in other "possible worlds". Such worlds, though non-actual, possess a kind of reality. For denotation is a kind of reference, and reference is a relation between linguistic element and mind-independent reality. To see that reference is a relation to mind-independent reality, consider the alternative. If "centaur" referred to a mere idea, as it does for the naive mentalist, "centaurs exist" would mean that the idea of centaurs exist, and it would be true. (For the sophisticated mentalist, the problem of intensionality never arises because reference is not meaning. "Centaur" expresses an idea, it does not denote an idea.)

For Russell, the ultimate elements of a sentence denote epistemologically accessible features of the world, and a sentence as a whole denotes a complex of such features, a proposition. If a proposition is identical to an existing state of affairs, it is true; otherwise it is false. For Frege, the elements of a sentence express functions that yield denotations of individual objects and other functions, and a sentence as a whole denotes a truth-value. Needless to say, the two strategies of re-analyzing logical form and postulating senses can be combined, and often are, the two strategies being fundamentally compatible because of their shared referentialism.

3.3   Realism and Verificationism

Commitment to reference, a relation to the world, naturally gives rise to realism, commitment to the existence of mind-independent entities, which yields classic, *realist* truth-conditionalism. Realist truth-conditionalism, however, appears to create an epistemological gap between word and world, which makes the world into an experience-transcendent realm. In response, "anti-realist" verificationism holds that because a theory of meaning is a theory of linguistic understanding, and human beings transition from not having such understanding to having it, meaning must be learnable. And so, it is claimed, the meaning of a statement P cannot involve classical truth-conditions but only the conditions under which P could be verified or falsified, in principle or in practice. This view has been advocated by the logical positivists, Quine (1969: 80), Dummett (1975, 1976), Peacocke (1986), Tennant (1987, 1997), Putnam (1988), and Wright (1993), and it comes in many varieties.

(25) VERIFICATIONISM, proof-theoretic version:
$P \equiv \Phi$ is demonstrably provable;
$\neg P \equiv \Phi$ is demonstrably disprovable.

(26) VERIFICATIONISM, confirmational version:
$P \equiv \Phi$ is confirmable (at a high probability);
$\neg P \equiv \Phi$ is confutable (at a high probability).

(27) VERIFICATIONISM, assertability version:
$P \equiv \Phi$ is warrantedly assertable;
$\neg P \equiv \Phi$ is warrantedly deniable.

One noteworthy feature of verificationism is that if there is neither proof/ confirmation/assertability of Φ nor disproof/confutation/deniability of Φ, then neither Φ nor $\neg\Phi$ holds; hence the law of excluded middle fails.

The law of excluded middle demarcates realism from irrealism, according to Dummett (1963). To a first approximation, if a theory affirms excluded middle then it uses realist truth-conditions, and if a theory denies excluded middle then it uses irrealist truth-conditions. According to this view, which posits (25/26/27) in addition to schema (T) rather than instead of (T), verificationism is a form of truth-conditional semantics. Thus, my animadversions against TC semantics will extend against verificationism so construed.

On top of that, verificationism faces its own unique problem stemming from the fact that the ability to do something (to prove, to confirm, to assert) is always *relative* to the doer. Thus, (25/26/27) are all logically incomplete and require added argument structure. Let's consider a few possibilities. To begin with, we might leave the left-hand side as is while making explicit the right-hand side's argument-structure.

(26′) $P \equiv \Phi$ is confirmable by S.
$\neg P \equiv \Phi$ is confutable by S.

The problem here is that if one subject has evidence confirming Φ while another has evidence disconfirming Φ, then we get the contradiction that P and that ¬P, which is unacceptable.[3] So let's try relativizing both sides of the equivalence.

(26″) P-relative-to-S ≡ Φ is confirmable by S.
        ¬P-relative-to-S ≡ Φ is confutable by S.

As a result we get both "The earth is round relative to us" and "The earth was flat relative to the Babylonians", which is formally consistent. Unfortunately these locutions make no sense to me. It is part of my very conception of something's being the case that it is the case, period; and until "P relative to S" is defined or explained, I have no grip on its significance.

As one explication of (26″), suppose that "P relative to S" is understood as "P is held by S", "P is believed by S", or "P is asserted by S".

(26*) S believes that P ≡ Φ is confirmable by S.
        S believes that ¬P ≡ Φ is confutable by S.

Now verificationism begins to look like attitudinal semantics. Despite similarities, however, there are two differences. First, I doubt that (26*) is what verificationists really have in mind; it's certainly not what they *say*. Second, (26*) uses a cognitive attitude on the left-hand side, and an epistemic attitude on the right. Attitudinal semantics, in contrast, would use the same attitude on each side. As a result, attitudinal semantics is invulnerable to the counterexamples which work against (26*). For instance, let Φ = "the parallels postulate is derivable from Euclid's other axioms". Then for some S, namely certain mathematicians prior to the 19th century, the left-hand side of (26*) is true. Yet for those same S, namely those who believed Φ on faith and without any good evidence, the right-hand side of (26*) is false. Therefore the equivalence fails.

3.4   Assertability Semantics

Verification-conditions, instead of yielding truth-conditions, may alternatively be understood as yielding assertability-conditions. Assertability semantics is prima facie attractive to me, and indeed it resembles attitudinal semantics. For the former, a statement may be assertable, unassertable, or neither; for the latter, a statement may be believed, disbelieved, or

---

[3] In its proof-theoretic version, verificationism can rightfully deny that it's possible for one subject to prove that P while another subject proves that ¬P. However, proof-theoretic verificationism meets its own reductio in its refusal to allow that I slept last night, which is true though no one can prove it.

neither. They both oppose the bivalence of classical truth-conditionalism, and furthermore there is a conceptual link between believing and asserting.

In detail, however, attitudinal and assertability semantics differ. According to the best version of assertability semantics that I know of, that of Gauker (2003), a conversation typically has a goal, and the goal relates to an action that accords with a set of sentences. For instance, if the goal is the getting of clean water then the relevant "context" set may be {Water is in the well, The well is next to Namu's house, Water is not in the barrel, *This* pail is not clean, *That* pail is clean}. A sentence is assertable, relative to a given conversational goal, iff it belongs to the relevant context-set.

Unfortunately, Gauker's example does not work. If dirty pails contaminate their contents, then a sentence describing this fact should be in the context-set, as indeed should indefinitely many others. The point is that context-sets are not so easily regimented as Gauker's discussion implies, one consequence being that the theory is hard to test. More fundamentally, I do not understand the basic concept of ACCORDANCE. Two speakers may be in accord with each other, when they agree; two propositions regarding the same topic may be in accord, when they are mutually consistent; and an action may accord with the facts when the action achieves its goal because of the facts. But what does it mean for an action to accord with a set of sentences? Surely accordance does not pertain to sentences understood as material *forms*, for a single form may have incompatible meanings. But if accordance pertains to sentence *meanings* then it looks like we may have the start of a vicious regress. Be that as it may, it moreover seems that we cannot map sentences onto facts without reverting to referentialism, which Gauker rightly abjures.

3.5   Technical and Formalist Semantics

In terms of *method*, formal semantics uses formal logic and set theory. It aims for formal rigor rather than casual or colloquial articulation. In terms of *subject matter*, formal semantics is the study of linguistic form (expressions such as words and sentences), in contrast to linguistic functioning (the use of expressions in speech acts). Typical TC theories are formal in both senses of the word, the methodological and the material, but I would like to keep the concepts distinct. Henceforth I shall call them "technical" and "formalist", respectively.

(i) THE TECHNICAL-INFORMAL DISTINCTION. Truth-conditionalism is a creed not just of deductive theories that spit out T-sentences; it is implicit in many theories that do not overtly invoke truth, for instance much of the componential analysis as it is practiced by anthropologists [e.g. Tyler

(1969: Part Three)], by linguists (e.g. the generative semanticists), and by philosophers [e.g. Katz & Fodor (1963), Katz (1990)]. In componential analysis, lexical meaning is broken into parts. For example, the meaning of "kill" is famously explicated in terms of either English or a metalanguage consisting of language-neutral concepts:

(27) X killed Y $=_{df}$ X caused Y to become not alive.
(28) X killed Y $=_{df}$ X CAUSED Y TO BECOME NOT ALIVE.

These, I take it, amount to:

(27′) The meaning of "X killed Y" = the meaning of "X caused Y to become not alive".
(28′) The meaning of "X killed Y" = X CAUSED Y TO BECOME NOT ALIVE.

But how do we know when two meanings are equal to each other? How do we test the adequacy of such equations? Although this question is rarely owned up to in the literature, the actual practice of componential analysis suggests an answer: the foregoing are accepted precisely when (29) is thought to hold:

(29) "X killed Y" is true $\equiv$ X caused Y to become not alive.

Thus, although truth does not explicitly occur in componential analyses like (27) and (28), nor is it explicitly acknowledged in the meta-theoretical commentary, it's a part of standard componential analysis. The real difference between the typical componential analyst and the logician truth-conditionalist, then, does not involve the role of "true" in semantics; it is a question of whether lexical meaning can be decomposed or not.[4]

Incidentally, I myself regard technical notation and punctilious rigor as sometimes useful and sometimes pedantically unnecessary. For instance, I shall often abbreviate T-sentences like (29) by means of:

(29′) X killed Y $\equiv$ X caused Y to become not alive.

(ii) THE FORMALIST-USE DISTINCTION. In contrast to formalist theories, pragmatic theories hang meaning on the functioning or *use* of sentence-forms. Attending to use naturally leads to giving context a larger role in semantic theorizing. Contextualism, an extension of formalist truth-conditionalism, ascribes highly variable truth-conditions depending on

---

[4] For notable exceptions to the generalization that componential analysts are truth-conditionalists, see Jackendoff (1983–2002) and Wierzbicka (1972–1999).

broad, multi-faceted, context that is hard or impossible to regiment (§3.6). Attending to use also may mean attending to some combination of assertability-conditions (§3.4), speech-acts (§3.7), intentions (§3.8), and computational role (§3.9).

3.6   Minimalism and Contextualism

According to minimalism, linguistic meaning is minimally or narrowly context-dependent. Relative to a narrow context, one that fixes the reference of pronouns, tense, and a restricted number of other obvious indexicals, and relative to a given state of affairs, a disambiguated sentence is determinately true or false. The truth-value of an expression is determined by its compositional articulation plus the facts of the matter. Such is the classical view (Stanley 2002, 2005, Borg 2004, Cappelen & Lepore 2005a).

Yet the understood import of an expression is typically richer than its compositional articulation allows:

(30) Sherri took out her key and unlocked the door.
(31) Dara's finished.

Sentence (30) by itself does not tell us that Sherri used her key in opening the door, nor does (31) tell us what it is that Dara is finished doing. Even when supplemented by indexed (narrow) context, sentence meaning thus underdetermines or UNDERSPECIFIES communicated truth-conditions (Atlas 1978, 1989, Searle 1978, Baker & Hacker 1984: 203–204, Sperber & Wilson 1986, Kempson 1988, Bach 1994, Travis 1996–2000, Bezuidenhout 1997, 2002, Levinson 2000, Carston 2002, Recanati 2004).

Nearly all underspecificationists, under the spell of truth-conditionalism, assume that if truth-conditions are not given by sentence meaning plus narrow context then they must be given by sentence meaning plus something else. CONTEXTUALISTS or TC PRAGMATISTS, then, hold that utterances have truth-conditions when "completed", "fleshed out", "enriched" (Recanati), or relativized to "broad context", to an "understanding" (Travis), to a "background" (Searle), or to a "set of assumptions" (Bezuidenhout).

Clearly not just any background set of assumptions will do. Relative to the assumption, say, that Dara lives in the twenty-first century, (31) still lacks truth-conditions. Presumably if any set of assumptions can fill in the truth-conditions of an utterance P, a total set could – a set describing a complete possible world, including facts about who tokened P, when, where, and why. (For me context, meaning that which co-occurs with the speech act, includes speaker intentions – and conversely speaker intentions, insofar as they point to elements in the surrounding discourse and physical environment, index relevant context.)

Contextual facts would indeed constrain the range of reasonable ascriptions of truth-conditions. Would they be completely determinative, though? Suppose that Dara has been typing out inventory orders, and your assistant manager reports (31) to you with the intention of prompting a new assignment. Does your assistant mean (a), (b), (c), or yet something else?

(a) Dara is finished typing out inventory orders.
(b) Dara is finished filling out inventory orders.
(c) Dara is finished doing whatever it is that I understand you to have assigned her.

In some cases, surely, total contexts do not choose among (a–c). For typically neither the speaker nor the hearer of (31) will distinguish among (a–c) and select one as the intended reading, not even covertly or tacitly.

My own position is that contextualists are right to deny that (30) and (31), either by themselves or supplemented by narrow context, express truth-conditions. At the same time, minimalists are right to deny that (30), supplemented by broad context, *says* or entails that Sherri used her key in opening the door. Such is not part of the truth-conditions of the communicative act, for neither sentences nor speech-acts nor even mental understandings have truth-conditions.

3.7   Speech-Act Theory

In his remarkable paper of 1940, J.L. Austin anticipates Wittgenstein's family-resemblance argument, he anticipates the proposal subsequently floated in cognitive semantics under the headings of *frames* and *scripts*, he anticipates Quine's assault on the analytic-distinction, he anticipates Gricean implicature, and he anticipates Putnam-style counterfactual reasoning about cats – with the exception that Austin's intuitions are sounder, in my judgment, than Putnam's. What these several discussions all point to is that words do not have necessary and sufficient conditions for correct application; TC semantics faces assorted EMPIRICAL PROBLEMS.

Austin (1962) emphasizes that performative utterances do not so much as aim at reporting truth, and he further suggests that declarative statements are performatives, from which it follows that statements do not aim at reporting truth. Austin does not put it this way, nor would he in view of his "Facts", but I would say that a statement *expresses a state* of believing, it does not *represent a content* of belief (Chap. 3.3.5).

Reinforcing Strawson, Austin makes clear that speech consists of acts, and that speakers are actors. This agent-centered conception of language is further articulated by Searle:

reference is a speech act, and speech acts are performed by speakers in uttering words, not by words. To say that an expression refers (predicates, asserts, etc.) in my terminology is either senseless or is shorthand for saying that the expression is used by speakers to refer (predicates, asserts, etc.) [1969: 28]

Such shorthand is indeed often legitimate. When we forget that it is shorthand, however, or when we deal with certain linguistic phenomena, it leads to error. It is only by remembering what the shorthand is for that we can solve problems of ambiguity, the liar paradox, and so forth.

Searle regards reference, predication, and assertion all as speech-acts, and for each he gives an analysis. "The speech act of referring is to be explained by giving examples of paradigmatic referring expressions" (p. 28), he writes, and "it is characteristic of these expressions that their utterance serves to pick out or identify one 'object' or 'entity' or 'particular' apart from other objects, about which the speaker then goes on to say something" (p. 26). Putting this in biconditional form, I think that Searle means that S typically uses term x to refer to object o iff S uses x to pick out or identify o.

Although I like the subject-centered logical form of Searle's analysis, I'm not completely satisfied. For one thing, if "pick out" is used literally then I don't think that referring amounts to picking out; you can refer to an apple in a bushel without physically removing it from the rest. If to pick out is to identify then it would seem that Searle advocates a kind of verificationism, which is not his intention. So I don't think that the concept of reference has really been at all explained or clarified. And when Searle states that S predicates F of x only if S successfully refers to x, his account seems to fall to examples like "gremlins are imaginary".

The speech-act program works better at explaining illocutionary force, which addresses the PROBLEM OF MOOD. On the face of it, imperatives and interrogatives are neither true nor false, which would contradict any general, unrestricted truth-conditional theory of meaning. The standard speech-act solution, due to Frege and Searle and Vanderveken (1990, 2004), posits truth-conditional propositions interior to the illocutionary force. This yields a kind of weak truth-conditionalism: meaning includes more than truth-conditions, but it does include truth-conditions.

Barker (2004) offers a more sophisticated version of speech-act theory, one built on *intentions* to refer rather than reference itself. Unfortunately, the theory seems to be too sophisticated for its own good; by my count, Barker's analysis of a single assertion invokes intention or other mental state ten times, many of them multiply embedded within others, which makes the whole account psychologically unrealistic (Saka 2007b).

3.8   Intention-Based Semantics

Any discussion of psychologized semantics raises the specter of Grice's intention-based semantics. Grice seeks to reduce word meaning, phrase meaning, and sentence meaning – in general, conventional linguistic meaning – to speaker meaning, which he does by invoking a complex of speaker intentions regarding the audience's mental state. Although this approach has fallen on hard times (Schiffer 1987), there is still life to it (Avramides 1989).

However, just because a theory invokes intentions – as virtually every theory of meaning does at some point – that does not automatically make it part of, or even necessarily compatible with, Grice's sort of program. Gricean semantics and my own are both mentalist, but mine more thoroughly so in that Grice's mental states contain objective truth-evaluable propositions whereas mine does not (Chap. 3.3.5).

Indeed, it is to support his truth-conditionalism that Grice develops the theory of implicature. According to Grice, participants in a conversation use a Principle of Cooperation, along with corollary maxims, to generate *implicatures* on the basis of what is *said*. For example, Grice holds that (32) says no more and no less than (33), that it implicates (34), and that the reasoning behind (34) is as sketched in (35).

(32) David did his homework and went to bed.
(33) "David did his homework" and "David went to bed" are both true.
(34) David did his homework and then went to bed.
(35) (a) S presumably speaks cooperatively, (b) therefore S speaks orderly, (c) therefore S relates events in the sequence as they happened.

By separating the meaning of (32) into statement (33) and implicature (34), and then explaining implicature in terms of language-independent principles of rationality, Grice is more plausibly able to ascribe truth-conditions to the core, literal meaning (33).

Gricean reasoning does take place, I believe, but not with the regularity that Gricean theory calls for. Right after an important date or interview you might consciously try to calculate the inferences that your interlocutor was making, but such occasions are rare and such calculations are highly uncertain. In everyday situations you might unconsciously calculate the inferences, but these cases too are rare and often lead to miscommunication. The trouble with Grice's program, covering both convention and implicature, is that it treats speakers as extremely rational agents whereas human beings in fact mostly act out of instinct and habit (Laurence 1996).

3.9   Conceptual Role Semantics

According to CRS, the meaning of a sentence is identified by its conceptual or cognitive role. The conceptual role of a sentence, in turn, is understood in terms of its computational (causal), normatively inferential, or functional relations to other sentences (and to the speaker-hearer's input/output states). For example, consider sentence p and its relations to q–v, where x ranges over humans:

(p) x has exactly two brothers.
(q) x is someone's offspring.
(r) x knows (at least) two males.
(s) x does not know x's brothers.
(t) x's parents have exactly three male offspring.
(u) x is female.
(v) x's parents have exactly two male offspring.

Sentence p entails q with virtual certainty; it also counts as a certain degree of evidence that r is true, since people usually but do not always know their close relatives. Sentence p hardly suggests s at all; but it would seem that p entails the disjunction (r or s). Sentence p is in turn entailed by the conjunction of (t & not-u) and by the conjunction (u & v). In short, the meaning of p is whatever proposition that entails q, probably-r, and (r or s); is entailed by (t & not-u) and by (u or v); and enters into an endless number of other relations as well.

Since conceptual-role representations of meaning can be posited within the constraints of methodological solipsism, CRS or something like it is popular in AI and in psychology, where it is often called procedural semantics (Miller & Johnson-Laird 1976, Eco et al. 1988, Fellbaum 1998). CRS also appears in linguistic structuralism (Saussure 1916, Lehrer 1974b, Cruse 1986, 2002), and it enjoys fair currency in philosophy (Quine 1951, Sellars 1963, Putnam 1975, 1978, Field 1977, Harman 1982, 1987, Lycan 1984, Block 1986, McGinn 1991, Horwich 1998, 2005, Brandom 2000).

CRS is often viewed as the leading rival of TC semantics, but this is incorrect; the two are not necessarily at odds at all. For starters, if the inferential relations among sentences manage to establish truth-values for the sentences – analogous to the way in which inter-sentence relationships manage to establish justification in coherentist epistemology – then CRS is simply a non-foundational, perhaps non-referential, version of TC semantics. Moreover, if foundations are provided for CRS in the form of inferential relations between some sentences and percepts [as advocated by Harman (1982)] then CRS looks very much like a TC or verificationist theory [cp. Fodor (1978)]. Finally, even if CRS by itself is non-truth-conditional, by far most CRS theorists want to admit truth-conditions on top of conceptual roles. If TC semantics is not built into CRS, as it is for Harman, and arguably Quine too (p. 250), then TC semantics is usually added as an independent supplement, as it is for Putnam, Field, Lycan, Block, and McGinn.

(36) DUPLEX TRUTH-CONDITIONALISM, also known as dual aspect, two-tier, double-factor semantics: meaning consists of at least conceptual role *and* truth-conditions as independent components (plus possibly force, tone, etc.).

Duplex theory has the virtue of being able to provide a solipsistic semantics for the use of cognitive scientists while at the same time giving a referentialist semantics to philosophers. Unfortunately, duplex theory faces what I shall call the COORDINATION PROBLEM: How is it that the conceptual-role content for a given proposition and the TC content for the same proposition always match each other so well? Why, for instance, do we never get a proposition Φ with the following contents?

(37) Φ is true $\equiv$ Honolulu is the capital of Hawaii; Φ possesses the same cognitive role as p does in the example (p–v) above.

In addition duplex theory inherits some of the separate problems of pure TC semantics and pure CRS.

Pure, monolithic CRS, free of substantive truth-conditionalism, appears to be held by Horwich, Brandom, and Field (2001). I believe that very much of what they say is correct, although I would not emphasize word-word relations so much as word-idea relations.

3.10 Cognitive Semantics

Classical TC semantics (minimalist and realist), TC pragmatics, verificationism, speech-act theory, Gricean intention-based semantics, Gauker's accordance-based assertability semantics, CRS, and attitudinal semantics issue forth analyses of the following respective forms.

(TC) Sentence Φ is true (relativized to narrow context c) $\equiv$ P.

(TC') Statement Φ is true in broad context c $\equiv$ P.

(Ver) Φ is verifiable $\equiv$ P.

(Act) General case: S's utterance is felicitous or satisfied $\equiv$ ...
        Special case: S's assertion Φ is true $\equiv$ P.

(IBS) In saying Φ, S means that P $\equiv$ S intends ... intends ... intends ...

(Acc) Sentence Φ is assertable in conversation c $\equiv$ Φ belongs to a set of sentences that accords with acting in pursuit of the goal of c.

(CRS) The meaning of Φ = the set of causal/inferential relations, of varying strength, that Φ bears to and from other sentences = $\{<\Phi,$ $\Psi, n_1>, <\Psi, \Phi, n_2>, <\Phi, \Theta, n_3>, <\Theta, \Phi, n_4> \ldots\}$.

(A) S thinks Φ (in context c) $\equiv$ S thinks that P.

Minimalism and contextualism treat the widespread intuition that language is *about* external reality, and they have generated a great deal of solid research. Each raises objections against the other, however; plus they stumble on the problems of intensionality, mood, and platonism. Verificationism gets around the worries of platonism, but seems to fall into an untenable form of relativism. When it is regarded as interpreting or qualifying truth-conditionalism rather than eliminating it, verificationism opens itself up to many of the problems that attend TC semantics. CRS, which provides a notion of narrow content for use in cognitive psychology, is almost always held as part of a duplex theory. As such, it too faces the problems of TC semantics, plus the coordination problem. Speech-act theory addresses the problem of mood, but its mainstream wing, represented by Strawson and Searle, incorporates classical truth-conditionalism as a proper part. In addition to their individual shortcomings, no TC semantics enjoys obvious resources for explicating diachrony, perspective, register, connotation, or ambiguity. Showing that at least some of these can be treated in a natural way by attitudinal semantics will occupy Part Two.

The attitudinal schema (A), by reference to S's thinking, provides an explicit bridge between linguistics and psychology. More specifically, I intend for it to provide entry to cognitive semantics, which understands linguistic competence in terms of prototypes, schemas, frames, idealized cognitive models, embodiment (Johnson 1987, Lakoff 1987, Talmy 2000); instantiation; metaphor (Lakoff & Johnson 1980); vantage (Taylor & McLaury 1995); mental models (Johnson-Laird 1983, Fauconnier 1997, Tomasello 2003); and generally the structure of the mind rather than the structure of the world (Jackendoff 1985, 1992, Pietroski 2003).[5]

The claims of cognitive semantics are motivated by a number of concerns. One comes from viewing the theory of meaning as a branch of human

---

[5] Jackendoff's "conceptual semantics" is often distinguished from the Lakoff wing of "cognitive semantics," but I see the difference as more sociological than substantive. While the two do differ in their attitudes toward Chomskyan syntax and in their use of Chomsky's "I-language" terminology, they are both (i) mentalist rather than referentialist, and (ii) distinctively informed by cognitive psychology.

linguistics, and human linguistics as a branch of human psychology. This combines with the idea that the correct methodology for psychology is solip-sistic, and it concludes that the correct theory of meaning must be solipsistic. Hence the proper object of inquiry, "I-language", is internal (Jackendoff 1985, Chomsky 1986, 2000). Such an approach may use counterparts to the ordinary notions of truth and reference, but only when such are construed as involving "narrow content" (Pietroski 2003).

Another motivation for cognitive semantics is internal to linguistics, driven by the language data. It is from looking at linguistic patterns, especially of metaphor, that Lakoff (1987: Chap. 11) and Johnson (1987) object to OBJECTIVISM. Objectivism, as I understand it, characterizes the regnant paradigm in semantics in several senses.

- The regnant paradigm is formalist, taking the subject matter of linguistics to be an object rather than some subject's act.
- Consequently it treats meaning as objective rather than subjective, "essentially indexical" [cf. Perry (1979)], and "embodied" (Lakoff & Johnson 1998).
- It is referentialist, committed to (explanatorily functional) relations between words or other units in the mind, and objects or other entities external to the mind.
- As one example of its referentialism, it is truth-conditional, where truth is substantive rather than deflationary.
- As another example, it assumes a set-theoretic ontology, a metaphysics of precise sets and elemental entities.
- As another example, it assumes that believings are relations to static belief-objects or belief "contents".
- Finally, it assumes that belief-objects are objective, or mind-independent, inasmuch as two believers can engage the same belief-object.

In the chapters to follow, I enlarge the brief against objectivism by considering the linguistic phenomena of vagueness, mood, connotation, ambiguity, quotation, and ascriptions of truth.

Chapter 2

THE CASE OF THE MISSING TRUTH-CONDITIONS

This chapter offers a two-step argument against the truth-conditional approach to meaning. First I argue against its epistemological wing, that to know the meaning of a sentence is to know its truth-conditions, and second I build upon the first step to argue against the ontological wing, that the meaning of a sentence is or determines its truth-conditions.

Strictly speaking, my two target theses – the ontological and the epistemological – both require qualification. To begin with, so as to accommodate the indexical nature of language, it is the meaning of an *utterance*, an assertoric *speech act*, or a sentence *plus context* that determines truth-conditions; the sentence by itself, one might say, merely determines truth-condition conditions. In addition, meaning must somehow be related to *relevant* conditions: "*the sky is blue* is true if, and only if, the sky is blue and $1 = 1$" fails as semantic analysis. Proposals for dealing with this problem of grain include identifying meaning not with truth-conditions simpliciter but with *derivational structures* of truth-conditions (Cresswell 1985) or with *designated selections* of truth-conditions (Larson & Segal 1995: 33), for instance those entailed by the simplest empirical and holistic theory (Davidson 1967). I mention all of this only to dismiss it; these problems of indexicality and hyperintensionality are independent of my present argument, and in what follows I shall often give casual formulations of TC semantics.

Against truth-conditionalism, I shall argue that in many cases and for a given sentence P:

(a) We know the meaning of P.
(b) We do not know the truth-conditions of P.
(c) Therefore knowledge of meaning $\neq$ knowledge of truth-conditions.
(d) Therefore the whole truth-conditional approach is untenable.

Section 1 cites examples where we know the meaning of a sentence yet do not know its truth-conditions, thus making a preliminary case for (a–c). Challenges thereto are considered and rejected in Section 2. Section 3, arguing from (c) to (d), draws wider consequences for the theory of meaning, in particular for ontological versions of truth-conditional semantics proper and for truth-conditional pragmatics.

1.   The Argument from Ignorance

Against epistemic truth-conditionalism, that knowledge of meaning entails knowledge of truth-conditions, vague language serves as a prima facie counter-example. Virtually every statement is vague, and for any vague statement P there are borderline conditions where one does not know whether P be true or false. Therefore, in knowing the meaning of P, one does not really know P's full truth-conditions. What's more, the argument can be extended against PARTIAL TRUTH-CONDITIONALISM, the thesis that knowledge of the meaning of a statement is knowledge of only some truth-conditions (Saka 2007a). To strengthen the case against partial truth-conditionalism, I turn from vagueness to non-declaratives (§1.1) and countless other constructions (§1.2).

1.1   Ignorance Regarding Non-Declaratives

On the face of it, only declarative sentences are true; imperatives, interrogatives, exclamatives, and sentences representing a variety of other moods found in the world's languages are never true or false. But given that non-declarative sentences are meaningful, this contradicts the TC thesis that the meaning of a sentence is its truth-conditions.

To this problem of mood there are three responses.

(i) REDUCTIONISM. The most developed TC strategy argues that imperatives are actually equivalent to declaratives, or to fragments thereof. According to some speech-act and Chomskyan deep-structure accounts, (1) below is equivalent to the tenseless or present-tense (a) (Searle 1969: 22, Liles 1971: 65) or to the future-tense (b) (Searle 1965: 42, Stockwell et al. 1973: Chap. 10, Baker 1978: 127); according to generative semanticists, (1) is equivalent to first-person performative (c), (d), or something similar [McCawley 1968, Lakoff 1972a; also Lewis (1970: §viii)]; according to some scholars of practical reasoning, (1) is equivalent either to a threat (e) (Bohnert 1945, Ross 1958) or to a normative statement (f/g), though (f) and (g) introduce fresh problems for truth-conditionalism; according to the paratactic theory, (1) is equivalent to an ordered sequence of declaratives (h) (Davidson 1979a).

(1) Eat your spinach!
 (a) You eat your spinach.
 (b) You will eat your spinach.
 (c) I order you to eat your spinach.
 (d) I request you to eat your spinach.
 (e) You will eat your spinach or something bad will happen to you.
 (f) You ought to eat your spinach.
 (g) It would be good for you to eat your spinach.
 (h) The following utterance has imperative force: You will eat your spinach.

Were I myself to favor reductive truth-conditionalism, I would propose taking (1) to be what it looks like, a bare predicate. Pragmatically it would be understood that if you address a bare predicate to me, you want me to satisfy it. Semantically the bare predicate, used as an imperative, would have the same value as a predicate used in a declarative: that which, when combined with a subject and maybe tense, yields truth-conditions.

Interrogatives too enjoy a number of reductive analyses. According to Belnap and Steel (1976), a *wh*-question (2) is equivalent to an infinite disjunction of its possible answers (a); according to Chierchia & McConnell-Ginet (2000: 102) and Lycan (2004: §3), (2) is equivalent to the answer that would make it true (b); and according to Frege (1918: 293), (2) is equivalent to an open formula (c).

(2) Who did you vote for?
 (a) I voted for Bush or I voted for Kerry or I voted for Mary Queen of Scots...
 (b) I voted for David Cobb.
 (c) I voted for x.

For polar questions like (3), Chomskyans propose a deep structure amounting to that of (a) while Aqvist (1965) proposes (b), which in turn is to be interpreted by one theory or another of imperatives.

(3) Did you hear the news?
 (a) You heard the news.
 (b) Make it true that either I know you heard the news or I know you didn't.

In short, many TC semanticists rest content because they think that in all cases of non-declarative sentences, crypto-equivalent declaratives can ingeniously be found.

Any genuine equivalence, however, should be neither ingenious nor cryptic if epistemic truth-conditionalism be correct. The fact that truth-conditions are opaque to those who understand non-declaratives establishes that knowledge of truth-conditions is not necessary for knowledge of meaning.

(ii) PROPOSITIONAL RADICALS. One alternative to the reductionist strategy is to treat sentences as made of two components, one expressing propositional (truth-conditional) content and one expressing illocutionary force (Frege 1918, Stenius 1967, Dummett 1993a, Vanderveken 2004). In this case imperatives and interrogatives do not reduce to declaratives, but nonetheless they do possess a truth-evaluable component, the propositional radical. Because attempts to identify truth-conditions for propositional radicals bump into the same range of possible positions that we have seen proposed by reductionists, the propositional-radical approach only exacerbates our state of ignorance.

(iii) DELIMITED TRUTH-CONDITIONALISM. The propositional-radical and reductionist approaches, which insist alike that sentences of *all* moods possess truth-conditions, both count as forms of GENERAL TRUTH-CONDITIONALISM. In contrast, DELIMITERS admit that non-declaratives lack truth-conditions. For them, imperatives possess compliance-conditions while interrogatives, exclamatives, and so forth possess their own analogous yet distinctive *satisfaction*-conditions or *felicity*-conditions. But this hardly solves the problem. If knowledge of meaning is knowledge of what truth-conditions a sentence has, and if interrogatives have no truth-conditions, then knowing the meaning of an interrogative should include knowing that it has no truth-conditions. Too, if knowledge of the meaning of an interrogative is knowledge of its felicity-conditions, then we should know what conditions make an interrogative felicitous. Yet as the numerous theories of mood prove, we know neither whether imperatives lack truth-conditions nor what their felicity-conditions might be.

The abundance of proposals for dealing with mood, far from saving the day, thus actually poses a problem for both general and delimited TC semantics. Indeed, reductive analyses can be turned on their head, as when declaratives were argued to derive from imperatives (the logical form of "P" being "Assume that P") – in which case it would seem that *no* sentence ultimately enjoys truth-value! From this I conclude first that, for any non-declarative P and *any* condition c, we do not know whether P is true in c, which contradicts even partial truth-conditionalism. Second, because it involves mood, the lack of truth-conditions is a systematic and pervasive fact about language.

1.2   Ignorance ad Nauseam

Ignorance of truth-conditions not only prevails for vagueness and non-declaratives, it permeates language. For instance, we are ignorant of the truth-conditions of ethno-racist slurs as in (4).

(4) Hitler was a kraut.

To anticipate Chapter 5: According to the Simple Conjunction Theory, (4) is equivalent to "Hitler was German, and Germans are despicable", which is false. According to the Indexical Conjunction Theory, (4) is equivalent to "Hitler was German, and I despise Germans"; its truth-value varies from speaker to speaker. According to the Bracket Theory, pejoration is a parenthetical side feature derogating all Germans, and (4) is truth-conditionally equivalent to just "Hitler was German"; it is true. According to the Multiple Proposition Theory, (4) is equivalent to the sequence <Hitler was German, Germans are despicable>, whose parts are true and false, respectively, and whose whole is neither. According to the Stereotype Theory, (4) is equivalent to "Hitler meets the negative stereotype of Germans", which is also true, though it differs from the Bracket Theory in treating "Einstein is a kraut" as false. According to the Disquotational Theory, (4) is true if and only if Hitler was a kraut, in which case the truth-value of (4) remains unknown to me. According to various Non-proposition Theories, (4) either rests on a false presupposition or functions expressively; it is neither true nor false.

The variety of theoretical positions establishes that no one knows the truth-conditions of "Hitler was a kraut". Not only that, the truth-conditions are so unspecified that we could stipulate *any* precisely defined world, and we would still not know its truth-value. We do not know any of its truth-conditions. There is no conceivable condition under which (4) counts as categorically true according to all theories (for the Indexical Theory treats truth as relative and some Non-proposition Theories treat truth eliminatively), there is no condition under which (4) counts as categorically false by all, there is no condition under which (4) counts as relatively true by all theories, and so forth. This means that not a single truth-condition is known.

This is not a case of borderline fuzziness; this is a case where the concept at its center is inscrutable, if concepts be truth-theoretic categories. But of course the concept or meaning of "kraut" is *not* inscrutable; we understand someone who uses the word, we understand who is being referred to, we understand what the speaker's attitude toward the referent is, we understand not only what the speaker's feelings are but something about the discourse's level of civility (or lack thereof). We know everything there is to know about the conventions behind the word. We know its meaning, though we do not know its contribution to truth-conditions, contrary to both total and partial truth-conditionalism.

Truth-conditionalists may reply that pejoratives are recherché. They may say that pejoratives represent a marginal aspect of language that can properly be ignored by semantic theory. This move, however, makes more than one mistake. First, it is a mistake to dismiss recalcitrant data or logical difficulties by equating either rarity or small size with inconsequentiality. Observational discrepancies at the sixth decimal place prove that Einstein's empirical theory is superior to Newton's, and Russell's single paradoxical sentence proves that a priori naive set theory is inconsistent. Likewise all linguistic phenomena, whether regarded as empirical or a priori, deserve consideration.

Second, it is a mistake to think of pejoratives as aberrations. Pejoratives proper exemplify connotation more generally, which is ubiquitous (Chap. 5). It is not just racist and sexist slurs, but all expressions having point-of-view content, that raise questions about truth-conditions. Pushing this idea further, it is a mistake to think that connotative expressions exhaust the cases where we are ignorant of truth-conditions. Indeed, given the utter inescapability of vagueness, we do not know the truth-conditions for any sentence.

Quite aside from vagueness, mood, and connotation, the case of the missing truth-conditions applies to almost every kind of sentence construction. It famously arises for definite descriptions (Russellians hold that under actual conditions "the king of France is bald" is false, Strawsonians that it is neither true nor false). The problem arises for plural generics and for indefinite generics and for definite generics – for instance, which if any of the following can be true if a few zebras are not striped?[1]

(5) Zebras are striped animals.
(6) A zebra is a striped animal.
(7) The zebra is a striped animal.

---

[1]   My own view is that the noun phrase in (5) is what it looks like: an NP without a determiner or adjectival qualification. It abbreviates neither "all zebras" nor "some zebras" nor "typical zebras", though of course a speaker may variously expect or hope the hearer-subject, S, to read in more than what is expressed. One natural expectation is for S to add STRIPED ANIMAL to S's concept ZEBRA; in other words, (5) is more likely to be used for informing rather than for being judged. Another natural expectation is for S to apply "are striped animals" to the first zebras that S thinks of, these normally being hypothetical constructs generated by S's concept ZEBRA, which is an image-schema or idealized cognitive model (Johnson 1987, Lakoff 1987). Because an arbitrary hypothetical construct generated by a given concept will have features typical of it, (5) can be used to convey genericness. Similar remarks can be made about (6) and (7).

The problem arises for reduplicative intensives. Inspired by Milton's lament after going blind, "Oh, dark, dark, dark amidst the blaze of noon", I ask: does statement (8) have the same truth-conditions, or not, of (a)? of (b)? of (c)? of (d)?

> (8) At noon it was dark, dark, dark.
> > (a) At noon it was dark.
> > (b) At noon it was very dark.
> > (c) At noon it was very, very dark.
> > (d) At noon it was dark, and I am choked up about it or hereby emphasize it.

The problem arises for so-called category mistakes [category errorists regard "rectangularity drinks procrastination" as *obviously* neither true nor false, others regard it as *obviously* false; Saka (1998a: Chap. 3.2)]. The problem notoriously arises for belief ascriptions, for subjunctive conditionals and causal statements and probability statements, for figurative language, and for quantified statements (in part because of questions about the domain of discourse). Absolutists like Unger (1975) deny the strict truth of statements like "my desk is flat", while others relativize to variable standards. In the realm of moral and esthetic philosophy, normative judgments are interpreted by Kantians as consistency-claims, by utilitarians as consequence-claims, by Stevenson (1944) as exclamations, by Hare (1952) as prescriptions, and by Phillips (1998) as indexical claims. Indeed, much of the history of philosophy starting with Socrates can be read as the attempt to find truth-conditions. It is a history that, fascinating and valuable though it is, has yet to yield knowledge of truth-conditions.

2.   Truth-Conditionalist Maneuvers

To sum up, my prior work on vagueness observes that for all sentences we're missing at least some truth-conditions; Section 1.1 (on mood) observes that for some sentences, and a good many at that, we have no truth-conditions at all; and Section 1.2 (on pejoratives and more) observes that the problem extends beyond vagueness, which is a shady character anyhow, and beyond non-declaratives, which have long been regarded as second-class citizens. It *permeates* language.

To all appearances, then, knowledge of meaning rarely if ever correlates with knowledge of truth-conditions: you can have the former without the latter (and also the latter without the former; §3.3). To this there are several possible replies. The Double Ignorance Defense admits that

we lack knowledge of truth-conditions but contends that we also lack
knowledge of meaning. The Double Knowledge Defense admits that we
know the meanings of the sentences we utter but contends, for example
by appeal to tacit knowledge, that we also know their truth-conditions.
A compromise between Double Ignorance and Double Knowledge, the
Half-and-Half Defense relates partial knowledge of meaning to partial
knowledge of truth-conditions. The Dialect Defense denies that there exists
any collective "we" to which the question of knowledge applies; a given
individual S understands a sentence P in one idiolect, in which case S knows
P's truth-conditions, but does not understand the homophonous P* from a
different idiolect, in which case S does not know P*'s truth-conditions.

Double Ignorance and Double Knowledge are rebutted in Saka (2007a).
In the present work, I wish to say more against them (§§2.1, 2.2), and also
argue against the Half-and-Half and Dialect defenses (§§2.3, 2.4). Then, in
Section 3, I will turn to the import of my Argument from Ignorance. Does
my claim, that knowledge of meaning is not knowledge of truth-conditions,
truly threaten truth-conditional semantics?

2.1   Ignorance of Meaning

The Double Ignorance Defense admits that we generally don't exactly
know the truth-conditions for a given utterance P, and concludes from this
that we don't exactly know the meaning of P either. However, there is an
epistemic difference between our relation to the words on this page and
our relation to a random Inuit utterance (at least there is for me). And this
difference is paradigmatically described by saying that we know commonly
used words in English (more precisely, we know what they mean) while we
do not know the meanings of words such as "kuviasuktuk". This claim is
buttressed by the fact that we have *learned* English vocabulary but not Inuit,
more precisely we have learned what "we" means but not "kuviasuktuk";
and to learn what a word means is, in the absence of forgetting, to *know* what
a word means (and not to have learned a word is, in the absence of innate
lexical knowledge, not to know its meaning). Likewise it's hard to deny that
we grasp the meaning of interrogativity and imperativity. [Indeed, children
learn imperatives at least as early as other moods (Bates & MacWhinney
1979); if we understand sentences at all, we understand imperatives.] There
is, then, a perfectly good sense in which all fluent speakers of English know
the meanings of my problem sentences.

In general, the notion that we do not understand a sentence P or know
its meaning, be it vague, non-declarative, or pejorative, is contrary to the
paradigm use of the words "we know its meaning". First off, we know
the conventions of use for P as well as we know the conventions of use

for any construction. If we do not know the meaning of P then we do not know the meaning of anything. Second, we know the conventions of use for P as well as anyone does. If we do not know the meaning of P then no one does, and if no one knows the meaning of P then P is not part of any actual language. (Granted, only some of the possible uses of the word "we" are governed by established conventions; but to the extent that a convention exists, subscribers to it know what it is.) Third, our knowledge of the meaning of P is supposed to explain our linguistic behavior relating to P. If we didn't understand P then we would never have reason to utter P or respond to others' utterances of it.

In fact, the Double Ignorance Defense appears to come down to an exercise in bad faith. The Double Ignorance Defense correlates knowledge of meaning with knowledge of truth-conditions, and all along it quietly holds that knowledge of meaning never exists. In this case the TC thesis is materially valid but only because it is vacuous; we could, with equal justice, maintain that to grasp sentence meaning is to grasp fairy dust.

2.2   Knowledge of Disquotational T-Sentences

Davidsonians will insist that we do know truth-conditions because (a) we know homophonic disquotational T-sentences and (b) disquotational T-sentences, such as that for (4), specify truth-conditions.

(4′) "Hitler was a kraut" is true iff Hitler was a kraut.

But T-sentences just do not specify truth-conditions, for otherwise knowledge of (4′), combined with relevant knowledge of the world, would yield knowledge of (4)'s truth-value. Yet it doesn't.

My interpretation of truth-conditionalism is explicitly backed by passages such as:

> What I want to put forward as the semantic competence of a native speaker is nothing more nor less than his ability, when presented with a sentence and a situation, to tell whether the sentence, in that situation, is true or false. [Cresswell 1978: 10; reaffirmed in 1994: 142]

> If someone knows the meaning of a sentence and is omniscient regarding physical facts (that is, is omniscient about all the non-semantic/non-intentional facts), then he knows whether the sentence is true. [LePore 1994: 197]

> If you know a sentence's meaning and you are omniscient as regards [non-linguistic] fact, then you know the sentence's truth-value. [Lycan 2004: §2]

Because we can be relevantly omniscient without knowing the truth-values of vague statements, non-declaratives, and pejoratives, knowledge of the relevant T-sentences does not give knowledge of truth-conditions.

Another reason for denying that disquotational T-sentences specify truth-conditions comes from the field of translation. Consider, for instance, how to translate (4) into Hawaiian. The Hawaiian language, due to its geopolitical history, does not lexicalize anti-German feeling; it has no word meaning "kraut" (though it has the broader quasi-pejorative "haole"). Yet given Davidson's rejection of conceptual relativity (1974), anything expressible in one language is expressible in another; (4) enjoys at least one truth-conditionally equivalent translation. Perhaps it is the Hawaiian counterpart of "Hitler was German", or of "Hitler was German and Germans are despicable", or "Hitler was German and I despise Germans", or "Hitler was a German haole"...Now assuming the Double Knowledge Defense, Anglo-Hawaiian bilinguals will know the meaning and hence truth-conditions of both (4) and all the proposed translations of (4). Knowing all this, bilinguals should then know which translation is truth-conditionally equivalent to the original. But they do not, for the same reason that anglophones do not know which paraphrases of (4) preserve truth-conditions.

For those already committed to TC semantics it may appear that T-sentences provide truth-conditions, but there is no available argument that they do. On the contrary, there are multiple arguments that they positively do *not*. My arguments, to repeat, are (i) that you can know that a T-sentence holds, and be omniscient as regards non-linguistic fact, and you will not know whether an object sentence is true; and (ii) you can know two languages, including the T-sentences that go with them, without knowing whether a proposed translation preserves truth-conditions.

2.3   Half and Half

Instead of taking such stark either-or positions on knowledge as I have been doing, one might maintain that we have partial knowledge of meaning and partial knowledge of truth-conditions, each in the degree right for maintaining an exact correlation between the two (partial knowledge of x being knowledge of part of x). Notice that this proposal differs from partial truth-conditionalism as scuttled elsewhere ("to know the [full] meaning of P is to know some of P's truth-conditions"). In some ways the half-and-half thesis is the more plausible, for it is natural, in hearing a vague statement, to say: "I have a general idea of what you mean, but not exactly".

Let's pursue this more carefully, though. If I say "it's hot in here" then, no matter what the temperature, regardless of the fact that "hot" is vague, you will probably be satisfied in your understanding of what I've said. To be sure, if it's freezing you might not be satisfied in your understanding of my motivations for saying what I did, but it is precisely because you understand what I did say that you wonder whether I am being sarcastic, playing a game of make-believe, deliriously falling into hypothermia, or whatnot; you might not understand *me*, but you understand my *sentence*. Only if someone were to ask whether my utterance of it is *true* would one begin to puzzle over its purported truth-conditions. Is *my* statement "it's hot" true so long as *I* feel hot; does it, in order to be true "for you", require that *you* feel hot; does it require that a "normal" person in my situation would feel hot – and if so, what is normalcy and how does one individuate situations ... ?

My point is twofold. First, I deny that our understanding of vague language is but partial. *Why* you say something may leave me in the dark, but *what* you say, insofar as we speak the same language, is something that I have full relevant knowledge of, to the extent that there is a fact of the matter. Second, successful communication, as when someone says "it's hot", far from conveying truth-conditions, normally does not even raise the question of truth-conditions.

Moving from vagueness to mood and pejoratives, the half-and-half thesis loses plausibility altogether. In the latter cases, recall, we do not know any truth-conditions. It follows, by the half-and-half thesis, that we would have *no* understanding of such constructions.

2.4   Dialects

Assuming that speakers enjoy privileged access to the truth-conditions of their own expressions, differences in intuited truth-conditions could come only from differences in language, dialect, or idiolect. Although all theorists I've cited belong to a community that can loosely be called anglophone, the community is far from monolithic in its customs and conventions. It might be said, then, that the Simple Conjunction Theory of pejoratives correctly describes one variety of English, the Indexical Conjunction Theory correctly describes another, the Bracket and Stereotype Theories yet others, and so on.

It's true of course that idiolects do differ. Otherwise language would never change over generations. But this fact does not save TC semantics. On the one hand, if competing theories of the pejorative are *all* correct, each one for a different dialect, then in some dialects meaning would be non-truth-conditional. For certain Non-proposition Theories, not to mention disquotational semantics, are non-truth-conditional. And if meaning is not truth-conditional in some languages then truth-conditions, instead of being the essence of *language*, are at best an accident of particular *languages*.

On the other hand, if some competing theories of the pejorative are incorrect then the problem remains: whoever subscribes to an incorrect theory does not know the relevant truth-conditions, yet does presumably know the relevant meaning; indeed, where multiple theories vie against each other, no one in the community of scholars can claim to know which theory is correct. What's more, one and the same individual will sometimes propose incompatible truth-conditions for a given statement. Stenner (1981) and Blackburn (1984), for instance, both do this (though perhaps Blackburn is not so much neutral between determinate analyses as he is committed to there being no fact of the matter). Finally, I present evidence that at least some of the proposed truth-conditions of pejoratives are just wrong (Chap. 5). But no one can get the truth-conditions wrong unless either they do not know the relevant meaning, or knowing the meaning is not the same as knowing truth-conditions.

In stressing interpersonal variation, the Dialect Defense also misses intrapersonal haziness. In the case of a vague question, for instance, Williamson (2006) correctly writes:

> If everyone found their own answer obvious, but different people found different answers obvious, then we might suspect that they were interpreting the question in different ways, talking past each other. But that is not so: almost everyone who reflects on the original question finds it difficult and puzzling. Even when one has settled on an answer, one can see how intelligent and reasonable people could answer differently while understanding the meaning of the question in the same way.

The same point is implied by Labov (1972: 197), who reports that "context can be controlled to produce . . . 'dialects' at will".

Finally, it's worth noting that the Dialect Defense stands in a certain tension to the overall truth-conditionalist position. For the acceptability of truth-conditionalism depends, at least indirectly and in part, on the rejection of its chief rival, mentalist (psychologized) semantics, yet the truth-conditionalists' favorite argument against mentalist semantics is that it admits too much linguistic idiosyncrasy [e.g. Frege (1918: 300), Fodor (1987), Putnam (1988: 80)]. If mentalist semantics were correct, so the argument goes, then every speaker would command a distinct idiolect, in which case, strictly speaking, there would be no such thing as a common language, hence no communication, which is absurd. For my part, I see nothing absurd in denying the existence of "the" English language, unless English be understood as an abstraction or collection which no one individual speaks. However, my immediate aim is not to defend mentalist semantics, only to point out a flaw in TC semantics. TC semantics cannot consistently criticize other theories for entailing pervasive idiolect variation while at the same time invoking pervasive idiolect variation as a reply to the Argument from Ignorance.

3.   Extending the Argument from Ignorance

I have argued against certain versions of truth-conditional semantics. Perhaps, however, I have argued against straw theses, despite the evidence adduced on p. 43f and extended in Saka (2007a). Perhaps real truth-conditionalists would happily accept everything I have said so far. Perhaps line (c) at the beginning of the chapter does not entail (d); perhaps ignorance does not contradict TC semantics as it's ordinarily construed or best construed. To explore these possibilities, I shall review and extend my taxonomy of truth-conditionalism. Nearly all varieties, I shall argue, fall to the Argument from Ignorance.

3.1   Depth of TCs: Total vs. Partial

We need to distinguish between "knowledge of P's meaning is knowledge of P's truth-conditions" and "knowledge of P's meaning is knowledge of *some* of P's truth-conditions". Although adopting the latter would call for revising official pronouncements and rewriting textbooks, at least it would preserve the spirit of TC semantics. However, I have already argued that the facts of vagueness, mood, and so on contradict partial truth-conditionalism as much as total truth-conditionalism (§1; Saka 2007a).

3.2   Breadth of TCs: General vs. Delimited

General TC semanticists, comprising both reductionists and propositional-radical theorists, ascribe truth-conditional content to all sentences regardless of mood or illocutionary force. Delimiting TC semanticists ascribe truth-conditions to some specially restricted fragment of language. Many delimiters profess to ascribe truth-conditions to just indicatives (as opposed to subjunctives); some ascribe truth-conditions to just declaratives (as opposed to imperatives, interrogatives, and exclamatives); and others still ascribe truth-conditions to just indicative declaratives or to just indicative declaratives consisting of non-moral vocabulary. On any delimitive view, truth-conditions are presumably a special case of satisfaction- or felicity-conditions.

General TC semantics, given the multiplicity of sincerely espoused proposals for non-declarative truth-conditions, easily falls to the argument from mood ignorance. Delimited TC semantics falls too, though less directly. To repeat Section 1.1, if to know the difference in meaning between a declarative and an imperative is to know that the one has truth-conditions and not vice versa, then to know the meaning of an imperative is to know that it lacks truth-conditions. But, as we've seen, we do not know this. And if that is not enough, delimited TC semantics falls to the arguments from vagueness ignorance, pejoratives ignorance, and so forth.

3.3   Strength of TCs: Strong vs. Weak

So far I've been working with the EPISTEMIC slogan, call it (9), that to know the meaning of a statement is to know its truth-conditions. This formula can be understood in at least two ways.

>   (9a) STRONG EPISTEMIC TRUTH-CONDITIONALISM (EQUIVALENCE):
>   S knows the meaning of a statement iff S knows its truth-conditions.
>   (9b) WEAK EPISTEMIC TRUTH-CONDITIONALISM (IMPLICATION):
>   If S knows the meaning of a statement then S knows its truth-conditions.

Additional readings can be spun off as we interpret "know" and "if". For now, suffice it to note the difference between (9a) and (9b). Strong truth-conditionalism is just a conjunction of the weak thesis (9b) and its converse (9c):

>   (9c) RETRO EPISTEMIC TRUTH-CONDITIONALISM:
>   If S knows the truth-conditions of a statement then S knows its meaning.

Davidson, Lewis, Cresswell, and Devitt advocate strong (biconditional) versions of truth-conditionalism, while many others are neutral or equivocate between biconditional claims and weaker theses.

Retro truth-conditionalism gets its name from the reversal of the usual TC formulation; I do not know of anyone who holds it, aside from those who automatically get it as a component of strong truth-conditionalism. And that may be for good reason. It seems that many linguistic properties, not contributing to truth-conditions, are features of meaning, at least according to ordinary understanding, where linguistic meaning encompasses everything of verbally conveyed *significance*. Non-truth-conditional features include register, broadly construed (whether a word is common or rare, archaic or slangy, formal or vulgar); other social markers (e.g. in languages like Koasati, whether a word is normally spoken by males or by females); perspective or vantage ("the roof slopes up" vs. "the roof slopes down"); and, relatedly, focus ("I baked the cake" vs. "it was the cake that I baked"). Against my examples, strong truth-conditionalists sometimes *stipulate* that meaning is limited to truth-conditions [e.g. Cresswell (1985: 145)]. Such a move admittedly preserves the thesis that giving the meaning (i.e. truth-conditions) of a sentence is equivalent to giving its truth-conditions – by making it empirically vacuous.

The evidence I've been citing counts directly against weak truth-conditionalism and therefore against strong truth-conditionalism as well. But it gets worse, for the same evidence turns against retro truth-conditionalism too. Recall that we do not know, by virtue of linguistic knowledge, whether pejorative (4) is truth-conditionally equivalent to (b); for all we know, it is.

(4) Hitler was a kraut.
(b) Hitler was German.

But now suppose we learn that in some language "pizzle Hitler" is true iff Hitler was German. Then we are still left wondering whether "pizzle Hitler" means (b), (4), both, or neither. The only way to know that "pizzle Hitler" means (b), given that it is true iff Hitler was German, is to know that something like the Bracket Theory is correct; and the only way to know that "pizzle Hitler" does *not* mean Hitler was German is to know that the Bracket Theory is incorrect. Since we do not whether the Bracket Theory is correct, we cannot know the meaning of "pizzle Hitler" simply from knowing its truth-conditions. Analogous arguments can be made for mood and vagueness. Suppose that we know that a sentence P, directed at you, is true if and only if you will eat your spinach. If the Searle-Stockwell-Baker view of mood is correct (p. 36), then P means "eat your spinach!", otherwise P does not mean "eat your spinach!" Since we don't know whether the Searle-Stockwell-Baker view is correct, we don't know whether P means "eat your spinach!" Knowledge of truth-conditions does not give knowledge of meaning.

In summary, the Argument from Ignorance, if correct, refutes the weak thesis. But if the weak thesis fails then the strong thesis does too. In addition I've reported prima facie evidence against the retro thesis and I've managed to turn the Argument from Ignorance against it as well.

3.4   Status of TCs: Epistemic vs. Ontic

The narrowly epistemic formula (9), which has been my focus so far, is similar to the CHIRIC formula, that to grasp the meaning of a sentence is to grasp its truth-conditions. This, I take it, metaphorically refers to factive cognition; hence it counts as epistemic, in the broad sense. Both differ from the ONTIC formula (10), that the meaning of a sentence *is* or *determines* its truth-conditions. It too comes in strong, weak, and retro varieties.

(10a) STRONG ONTIC TRUTH-CONDITIONALISM:
A statement Φ means that P iff Φ is true under conditions where P.

(10b) WEAK ONTIC TRUTH-CONDITIONALISM:
      If statement Φ means that P then Φ is true under conditions
      where P.

(10c) RETRO ONTIC TRUTH-CONDITIONALISM:
      If statement Φ is true under conditions where P, then Φ means
      that P.

Most TC semanticists appear to hold both epistemic and ontic theses,
although sometimes it's hard to tell. Most usually one hears that to "give"
the truth-conditions of a statement is to "give" its meaning. This is elliptical
and metaphorical, I take it, for either *give knowledge of*, which amounts to
narrowly epistemic truth-conditionalism, or *give voice to*, which evidently
expresses a more broadly cognitive truth-conditionalism.

Given the distinction between ontic and epistemic/cognitive truth-
conditionalism, the full significance of the Argument from Ignorance can
now be spelled out: (i) It immediately contradicts the epistemic thesis, which
represents the vast bulk of the TC literature; (ii) it indirectly contradicts the
ontic thesis, assuming the intrinsically plausible and widely shared inference
from "meaning = x" to "knowledge of meaning = knowledge of x"; and
(iii) it undermines the ontic wing according to the argument given below.

(i) THE EPISTEMIC WING. Because the Argument from Ignorance primarily
targets epistemic truth-conditionalism, it is important to see just how popular
that view is. It can be gathered from Frege, and it is perfectly explicit
in, for example, Wittgenstein (1921: §4.024), Carnap (1947: 22), Davidson
(1967: 64), Dummett (1978: xxi), Lycan (1984: 18), Recanati (2004: 21),
Stanley (2005: 221), Higginbotham (2006), and in textbook after textbook:
Dowty et al. (1981: 4), Cann (1993: 15), Larson & Segal (1995: 33),
Stalnaker (1997: 172), Heim & Kratzer (1998: 1), Swart (1998: 33), Luntley
(1999: 89), Lycan (1999: 131), Chierchia & McConnell-Ginet (2000: 72),
and Portner (2005: 13). The position also appears in surprising quarters, for
instance in the works of the anti-logicist communication-theorist Strawson
and the anti-propositionalist behavior-theorist Quine:

> It is indeed a generally harmless and salutary thing to say that to know
> the meaning of a sentence is to know under what conditions one who
> utters it says something true. [Strawson 1970: 189]

> A man understands a sentence in so far as he knows its truth-conditions.
> [Quine 1975: 88; cp. 1980: 9, 21]

Others, not asserting epistemic truth-conditionalism outright, nonetheless
commit themselves to it. For example, Lewis (1970: §i) criticizes the

Katz-Postal-Fodor theory, which identifies meanings with translations into Semantic Markerese, by observing: "we can know the Markerese translation of an English sentence without knowing the first thing about the meaning of the English sentence". Because this claim is relevant only if Lewis accepts the inference from "meaning = x" to "knowledge of meaning = knowledge of x", Lewis's ontic truth-conditionalism entails epistemic truth-conditionalism.

(ii) THE ONTIC WING. The epistemic thesis is not only widely held, it is widely held as being more certain than the ontic:

> A system of rules...determines a truth-condition for every sentence...because to understand a sentence, to know what is asserted by it, is the same as to know under what conditions it would be true...the rules determine the meaning of the sentences. [Carnap 1947: 22]

> For certain sentences, anyway, to know their meanings is to know their truth-conditions and to know their truth-conditions is to know their meanings. So, the meanings of these sentences are their truth-conditions... [Harman, commenting on TC semantics, not advocating it, 1974: 195]

> To know the meaning of a sentence is to know its truth-conditions... A theory of meaning, then, pairs sentences with their truth-conditions. [Heim & Kratzer 1998: 1]

> Various philosophers have argued...that knowing the meaning of S is just knowing its truth-conditions. If that is so, one could propose the following definition: S means p = df S is true in (context) v iff p. [Chierchia & McConnell-Ginet 2000: 73]

The foregoing six authors, in deriving ontic truth-conditionalism from epistemic truth-conditionalism, evidently regard the former as dependent upon the latter.

(iii) MORE AGAINST THE ONTIC WING. Some critics may accept the Argument from Ignorance against epistemic truth-conditionalism while denying that it touches ontic truth-conditionalism. To show that my argument is relevant to the ontic issue I would need to show that the ontic thesis entails the epistemic; for only in that case would a refutation of epistemic truth-conditionalism work against ontic truth-conditionalism. In order to do this, I shall have to discuss attitude ascriptions, in particular the difference between *de dicto* and *de re* readings.

The following inference is said to fail when attitude ascription is construed de dicto, the reason being that de dicto ascriptions purport to present attitude contents in a guise, or under an aspect, recognizable by the attitude subject.

   (11) Superman = Clark Kent
   (12) ∴ Lois Lane knows that Superman can fly ≡ Lois Lane knows that Clark Kent can fly.

The inference succeeds, however, when attitude ascriptions are construed de re. "S knows, de re, that P" holds so long as there exists *some* possible guise of P, g(P), such that S knows, de dicto, that g(P). For instance, given that "Clark Kent can fly" is a guise of "Superman can fly" and that Lois Lane knows Superman can fly, it follows that Lois Lane knows that Clark Kent can fly, though she wouldn't put it that way herself. Conversely, there is some guise g(P) such that S knows, de dicto, that g(P) if S knows, de re, that P, assuming that S is linguistically competent.[2]

   Accordingly, the following inference is valid so long as we construe (14) de re.

   (13) The meaning of Φ = the truth-conditions of Φ.
   (14) ∴ S knows the meaning of Φ ≡ S knows the truth-conditions of Φ.

Ontic truth-conditionalism as expressed in (13) entails epistemic truth-conditionalism as expressed in (14), if the latter is construed de re. Consequently, refuting the latter entails refuting the former.

   Because the clauses of (14) appear to report acquaintance knowledge rather than propositional knowledge, one might wonder exactly how the dicto/re distinction even applies. In answer to that, I shall assume, as I have been assuming all along, that (14) amounts to (15):

   (15) S knows (Φ means that P) ≡ S knows that (Φ is true iff P).

My task now is to show that (15) fails *while construed de re*; to rule out *any* guise of the proposition that P, g(P), such that we know, de dicto: Φ is true iff g(P).

   But this is just what I've argued all along. When I denied that we know the truth-conditions of (say) an imperative, I was not merely denying that we know them under a particular guise. I was denying that we know them under any guise. To put the point in traditional jargon: Lewis believes *of*

---

[2] Traditional doctrine treats dicto/re as a case of lexical or structural ambiguity, but this is surely a mistake, as is now widely recognized (p. 73). I count the distinction as pragmatic, though my discussion here is neutral on the question.

(c) that it gives the truth-conditions of (1) whereas Davidson believes *of* (h) that it gives the truth-conditions of (1).

(1) Eat your spinach!
(c) I order you to eat your spinach.
(h) The following utterance has imperative force: You will eat your spinach.

These are not merely two different reports of belief, they are reports of two different beliefs, and incompatible ones at that. Hence, (i), neither can count as knowledge or true justified belief; and (ii) they cannot both count as graspings or as true belief. More generally, (i) it's never true that to know the meaning of a sentence is to know its truth-conditions, and (ii) it's not always true that to grasp the meaning of a sentence is to grasp its truth-conditions. From either (i) or (ii) it follows that truth-conditions do not constitute meaning.

Prominent writers who come close to rejecting the epistemic thesis while maintaining the ontic are Field (1978), Devitt (1981), and Soames (2002).[3] I say they come close because they do not, technically speaking, reject epistemic truth-conditionalism; they dismiss it. They do not treat it as false, they treat it as vacuous and irrelevant. They hold that semantics is not a theory of linguistic knowledge, understanding, or competence; it is a theory of the relation between language and the world, and nothing else. Field, Devitt, and Soames can thus hold (i) the ontic thesis, that meaning is truth-conditions, and (ii) the epistemic thesis, that knowledge of meaning is knowledge of truth-conditions, while admitting (iii) that we lack knowledge of truth-conditions. They can do this by holding also (iv) that we lack knowledge of meaning. This amounts to a variant of the Double Ignorance Defense, but it's more interesting. Instead of *simply* holding onto the epistemic thesis as irrefutable yet irrelevant – as is, for example "all unicorns are purple" – it accepts the epistemic thesis as a consequence of the ontic thesis, which presumably is *not* irrefutable yet irrelevant.

A purely ontic position, as I see it, is untenable for two reasons. First, as already mentioned in my reply to the Double Ignorance Defense (Saka 2007a), to deny that we know the meanings of English sentences is to use language in a non-standard way. Not only do we know the conventions of English, we can often recognize ambiguity, draw inferences, and paraphrase. This, to me, proves that we have at least some grasp of meaning. Second,

---

[3] Some Montagovians write exclusively in the ontic mode, but few if any discuss and defend their doing so.

if semantic theory is not a theory of competence then I do not understand what it is a theory of. One can say it's about word-world relations, but there are infinitely many word-world relations, and it is capricious to select one in particular for study unless you can show how it hooks up to something of independent interest. As far as I can tell, the only motivation for the Field-Devitt-Soames account of reference and truth comes from linguistic judgment, which threatens to make their theory one of competence.[4]

In a nutshell, the substantive epistemic thesis (that we have knowledge of both meanings and truth-conditions) is far more popular than the vacuous epistemic thesis (that we have knowledge of neither meanings nor truth-conditions). The substantive thesis is refuted by the Argument from Ignorance, while the vacuous thesis is refuted by two arguments. One, call it *competence*, asserts that we understand the sentences in our own language, and that understanding a sentence is nothing more and nothing less than knowing its meaning. The other, call it *naturalism*, complains of God's-eye metaphysics and all other schemes that arbitrarily and without evidence privilege some relations at the expense of others. To give up the epistemic thesis, many already agree, is to lose support for the ontic thesis. More dramatically, I have argued, insofar as both substantive and vacuous forms of the epistemic thesis are untenable then the ontic thesis too is untenable.

3.5   Modality of TCs: Explanatory vs. Nominal

Some critics express optimism about future prospects. We do not currently know the truth-conditions for definite descriptions, generics, conditionals, and so forth, but we have certainly made progress in our understanding of such phenomena, we already have good reason for rejecting some analyses, and it is only a matter of time before we arrive at the right theory, whereupon we *will* know the truth-conditions.

But this doesn't fix the problem, for the TC thesis has modal force. If knowledge of meaning fails to align with knowledge of truth-conditions at *any* point in time then TC semantics is mistaken. To understand why, we need to distinguish among the following theses.

(16) CONSTITUTIVE TRUTH-CONDITIONALISM:
knowledge of meaning is (at least in part) constituted by knowledge of TCs.

(17) CAUSAL TRUTH-CONDITIONALISM:
knowledge of meaning is (at least in part) caused by knowledge of TCs.

---

[4] Further discussion can be found in Barber (2003), especially the papers by Antony, Laurence, and Devitt.

(18) EXPLANATORY TRUTH-CONDITIONALISM:
knowledge of meaning is (at least in part) explained by knowledge of TCs.

(19) NOMINAL (LAME) TRUTH-CONDITIONALISM:
knowledge of meaning merely happens to be (at least in part) knowledge of TCs.

I take it that proponents of truth-conditionalism all subscribe to the constitutive thesis, and that if either it or the causal thesis is true then the explanatory thesis is true. I further take it that the explanatory thesis is significant, but I deny any significance at all to the nominal thesis. One could grant nominal truth-conditionalism while denying that truth-conditions play any role in linguistic theory, as Field (1994) and Horwich (2005) do. In that case opponents of TC semantics – who do not *necessarily* deny the existence of truth-conditions, only its relevance to understanding the nature of linguistic meaning – would actually be vindicated.

3.6   Role of TCs: Flat, Structured, Holistic

Some critics complain that I overlook the sophistication of any serious TC semantics when I target FLAT truth-conditionalism, according to which the meaning of a statement is given, point-blank, by its truth-conditions. According to STRUCTURED truth-conditionalism, the meaning of a statement is given not by a T-sentence, but by a *derivation* of a T-sentence. According to HOLISTIC truth-conditionalism, the meaning of a statement is given not by a single T-sentence, or even derivation thereof, but by a whole truth-theory that simultaneously gives all T-sentences (or derivations thereof). These twists on the flat thesis fail to save TC semantics, however, for it is not just atomistic truth-conditions that we are ignorant of, it's also derivations thereof as well as the whole containing truth-theory. Similar remarks extend to the interpretive truth-conditions of Larson & Segal (1995: 33).

3.7   Nature of Truth: Realist vs. Verificationist

For some, truth is non-epistemic, and truth-conditional semantics stands opposed to verificationist semantics. For others, TC semantics encompasses classical and verificationist varieties, the two differing not in whether to accept truth-conditions but in whether to regard truth realistically or epistemically. For current purposes, the disagreement is parochial; verificationism as well as classical truth-conditionalism succumbs to the Argument from Ignorance. Just as we do not know exactly what conditions will make true a given vagary, to coin a new use for an old term, so we do not know what evidence is necessary and sufficient for warranting its assertion. Just as we do not know what conditions make non-declaratives and pejoratives true, we do not know what would count for their verification.

3.8   Locus of TCs: Semantics vs. Pragmatics

According to formalist truth-conditionalists, TCs are borne by sentences, or by sentences relativized to narrow context; for speech-act theorists, TCs are borne by assertions and statements and such; and for contextualists, TCs are borne by sentences or speech-acts relativized to broad context, or by "understandings" (Chap. 1.3.6).

Now the Argument from Ignorance, as presented in Section 1, speaks primarily of sentences and rarely of contexts. This is only for expository simplicity, however. Add as much contextual information as you care to, and still you generally will not know exactly which worlds your understanding is true of. For example, contextualist theories of "completion", "enrichment", and "fleshing out" may tell us that a particular token of (20) refers to a throne rather than a highchair and it may tell us that the speaker thinks of thrones as chairs –

(20) The Queen of England is sitting in her chair.

– but it is unclear how context can always determine whether the given throne *actually is* a chair.

Even if the chairiness of thrones be determined by some contexts, it is not determined by all. Given a context where the speaker thinks of thrones as chairs, but no one else in the room does, is a throne a chair? Given a context where the speaker can't decide whether thrones are chairs, but affirms (20) out of expediency, are thrones chairs? In the context of having the conversational purpose of deciding whether thrones are chairs, is a throne a chair, or is it not? The examples multiply endlessly. At best, contextualism narrows the range of admissible truth-conditions for (20), getting us closer to truth-conditionalism but never quite there. We lack truth-conditions not just for (20) in the abstract, but also for particular utterances of (20) and for the thoughts or understandings that go with them.

Likewise, pragmatics may tell us that a particular token of (1) is encouragement to eat the spinach on your plate and not a command to eat the spinach in your garden,

(1) Eat your spinach!

But knowing the exact reference and speech act of (1) does not solve the problem of the imperative. It does not matter whether (1) is a command or a request or a reminder, it is not just sentence-type truth-conditions that we are ignorant of. We do not know when, or whether, the thought behind a token utterance of (1) is ever true.

As with vagueness and mood, so with pejoratives and generics and intensives and conditionals and normative statements and on and on. The Argument from Ignorance applies not only against formalist TC semantics, it applies against TC pragmatics, in particular that version of underspecificationism which uses rich contextual and cognitive principles to assign truth-conditions to utterances or thoughts.

Chapter 3

FOUNDATIONS OF ATTITUDINAL SEMANTICS

My thesis is that meaning is given not by truth-conditions but by attitude-conditions; that semantic analyses of the form (TC) ought to be dropped in favor of semantic analyses of the form (A).

(TC) Φ is true ≡ P.

(A) S thinks Φ ≡ S thinks that P.

In this chapter I develop my thesis by addressing some foundational issues. Section 1 offers broad motivation for an attitudinal approach to the theory of meaning, Section 2 details my particular analytic framework, and Section 3 reflects on the theory of belief that is assumed in the background.

1.   Motivating Attitudinal Semantics

According to empiricism, the object of linguistic inquiry is to predict and explain those linguistic facts that are observable, namely linguistic behavior. The theory of language, therefore, ought to generate all and only true biconditionals of the following form for any given speaker S and expression Φ.

(1) S utters Φ ≡ ...

In other words, in specifying the conditions under which an expression is manifested, empiricist theories of language are *speech-conditional* [as in Bloomfield (1933), Quine (1960)]. This much holds, at any rate, as a crude first approximation. A more refined view recognizes that to be an empiricist is not necessarily to be a behaviorist. And for good reason;

filling in the necessary and sufficient conditions for (1) would be unillumi-
nating and practically impossible given the vagaries of linguistic behavior.
People say things, in the sense that they utter the words, under all sorts of
conditions: when sincere, when lying, when joking, when confused, when
sleep-talking, when ordered to at gun-point... Conversely, they may fail to
give expression to something they do mean: when they have laryngitis, when
trying to be polite, when tired, when alone... For these reasons I follow
Chomsky's cognitivism, which shifts attention from performance to competence (analogous to, but distinct from, Saussure's structuralist shift from
"parole" to "langue") – so long as we keep it within naturalist param-
eters. That is to say, we are to understand competence not as a platonic
entity, as Katz (1981) for instance does, but as a theoretical construct that
yields predictions and explanations of observables when integrated with
other theories (of memory, attention, politeness, the effects of inebriation,
deafness, etc.).[1]

In shifting from performance to competence, we need to shift from the
behavioral explanandum as given in (1) to a corresponding mentalistic one.
In particular, I suggest that utterance (a purely behavioral phenomenon) be
understood in terms of illocutionary acts, for example asserting, ordering,
and questioning, as modulated by some performance factors; and that
illocutionary acts, which mix mental and behavioral features, be understood in terms of propositional attitudes such as thought, belief, desire,
and wonderment, plus or minus other performance factors. (This move is
justified given the analytic relation between belief and sincere assertion.)
Propositional attitudes, which are purely intentional, will then serve as
the object of inquiry for empiricist semantics as guided by the compe-
tence/performance distinction. Therefore a preliminary aim of semantics is
to complete the likes of:

(2) S thinks $\Phi \equiv \ldots$

If we can fill in the necessary and sufficient conditions for (2) and for all
the other propositional attitudes as well, and if our auxiliary physiological

---

[1]   I do not mean to suggest that linguistic competence is altogether divorced from psychological processing mechanisms. Indeed, the impressive work of Deane (1992) argues that
syntactic island constraints result from attentional limitations. For further exploration of this
topic, see Hawkins (1994) and the mentalists cited in Chapter 1.3.10. Similarly, biology is
ultimately important, and my work may be seen as a way station to the sort of theorizing
found in Jennings (2005).

and psychological theories are otherwise perfect, then we should be in a position to predict and explain linguistic behavior.

Of course the project of filling in the necessary and sufficient conditions for (2) looks about as daunting as the project for (1) did. Dualism, behaviorism, the materialist identity theory, functionalism, and eliminativism all face discouraging difficulties. Nevertheless, replacing (1) in favor of (2) opens up a powerful strategy: for we can now, I suggest, simply leave thinking and the other attitudes unanalyzed. Instead of giving a complete analysis for (2) – one which elucidates "S", "thinks", and Φ – we can repeat "S thinks" and focus on elucidating just Φ:

(3) S thinks Φ ≡ S thinks . . .

So long as we finish the right-hand side with something other than Φ, we will have a substantive biconditional. For example, (4) analyzes the meaning of "misology is common".

(4) S thinks "misology is common" ≡ S thinks that scorn for reason is common.

Even though it is mostly circular, analysis (4) tells us something instructive. While (4) conveys nothing to speak of about the repeated elements "S", "thinks", and "is common", the meaning of "misology" is partly explicated. It is more fully explicated when combined with attitudinal analyses of other sentences that contain "misology".

The line of thought just traced out represents one entrance to attitudinal semantics. But although reasonable so far as it goes, it is not meant as a conclusive deduction. Rather, the proof is in the pudding: will this approach, suitably elaborated, result in solutions to recalcitrant problems in the theory of meaning? It is the burden of Part Two to demonstrate that it will. Before turning to those chapters, however, I will want to lay some more groundwork and respond to objections. To begin I clarify what the attitudinal framework (A) amounts to, providing further motivation for it in the process.

2. Elaborating Attitudinal Semantics

So far I've given a loose presentation of attitudinal semantics, and it is now time for me to tighten it up. Attitudinal semantics, I have claimed, represents meaning by issuing instances of the following biconditional.

(A) S thinks Φ ≡ S thinks that P.

Although I shall continue to use this formulation in subsequent chapters, it is intended as an abbreviation for something more elaborate. I shall now explain more precisely some of the features of my framework, and I shall motivate them by appeals both to principle and to practice.

2.1   The Analytic Framework

To begin with, (A) does not purport to analyze directly the concept of meaning. That is to say, I do not suggest the following.

(5) Φ means (to S) that P ≡ (S thinks Φ ≡ S thinks that P).

In the first place, analyses of form (5) are *insufficient* because meaning generally cannot be given in *that*-clauses. Where Φ is an interrogative sentence, for instance, the analysis is either false (6) or ungrammatical (7):

(6) "Is misology common?" means that misology is common.
(7) "Is misology common?" means that is misology common.

In the second place, analyses of form (5) are arguably *unnecessary*. If we knew that Φ means P, then we would know the meaning of Φ, and semantic theory regarding Φ would be complete. In other words, the left-hand side of (5) is itself an ostensibly complete analysis, including as it does both analysandum Φ and analysans P, and therefore it is pointless to place it within a larger biconditional.

Rather than (5), I suggest that meaning can be understood only as the object of some cognizant subject, that is only as embedded under some attitude like "specify" (8) or "grasp" (9) or "understand" (10), where Σ = some subject who may or may not be identical to S.

(8) Theory θ specifies the meaning Φ has for S ≡ θ specifies that (S thinks Φ ≡ S thinks that P).
(9) Σ grasps what Φ means to S ≡ Σ grasps that (S thinks Φ ≡ S thinks that P).
(10) Σ understands S's utterance Φ ≡ Σ understands that (S thinks Φ ≡ S thinks that P).

Formula (8), I take it, is metaphorically elliptical for "some Σ uses θ to specify...", since it is agents rather than atemporal objects that make specifications. Claims like (8), therefore, seem to be derivative upon some claim like (9) or (10). One attraction of (9) is that it explicitly refers to meaning, which is after all our object of inquiry. But this attraction is probably deceptive: as Alston once observed, just as chemistry explains the chemical facts of oxygenation, ionization, and crystallization without needing to use or analyze the term "chemical", so too semantics might explain facts about meaning without using or analyzing the term "meaning". My own preference is for (10), which treats a theory of meaning as a theory of understanding. One reason for wanting this is that understanding is empirically more accessible than meaning.

Claim (10) entails that you cannot understand the meaning of someone's words unless you possess the concept of their having a thought. This consequence, reminiscent of the Gricean position that you cannot understand the meaning of someone's words unless you possess the concept of their having an intention, strikes me as intuitively plausible. For while you can understand that grass is green without understanding that someone thinks that grass is green, you can hardly understand that "grass is green" means that grass is green, unless you understand that "grass is green", the ink marks or soundwave, is an artifact that is coordinated with someone's thought.

The full version of my analytic framework must make explicit what is tacit in (A), namely quantification over speakers of a given language. The reason for this is that the attitudinal framework is supposed to apply to the explication of linguistic meaning, and linguistic meaning is relative to languages. Thus, (A) is to be understood as an abbreviation for:

(11) (∀S: S speaks L) (S thinks Φ ≡ S thinks that P),

where L is the language of the clause, Φ, that is under analysis. (The Greek letter Φ mnemonically indicates that L may be foreign.) For instance, if we didn't restrict S to speakers of the right language then analyses like (12) and (13) would erroneously be possible.

(12) (∀S) (S thinks "Der Schnee ist weiß" ≡ S thinks that snow is white).
(13) (∀S: S speaks French) (S thinks "Der Schnee ist weiß" ≡ S thinks that snow is white).

These biconditionals are false; the right-hand side fails to imply the left-hand side since thinking that snow is white does not entail thinking in German except sometimes for speakers of German.

If one had a naive notion of language, it would be easy to disprove my claim (11), given that speakers differ in how much they know about their common language.

(14) (∀S: S speaks English) (S thinks "Bucky is erinacious" ≡ S thinks that Bucky is hedgehog-like).

Isabella thinks that Bucky looks and acts like a hedgehog, but she bears no (appropriate) cognitive relation to the sentence "Bucky is erinacious" because she has never heard the word "erinacious". Hence, as a generalization about speakers of English, (14) is mistaken. To correct for this, we might adopt one of two different strategies. On the one hand, we might restrict "S" to ranging over *ideal* speakers of the language. Although Isabella is ignorant of the term "erinacious", anyone who had full mastery of English vocabulary would certainly satisfy biconditional (14). Alternatively, we might take L as an *idiolect*, in which case "S" would range over a single suitable individual at a single time. (The value of understanding a given idiolect L would depend partly on how important the speaker of L was, and partly on how much L resembled other important idiolects.) Personally, I am inclined toward the latter solution, since I do not think that supra-individual, community-wide languages exist except as sums of idiolects. This is not to deny that the notion of a community-wide language may be a regulative posit in the minds of speakers, but only to insist that the locus of causal agency is to be found in the individual. However, if you prefer to think in terms of reified languages and ideal speakers, I see no immediate harm in doing so.

The approach that invokes the ideal speaker may be charged with circularity. If meaning is explained via reference to ideal speakers, and if ideal speakers are defined as those who know the meanings of all the relevant words, then meaning is explained by reference to meaning. In reply, I would like to say that the characterization of an ideal speaker as one who possesses certain semantic knowledge is not an axiom, but rather a fall-out, of the attitudinal framework. Axiomatically, an ideal speaker of L is simply any subject for whom the semantic theory of L truly applies. (Thus, "S" refers not just to speakers but to all *subjects* who understand a language, be they speakers, hearers, or overhearers.) L, in turn, is defined a priori by the theory, just as geometries are by axiomatic systems. Whether a given definition is useful or applicable is where the theory makes empirical contact with reality. I conclude that although the concept of an ideal speaker entails that there are no ideal speakers of English or of any other literary language possessing lexicons too large for any individual to know, the concept itself is sufficiently clear and involves no question-begging within the semantic theory.

The attitudinal analysis represents more than a material biconditional that holds whenever the left-hand and right-hand sides just happen to coincide in truth-value; it expresses a modal connection.

(15) $\Box$ (S thinks $\Phi \equiv$ S thinks that P).

The use of some necessity operator is motivated in principle by the idea that semantics, like all other sciences, is interested in nomic connections, not chance connections. It is motivated in practice by the undesirability of equivalences such as:

(16) S thinks "grass is green" ≡ S thinks that snow is white.

This material equivalence arguably holds for all adult native speakers of English, yet intuitively it does not analyze the meaning of "grass is green".

Still, the necessity operator might be questioned on two grounds. First, is it really called for? In Davidson's theory, for instance, the biconditionals purportedly use simple material equivalence, the rationale being that any comparatively simple, recursively correct and complete theory of meaning will never allow for the deduction of equivalences analogous to (16). But this claim strikes me as an implausible article of faith. Even if the monstrous complexity of adult English, compounded by the heterogeneous beliefs of the subject population, were to impose limitations on semantic theory that resulted in only legitimate equivalences, such is surely not the case for a primitive language with few kinds of sentences and only one speaker. Indeed, in a late footnote Davidson himself (1984: 26) acknowledges the need for regarding T-sentences as lawlike.

The second challenge to the necessity operator asks whether it's circular. For in the context of (15), doesn't "□" mean "it is analytically true that...", that is "it is true by virtue of *meaning* that..."? If our task is to eliminate the concept of meaning from the analytic framework, then we fail when we invoke analytic necessity! This matter merits close scrutiny, and I am not sure exactly what the best response to it is. For the present, I rest with my reply to the more general concern about circularity in Chapter 4.14.

Incidentally, there is a pragmatic asymmetry in the equivalence sign [probably due to topic-comment ordering; cf. Haiman (1978)]: the left-hand side represents the analysandum, the right-hand side the analysans. It is presumed that the left-hand side is what is being explained, and that the right-hand side is what is doing the explaining. This asymmetry, however, need not be formally stated in the analytic biconditional itself, for switching the order does not affect the purported validity of a given analysis one way or the other.

Although the simple formulation (A) refers to thinking, thinking is only one representative case provided for the sake of concreteness. My official formulation extends – with qualifications to be noted – to all mentalistic propositional attitudes, be they strictly cognitive, volitional, or affective (thinks, believes, judges, supposes, wonders, hopes, wants, intends, ...).

In addition, it includes perceptual propositional attitudes (sees, hears) and speech-act attitudes (says, states, asserts, asks, orders, ...).[2] Indeed I would go even further and say that semantic analysis may deal with *sub-propositional* attitudes too, that is any attitude whose object is less than a clause (think of, refer, call).

The propositional attitudes ordinarily take *that*-clauses or *whether*-clauses as direct objects rather than quotation clauses. (17) seems a little odd, (18) even odder:

(17) S thinks, "Grass is green."
(18) S believes, "Grass is green".

These sentences are well-formed and interpretable, however, if my account of quotation be right (Chap. 7). Besides, it's possible to stipulate technical uses of the ordinary propositional attitudes. In the case of belief, we might say that S believes the sentence "P" iff S holds a belief linguistically encoded by "P", S believes "P" iff S bears an accepting attitude toward "P", or S believes "P" iff S believes that "P" is true. At any rate, I take the ill-formedness of (18), if ill-formed it be, as an accidental defect of English that lies within our power to remedy as we build a meta-language.

The various psychological attitudes can be schematized by ψ, which yields a generalized form of (A):

(A') $S \psi \Phi \equiv S \psi P.$

The grammatical nature of Φ will constrain the range of possible attitudes ψ. If Φ is a declarative sentence, ψ must be selected from the set of declarative attitudes {thinks, believes, states ...}; if Φ is an interrogative sentence, ψ must be selected from the set of interrogative attitudes {wonders, asks, ... }; if Φ is an imperative sentence, ψ must be selected from the set of imperative attitudes {wants, orders, demands, ... }; if Φ is a term, ψ must be selected from the set of sub-propositional attitudes {thinks of, refers to, calls ... }. The choice of ψ in turn will dictate the form of P. If ψ is a declarative attitude, P will take the form of a *that*-clause; if ψ is an interrogative attitude, P will take the form of a *whether*-clause; if ψ is an imperative attitude, P will take the form "NP to VP"; if ψ is a sub-propositional attitude, P will take a sub-sentential form. The principles just sketched are illustrated below.

---

[2]   The term "propositional attitude" stems from Russell (1940). For what is both a dictionary of speech-act verbs and a contribution to theoretical semantics, see Wierzbicka (1987).

(19) S thinks "x is an oncologist" ≡ S thinks that x is a cancer specialist.
(20) S wonders "Is x an oncologist?" ≡ S wonders whether x is a cancer specialist.
(21) S advises x, "See an oncologist" → S advises x to see a cancer specialist.
(22) S refers to x as an "oncologist" → S refers to x as a cancer specialist.

There is an important difference, note, between the strictly mental attitudes in (19, 20) and the mental-behavioral attitudes in (21, 22). In the latter cases the analysis fails to hold from right to left. Consequently, my claim that ψ ranges over all sorts of attitudes must be qualified: while ψ ranges over mental propositional attitudes to produce complete biconditional analyses, ψ ranges over speech-act attitudes to produce unidirectional semi-analyses. The latter may be all that the theory of competence is responsible for, depending on how competence is ultimately made to link up with performance; they are, at any rate, a start. (A different tack would aim to restrict S somehow to those subjects who express, in L, their attitudes. The problem here is that this restriction is insufficient, since S may express an attitude in a variety of ways, given the existence of synonymy, even when the expression is limited to L.)

My principled motivation for allowing ψ to range as it does is that if meaning is tied up with thought – either as I think it is or as others, like Davidsonians, think it is – then surely it's implicated with other propositional attitudes too, and in similar ways. My practical motivation is that the generalized formulation works better than the original. For one, it allows for the semi-analysis of subsentential expressions as in (22). For another, it allows not only for (19) but also (23).

(23) S believes "x is an oncologist" ≡ S believes that x is a cancer specialist.

If (19) is valid, then surely (23) is too. For ease of exposition, however, from now on I shall usually restrict discussion to the case where ψ stands for "thinks".

Attitude ψ occurs twice in the attitudinal formula. On the left-hand side it represents an attitude toward an *expression* (understood as a form); on the right-hand side it represents an attitude toward a so-called *content*. Structurally, therefore, the attitudinal formula bears some resemblance to meaning statements like:

(24) "Sticky" means STICKY.

The resemblance is not surprising, given the common aim of meaning statements and attitudinal analyses.

It's possible to quote either an expression's form or an expression's content, and either an expression token or an expression type (Chap. 7.2iii). It is necessary, therefore, for me to specify how Φ is supposed to be understood. My position is that it depends on the purpose of our analysis. For instance, we can focus on "paper" either as a form that is open to multiple readings, or as a particular interpreted form-cum-content. In the former case we analyze the expression as (25), and in the latter case as, say, (26).

(25) S thinks "x read the paper" $\equiv$ (S thinks that x read the newspaper or S thinks that x read the academic article or S thinks that x read the sheet of paper).

(26) S thinks "x read the paper" $\equiv$ S thinks that x read the newspaper.

The full analysis (25) is demanded by linguistic theory, which aims to specify every legitimate reading of every possible expression. The truncated analysis (26) is appropriate in various practical contexts where the interlocutors are agreed that one particular reading is relevant to the discussion.

To summarize, I have elaborated upon the simple formulation (A) in five ways. First, the analytic biconditional (A) is but a subordinate component in the more complex analysis of linguistic understanding (10). Second, every analysis of language L is a claim only about speakers of L. (Here we either restrict L to an idiolect or we restrict S to ideal speakers.) Third, semantic analyses are true by virtue of the meaning equivalences that are offered and therefore involve some kind of analytic status as relativized to a language. Fourth, attitudinal analyses are not just about thinking but can be couched in terms of other attitudes, as schematized by ψ. (Getting things just right will require a detailed syntacto-semantic theory of mood.) Fifth, the analysandum of (A) involves a speaker's relationship to an expression form, not content. Taking these separate pieces together yields the following format for attitudinal semantics:

(A″) Σ understands utterance Φ in language L $\equiv$
    Σ understands that $(\forall$ S: S speaks L$) \, \Box \, (S \, \psi \Phi \equiv S \, \psi P)$.

As we shall see in later chapters, this formulation will need to be modified yet further in order to represent other complications of natural language. Those modifications, however, will represent but variations on the underlying theme as presented here.

2.2 The Propositional Attitudes

In the remainder of this section I would like to focus more on the heart of my analytic framework, the propositional attitudes, with an emphasis on belief and thought. To begin with, questions arise in connection with the distinction between occurrent and dispositional beliefs, and the similar distinction between explicit and tacit beliefs. Before turning to this page, did you or did you not think that fleas never play the harmonica? The question does not enjoy a clear-cut answer. But this equivocacy poses no problem for us, for we can easily stipulate that whichever understanding applies to the left-hand side of the analytic framework applies as well to the right-hand side. Another distinction that makes no difference is that between states and events. "Think" is ambiguous this way, denoting either an enduring state or the incipient entry into such a state. It does not matter how we understand this propositional attitude, so long as we take it the same way in both the analysandum and the analysans. This is one reason why the stative "believe", if it appears on the left-hand side, must be balanced by "believe" on the right; and why the event verb "judge", if it appears on the left-hand side, must be balanced by "judge" on the right.

In a related vein, there is the case of intellectual uncertainty. You might have no opinion, for instance, whether God exists. Although this seems to me to be a clear case of neither believing that God exists nor believing that God does not exist – that is it's a clear case of agnosticism as a neutral alternative to both theism and what I call positive atheism – others, such as William James, would insist otherwise. James, denying the possibility of neutral unbelief in "The Will to Believe" (at least sometimes as regards to religion), holds that the only options are full belief and full disbelief. Therefore the agnostic who says, "I don't know whether or not God exists" actually either believes in God or does not. Assuming that James is right, then, how do we determine the real belief of the agnostic? Although I don't think James's position is tenable, I do accept that in some cases the sincere profession "I don't know whether P or ¬P" is compatible with the speaker actually believing at least one, for first-person reports are fallible. However, any indeterminacy regarding what a subject believes is irrelevant to the purpose of semantic analysis. For suppose some particular analysis (27) is correct.

(27) S thinks $\Phi \equiv$ S thinks that P.

Then it doesn't matter whether S or anyone else can tell whether S in fact thinks that P; all that matters is that S would think that P if and only if S were to think Φ. And this is something that we can tell by establishing whether (27) holds in cases where beliefs are clear.

I conclude then that many of the problems surrounding our understanding of thinking (and propositional attitudes more generally) do not affect my program. Because attitudinal analyses refer to propositional attitudes twice, once in the analysandum and once in the analysans, some issues involving the mind cancel themselves out.

Not all problems drop out of the picture, however, partly because the left-hand and right-hand beliefs do differ from one another: on the left hand, "believe" is a relation to an expression, as given in some language, perhaps one foreign to us; and on the right hand, "believe" is a relation to an expression in use in the analyst's language. (When I speak of "believe" as a relation, I am not making any metaphysical claims. In particular, I am not making the popular metaphysical claim that belief is a relation to either a sentence or a proposition; the sententialist and propositionalist theories of mind, I am convinced, are both mistaken. Rather, I am making the prosaic claim that "believe" is a two-place predicate, and that in a complete grammatical sentence it combines with a subject on the one hand and an object on the other. I emphatically do not deduce the real structure of the external world from linguistic structure.) To repeat, there is a difference between the left-hand belief and the right-hand belief. Explicating it is a matter of some delicacy.

As it appears on the left-hand side of (A), belief might be taken as a disposition to utter a language-specific expression. Variations on this theme appear in Carnap (1947), Ryle (1949), and Sellars (1963), in Field (1978: 33ff) under the rubric "belief*", in De Sousa (1971) as "assent", and in Dennett (1978: 303ff) as "opinion". The basic idea is familiar, then, albeit undeveloped.

As it appears on the right-hand side of (A), the operative conception of belief is troublesome because it is entangled among a host of confusing theoretical contrasts:

(a) opaque versus transparent
(b) intensional versus extensional
(c) sense versus reference
(d) connotation versus denotation
(e) de dicto versus de re
(f) notional versus relational
(g) general versus specific
(h) by description versus by acquaintance
(i) sentential versus propositional
(j) attributive versus referential

Some of these contrasts seem to represent uncontroversial variation in terminology, as with (a, b) and also (e, f). In other cases the interrelationships are not at all clear. For instance, the distinction made in (e) appears to come into play only in opaque contexts, which isn't true for the distinction made in (j); yet some scholars have justifiably seen a connection between the two [e.g. Searle (1979b)].

The contrasts in (a–j) are related in that they each involve (I) a difference in existential import, and (II) a difference in substitutability of coreferential terms. As for (I), the de re construal of (28) presupposes that I have a sister, whereas de dicto it carries no such significance.

(28) Kris thinks my sister is a spy.

Similarly, if the subject noun phrase in (29) is interpreted referentially then it necessarily refers to something that exists, whereas if (29) is interpreted attributively then it does not.

(29) The man in the corner drinking a martini is my friend.

As for (II), if (30) is construed transparently then it is equivalent to (31) when also construed transparently, whereas the opaque readings of (30) and (31) do not entail each other.

(30) Lois Lane thinks that Superman can fly.
(31) Lois Lane thinks that Clark Kent can fly.

With distinctions (I) and (II) in mind, it is clear that the attitudinal framework requires that the explanans be construed opaquely/intensionally/notionally. (I) Our solipsistic methodology demands that semantics have no bearing on metaphysics. Analyses of the meaning of "sister", "spy", "Superman", and so forth cannot commit us to the existence or non-existence of sisters, spies, Superman, etc. (II) We cannot accept substitution of coreferential terms on pain of accepting:

(32) S thinks "the largest holder of private property ought to pay property taxes" ≡ S thinks that the Catholic Church ought to pay property taxes.

Since the right-hand side fails to gloss the left side, analyses are not to be construed transparently.

In order for an analytic biconditional to represent the meaning of an expression, it must not only be true as (33) is, but meaning-preserving, like (34).

(33) (∀S: S speaks German) (S thinks "das Wasser ist naß" ≡ S thinks
that grass is green).

(34) (∀S: S speaks German) (S thinks "das Wasser ist naß" ≡ S thinks
that water is wet).

But now the question arises as to just what counts as meaning-preservation.
What, for instance, can legitimately go into the right-hand slot in (35)?

(35) (∀S: S speaks German) (S thinks "das Wasser ist naß" ≡ S thinks
that _____ is wet).

Would "H_2O" make (35) analytically true? Would "melted snow and other
instances of the same kind of substance"?

The answer, I suggest, is doubly contextual and furthermore a matter of
degree, and a multidimensional one at that. In the first place, we need to
consider S's context, the context of the original German expression. Who
uttered it, and why? If we are analyzing a token of "das Wasser" that was
made in this century by someone cognizant of elementary chemistry, then it
would be more justifiable, though not completely so, to accept "H_2O" than
if we were analyzing a token of "das Wasser" made prior to the time of
Lavoisier. In the second place, we need to consider Σ's context, the context
of the analyst. Who is conducting the translation, and why? Whether the
purpose is poetic, scientific, or commercial will affect our decision. Suppose,
for instance, we want an adequate analysis of the German meaning in order
to telegram it to someone who does not know German. Then it might not
matter if we used "H_2O", and it may well save money.

It's easy to find examples where "H_2O" is an adequate translation of "das
Wasser", but only in highly unusual cases might it ever be the best. The usual
translation is "water", but there is no *perfect* translation: even "water" fails
in some contexts where rhyme matters. Or imagine that Martians possessed
a molecular description of water – something intensionally isomorphic to
"H_2O" – yet lacked a corresponding colloquial term. Then their best translation for "das Wasser" would be farther from perfect. Similar remarks can
be made for terrestrial languages, where political, religious, and culinary
terms rarely translate well across civilizations (that's why English borrows
so many words like "raj", "ayatollah", and "sushi"); also terms from
science and technology do not translate well into the languages of prelit-
erate societies (how would you translate "capillary" into a language whose
speakers are ignorant of microscopic anatomy?); even translating basic
perceptual terms is problematic (Hopi, Japanese, Somali, and many other
languages each uses a single basic term for green and blue).

That said, if we can understand a foreign language at all then we can find at least one imperfect though adequate context-specific translation, and once we have that translation we can use it to ascribe an appropriate belief to the original speaker. (The question arises: since we are dealing with translation anyhow, why don't we drop the "S thinks" frame? The answer is twofold. First, embedding under attitudes is necessary for getting analyses right, as Part Two will show. Second, the attitudinal framework purports to reveal the structure of meaningfulness, just as Davidson's truth-theoretic framework purports to. To ask for the relevance of "S thinks" within my paradigm is akin to asking for the relevance of "is true" within Davidson's.)

The distinction between de dicto and de re beliefs, as traditionally understood, is now widely and rightfully regarded as untenable.[3] If the other contrasts on the list (a–j) share the same lot as de dicto and de re, then one might question my reliance on that kind of distinction. But my position is doubly safe. For one thing, my gloss on attitudinal analyses does not rely on the opaque/transparent distinction. Though I do rely on some understanding of opacity or intensionality, I make no use of transparency or extensionality – after all, I oppose referentialism. (Apparent transparency, I would argue, is just the case of opacity on the part of the ascriber.) For another thing, the attack on the de dicto, de re distinction must be understood for what it is. The arguments are compelling if you construe "belief" realistically: regardless of whether we ascribe to S a belief de dicto or de re, S possesses a single unambiguous brain state, objectively speaking. What differs is our way of reporting it. Yet, since there are distinct ways to report a mental state, if "belief" is understood as the subjective imposition as given by our reports then there does remain a difference between de dicto and de re.

The most difficult problem for my program lies in knowing just which attitudinal biconditionals are correct. I think the problem is not fatal, however, as is the corresponding problem of ignorance for TC semantics (Chap. 2). In the first place, as an opponent of truth-conditionalism I reject the truth-conditional reading of equivalence. Instead of understanding "P if and only if Q" as a line in a truth-table or as a rule that moves us between P and Q while necessarily preserving truth, we might take the biconditional as a *default* rule that preserves assertability. (Whenever possible, however, I prefer a conservative reanalysis of equivalence, one that maintains a crisp live-together, die-together relation between the biconditional components.)

3   Searle (1979b: §4), Dennett (1982), Stich (1986), Grandy (1986), Bach (1987: §9.4), Fauconnier (1997); cf. Lewis (1981), Marcus (1981, 1990).

Aside from the significance of "if and only if", the (TC) and (A) schemas differ in their appeals to mental states. As a result, I shall argue, attitudinal equivalences enjoy plausibility where TC equivalences do not.

To begin with, in the case of vagueness we disagree over truth-conditions because we disagree over how to reconcile two conflicting intuitions, namely that truth is bivalent and that vague predicates are not. In contrast, the intuition that vague predicates are polyvalent matches the intuition that belief both comes in degrees and is indeterminate. By talking about degree-of-belief we end up with formulas that are intended to be uncontroversial:

> (36) S thinks "x is bald" to the extent that S thinks x is missing hair.
> (37) The more S thinks "x is bald", the more hair S thinks x is missing, and vice versa.

The controversy is not over the acceptability of (36) and (37) but over their role in the theory of meaning: TC semanticists will deny that (36, 37) offer analyses of linguistic vagueness, insisting that they are analyses only of degree-of-thought; mentalists, countering that the analysis of meaning is always the analysis of the mind, will regard the form of (36) or (37) as a key to understanding scalar vagueness.

In the case of mood, TC semanticists are torn between their theoretical commitment to seeing truth-conditions everywhere and the ordinary intuition that interrogatives lack truth-value. As a result, collectively, they don't know what to say about non-declaratives. In contrast, the following seems to be right so far as it goes:

> (38) S wonders "Did the cow jump over the moon?" $\equiv$ S wonders whether the cow jumped over the moon.

Again, the issue is not whether (38) is correct. It is correct, the only question being whether it conveys the significance or meaning of the English inter-rogative construction. If you knew the meta-language, in this case that which includes "wonders", "cow", "jumped", and "moon", and if you knew nothing of "did" or subject-aux inversion, would you learn the significance of "did" and subject-aux inversion from (38)? The attitudinal semanticist answers *yes*.

Likewise for the attitudinal analyses of Part Two, where the proffered biconditionals are not expected to be tendentious. Attitude-conditions are in fact known for adequately specified contexts, the controversial part being only whether they explicate meaning.

3.   Matters of Interpretation

The question presses, How do we determine whether an analytic biconditional holds? More especially, how do we assign so-called content to the
propositional attitudes? My own provisional view is that belief is an instru-
mental construct determined by the functional-holistic considerations of an
interpreter. (Belief-ascription is therefore very much like translation, which
lends further support to attitudinal semantics.) My interpretationism has
been heavily influenced by Quine (1960), Davidson (1984), and especially
Dennett (1987), but departs from theirs in notable ways. Most importantly,
I reject the principle of charity (henceforth "Charity"). This point is crucial,
for Charity forges a link between belief and truth that threatens to collapse
together truth-conditions and belief-conditions (Chap. 4.3).

Section 3.1 makes more precise exactly what it is that I reject, Section 3.2
argues that Charity is false to the extent that it is even clear, Section 3.3
rebuts arguments in support of Charity, and Section 3.4 speculatively
concludes with consequences for traditional Christianity, animism, and
container-content dualism as a theory of mind. Finally, Section 3.5 turns
to a very different view, due to Christopher Gauker, that also threatens my
project. Even though it is not so well know as Charity, it is more promising
and so deserves attention.[4]

3.1   Versions of Charity

The principle of charity takes many different forms. To begin with, it
comes in different degrees of strength.

(39) MINIMAL CHARITY: If S is an intentional system then at least some
of S's beliefs must be true.

(40) PREPONDERANT CHARITY: If S is an intentional system then most
(more than half) of S's beliefs must be true.

(41) REGULAR CHARITY: If S is an intentional system then nearly all of
S's beliefs must be true; true beliefs are the rule, false beliefs the
rare exception.

(42) TOTAL CHARITY: If S is an intentional system then all of S's beliefs
must be true.

---

[4]   Any rejection of Charity not only undermines one argument for truth-conditionalism, it
has other consequences as well. For instance, it undermines the anti-skeptical argument of
Davidson (1977a, 1995), and it undermines the pretences of a priori philosophy [as noticed
by Baghramian (2004: 259)].

Variations on Minimal Charity are held by Putnam (1975), Cherniak (1986), and Stich (1990: Chap. 2). Variants of Regular Charity are held by Lewis (1974), Davidson (1984), Dennett (1987), Travis (2000: 64), Jackman (2003), and Ludwig (2004). Although Regular Charity is the vaguest of the lot – its defenders never quantify just what fraction of S's beliefs must be true in order for S to count as an intentional system, and would in fact resist posing the question in this way – it nonetheless is popular [Henderson (1996) calls it "the received view", the few critics including Baghramian (2004: Chap. 8) and Sorensen (2004)]. Total Charity is not held by anyone, so far as I know, though later on we shall have to wonder why.

The foregoing principles, formulated in terms of *true* beliefs, express the ur-version of Charity, call it Verity. Variants of Verity refer instead to *rational* beliefs and to rational systems of belief-desire-action [held for instance by Cherniak, Stich, Cohen (1981), and Devitt (1991: §10.5)].

   (43) RATIONALITY: If S is an intentional system then S must be somewhat/
        mostly/usually/entirely rational.

We also need to distinguish between objective, "transcendent" forms of Charity, which ascribe beliefs that are in fact true or rational, and *projective* or "immanent" forms, which ascribe those beliefs that interpreters hold or would hold if they were in S's position.

   (44) HUMANITY: If S is an intentional system relative to you then some/
        most/all of S's beliefs must be those that you would have if you were
        in S's position.

The principle of humanity is held by Quine (1960: 219), Grandy (1973), Davidson (1975), Harman (1990), and Stich (1990: §2.3.1). Verity, Rationality, and Humanity, one might very well argue, are linked, so that they all stand or fall together.[5]

In addition to considering the different forms of Charity – which vary on the dimensions of quantity (Minimal, Preponderant, Regular, Total) and quality (Verity, Rationality, Humanity) – we need to consider the different roles that Charity might play in the theory of interpretation. On the one hand, the principle of charity may be taken as a description of interpretive practice; on the other, it may be taken as normative.

---

[5]   For one argument to the linkage thesis, consider the omniscient interpreter of Davidson (1977a, 1983).

(45) DESCRIPTION: Interpreters *do* ascribe beliefs according to some principle of charity.

(46) PRESCRIPTION: Interpreters *should* ascribe beliefs according to some principle of charity.

Now what is the case for (46)? Why think that interpreters should accept Charity in any of its prescriptive forms? One possible motivation is *prudential*: interpreters should accept Charity because Charity provides a cognitively efficient means of representing other people's intentionality. The purer motivation is genuinely veridical: interpreters should accept Charity because Charity yields knowledge of truths.

(47) PRUDENTIAL CHARITY: Finite interpreters like ourselves should exercise Charity because doing so saves cognitive resources.

(48) GENUINE CHARITY: Interpreters should accept Charity because every intentional system does in fact possess beliefs that are somewhat/mostly/usually/entirely true, rational, or like ours.

So far as I can tell, every proponent of Charity holds that Charity gets at the truth. Davidson (1973b) and Lewis (1974) represent Charity as a priori and necessarily valid; Davidson (1977a) holds that an omniscient interpreter, one for whom prudential considerations would presumably not exist, would still exercise Charity; and Dennett insists on the non-relativity of belief-ascription, which again means that prudential concerns are not at issue.

My own position admits to Charity some merit when it is construed either as description or as prudential prescription. Indeed it might even be necessary regarding human cognition if the Simulation Theory is correct [Gordon (1986), Goldman (1989)]. However, I oppose genuine Charity. Just as it is the hallmark of childlike egocentricity to assume that everyone else knows, believes, and values as one's own self does, so too the more sophisticated and qualified versions of Verity, Rationality, and Humanity are mistaken. To make my case, I shall first argue that (genuine) Charity is untenable and then address why it is so. My explanation shall then lead to some implications for our understanding of the nature of belief, and of the ascription of propositional attitudes more generally.

3.2   Charity is Untenable

Charity simply does not seem to be a conceptual truth. In his essay on liars, Montaigne mentions a lad "whom I have never heard to utter a single truth, even when it would have been to his advantage". We have no difficulty understanding Montaigne's thought, despite its incoherence according to Charity, and indeed we have no difficulty believing that such pathological liars may literally exist.

But there is another argument as well. If you subscribe to Preponderant Charity then you think that most of one's beliefs must be true. (If you subscribe to Preponderant Rationality then you think that most of one's inferences must be valid, or that most of one's beliefs must be consistent, or that most of one's actions follow from one's beliefs and desires.) And if you think that most of one's beliefs must be true or most inferences valid, you must think that one has a number of true beliefs or valid inferences N and a number of false beliefs or invalid inferences M, such that N>M. But the individuation and counting of beliefs and inferences is not only indeterminate but so vague as to make M and N incommensurable. Therefore to claim that true beliefs outnumber false beliefs seems to be fishy from the get-go, even irresponsible.

It's not just that we lack a generally agreed upon criterion for counting beliefs. We don't even have one on offer. Furthermore, the possibilities that do suggest themselves fail to serve the charity advocate's interests. Let's consider a few.

(i) At the parsimonious end, we might say that our beliefs are exhausted by our explicit and occurrent beliefs. Aside from the worry that there are no explicit beliefs [Dennett (1987: 55ff)], this view mistakenly denies that (49) was one of your beliefs while you were reading the previous page.

(49) Beijing is the capital of China.

In fact, the parsimonious view would seem to suggest that at any one time you typically have at most one belief. In that case, if most of your beliefs at any one time are true, then *all* of your beliefs at any one time would have to be true, in which case Minimal, Preponderant, and Regular Charity all tend toward Total Charity. Yet Total Charity is not what charity proponents advocate. Look at it another way: you could never have a single false occurrent belief, given the parsimonious view, for in that case all of your beliefs would be false.

(ii) Alternatively, at the liberal end, we might say that beliefs include implicit and dispositional beliefs. But if we count implicit beliefs, then those who know the basic axioms of mathematics would know all mathematical theorems, which I take to be a reductio. More damaging for the charity advocate, the liberal view entails that we possess an infinite number of beliefs. If we have a single true belief then, taking its logical consequences, we would have an infinite number of true beliefs; and if we have a single false belief then, taking its logical consequences, we would have an infinite number of false beliefs. Unless we had nothing but true beliefs or nothing but false beliefs, therefore, we would have an *equal* number of true and false beliefs.

(iii) The key is to find some middle position between the parsimonious and liberal ends. We might say, for instance, that beliefs are constituted by explicit beliefs plus occurrent beliefs plus those beliefs that *immediately* follow. Unfortunately, this middle position too results in an infinity of beliefs. For consider V_iP, which schematizes i many disjunctions of P. If you explicitly or occurrently believe that the schema $\forall i\ (V_iP)$ holds for some proposition P, then you also believe that V_1P, i.e. PvP; and V_2P, i.e. PvPvP; and V_3P, i.e. PvPvPvP... To be sure, as i gets large, the number of iterations will not and cannot be explicitly represented. But explicitness, according to criterion (iii), is not necessary for beliefhood.

(iv) We might deny that "PvP" and "PvPvP" represent distinct beliefs; rejecting the sententialist theory of mind in favor of a simple propositional theory, we could say that they are two representations of the same belief because they pick out the same set of possible worlds. But this position, because mathematical truths hold in all worlds, means that if you believe one mathematical truth then you believe all mathematical truths – which I still take as a reductio. Nor does it help to appeal to structured propositions, which would return us to the problem in (iii).

(v) Finally, suppose we limit the principle of charity to "core" beliefs, for example to foundational or to perception-based beliefs. Perception, for current purposes, is to be understood non-factively, so that "S sees a dog" entails not (50) but (51).

(50) S stands in a certain causal relation to a dog, thus entailing that some dog exists.

(51) S stands in some solipsistically describable state, for example S is having the sort of qualitative experience that S would have if S really were in a certain causal relation to a dog, or S's retinas are in such-and-such a state.

If we construed perception factively, then our delimited principle of charity – "If S is an intentional system then most of S's perceptual beliefs must be true" – would simply amount to the claim that most factive beliefs are true – i.e. that most true beliefs are true – which is vacuous. It would also make Davidson's charity-based anti-skepticism argument question-begging.

Non-factively construed, however, criterion (v) avoids both vacuity and the infinity problem which plagues (ii, iii, iv). Yet it invites the following counter-example. Imagine a fervent theist who believes not only that God exists, but that the most important fact about anything is that it exists by the grace of God. [Schlesinger (1994: 91) writes, "The most important task is to do everything in one's power to adjust and attune one's soul so that it has the capacity of fully resonating with the celestial [divine] radiance ... such a view is bound to permeate every act and every thought of its adherent."] Thus, for each atomic proposition P that the fervent theist believes, the fervent theist also believes that God made P the case. In contrast, for each atomic P that the fervent atheist believes, the fervent atheist also believes that P is true naturalistically. At this point in our reckoning, then, half of the theist's beliefs are false as judged by the atheist. In addition we can safely assume that at least a few of any mortal's mundane atomic beliefs are false, thus making the fervent theist's total belief system mostly false.

Of course the defender of Charity might try to separate beliefs from their logical consequences. On this view, the theist believes atomic propositions and also the complex proposition (52), but does not believe many of the instantiations of (52).

(52) ∀P (If P is true then P is true by the grace of God).

In reply, I note first that it strikes me as extraordinarily artificial. If we deny that the immediate logical consequences of our attitudes are themselves attitudes, unless they are consciously apprehended by us, then I must say that until two minutes ago I did not realize that sport cars contribute to air pollution, even though I frequently think that cars pollute. Second, this line misses the point that, for the fervent theist, instances of (52) may count not as deductions but as foundational beliefs and as perceptual beliefs. They are foundational insofar as the fervent theist will hold to theism come what may; for the utterly faithful, the truth-values assigned to theistic statements are unrevisable. And they can be perceptual in the non-factive sense just laid out: "God sustains me in pouring out His creative love into me" and "This flower was created by God" are reported as examples of perceptual experiences by Alston (1983: 3, 36, 43), (1991: 43), and Plantinga (1983: 80). For some theists, it seems that every mundane belief is conjoined by the (non-factive) perceptual belief that God is wonderful. Whether or not this is actually the case, it's surely conceptually possible, in which case Preponderant Charity is untenable.

Advocates of charity tend to protect their claims by limiting their doctrine to "core" cases or by introducing ceteris paribus clauses or defeasibility clauses. But such maneuvering must trace a fine line between the surrender of Charity on the one hand, and insistence on Total Charity on the other. For if beliefs may go wrong where going wrong is explicable, as in the case of religious indoctrination, then it looks like beliefs may go completely wrong wherever the right story might be told (e.g. involving a Cartesian demon). The easiest way to avoid such an anti-Charity result is probably to allow the ascription of explicable error *only as a last resort*. But the ascription of explicable error is never a last resort, for it is *always* possible to ascribe nothing but true beliefs to any given subject. Thus if you are going to defend Charity at all, it seems to me, you ought to defend Total Charity.

To recapitulate, the charity advocate must both identify and motivate some manner of individuating beliefs which results in there being more true beliefs than false beliefs. So far I have illustrated the unlikelihood of achieving the right kind of delineation. Even if we granted that it were possible, however, the second part of the task, justifying it, would remain. In short, the principle of charity is, on the face of it, implausible. Human beings are separated from each other by all sorts of profound and systematic ideological dissent (or at the very least they could be), but this does not keep them from being intentional systems.[6]

3.3   The Case for Charity is Untenable

Charity is often based on a panglossian appeal to natural selection. If beliefs were not mostly true, so the claim goes, people would not survive; people obviously do survive, so the enthymeme continues; therefore people have mostly true beliefs [Quine (1969: 126), Bennett (1976: 48), Fodor (1981: 121), Dennett (1987: 33)]. This evolutionary argument does not have legs, however, because its leading premise is a naked, unsubstantiated assertion [Gauker (1986: 3), Stich (1990: Chap. 3), Devitt (1991), Plantinga (1993: Chap. 12)]. What's more, the leading premise *can't* be substantiated, for the reason given in the previous section: there is no metric for beliefs. Because the evolutionary argument is fishy, the principle of charity reeks.

In order to identify the correct criterion for the individuation of belief, we need to consider the significance of belief. *Why* do we speak of beliefs? A leading answer to this question is that beliefs possess the property of making behavior *intelligible*. The answer to "Why did S do that?" is sometimes facilitated by the intentional stance, where beliefs and desires

---

[6]   Another consideration against the case for Charity is that our theory of truth, like Euclidean geometry, is conceivably not precisely descriptive of reality (Nozick 2001: 52). Hence it's hardly a *conceptual* truth that most beliefs are true.

are holistically and functionally ascribed to a subject along with the sort of belief-desire psychology illustrated in the following practical syllogism.

> (PS) PRACTICAL SYLLOGISM, STANDARD VERSION
>   S believes that state-of-affairs P obtains.
>   S desires that state-of-affairs Q obtain.
>   S believes that action A would effect a change from state P to state Q.
>   Therefore, ceteris paribus, S performs A.

Assuming that (PS) provides for the individuation of belief, a proposition counts as a belief only if it plays the right role in an appropriate (rational) belief-desire-action economy.

At first sight, the intelligibility argument appears to take the following form.

(a) If human beliefs are mostly true then human actions are mostly intelligible.

(b) Human actions are mostly intelligible.

(c) Therefore, human beliefs are mostly true.

Premise (a), however, is questionable, given that (PS) is loaded with a ceteris paribus clause; premise (b) is untenable for reasons analogous to those given in the previous section (just as there is no metric for belief, there is no metric for action); and the inference to (c), as it stands, commits the fallacy of asserting the antecedent. To repair the fallacy, we could reconstrue the argument from intelligibility as an inference to the best explanation. This requires changing the first premise to "that human beliefs be mostly true is the best explanation of the intelligibility of human actions". However, I know of no reason to assert this, and I can think of more than one reason to reject it. In particular, predictions based on rational psychology do not require that beliefs be true.

In order to demonstrate this, I propose to examine an exceedingly simple case, that of a thermostat [my inspiration here comes from Dennett (1987)]. Suppose that thermostat θ turns the furnace on whenever the temperature falls to 74°. Then using (PS) we could predict the behavior of θ by ascribing to it any of the following.

(53) The belief that the temperature has just fallen to 74°, the desire to maintain the temperature at 75°, and the belief that turning the furnace on would change the temperature from 74° to 75°.

(54) The belief that the temperature has just fallen to 174°, the desire to maintain the temperature at 175°, and the belief that turning the furnace on would change the temperature from 174° to 175°.

(55) The belief that a burglar has just broken in, the desire to thwart burglars, and the belief that the furnace "on" switch activates an alarm, thus scaring off burglars.

(56) Ad infinitum.

Evidently there is no fact of the matter. *Any* ascription of belief, so long as it is matched by the right collateral beliefs and desires, will correctly predict and render intelligible θ's behavior. (In the case of false-belief systems such as (54), satisfaction of desire will always be thwarted. Nonetheless we can coherently imagine such systems tragically desiring, believing, and exercising rationality, and we can predict their behavior from adopting the intentional stance without adopting any principle of charity whatsoever.[7])

This argument extends to the ascription of linguistic content as well. Suppose that θ has a broken read-out which always reports the temperature as being 10° higher than it actually is. Suppose further that θ turns the furnace on whenever the real temperature drops below 65° (whenever the read-out registers less than "75°"). Then how would you describe its behavior? You might say:

(57) It wants to keep the temperature at 75°, but unfortunately it fails because it mistakenly thinks that the house is 10° warmer than it actually is.

Alternatively you might say:

(58) The thermostat wants to keep the house at 65°, and it succeeds.

The former line of reasoning might be more natural if the owner of the thermostat, unaware that the read-out is broken, sets the gauge with the intention of keeping the house at 75°; the latter line might be more natural if the owner knowingly translates the read-out into true reports about the temperature. The important point to notice, however, is that neither description is more adequate than the other; neither interpretation scheme

---

[7] Interpretationism and the indeterminacy thesis thus carry grave moral implications. If happiness is defined as preference-satisfaction, or if tragedy is defined as the constant thwarting of good or great desires, then the life of *every* intentional system is both happy (interpreted in some scheme) and tragic (interpreted in another). There is no absolute fact of the matter, and it all depends on the assessment of interpreters other than the subject.

enjoys objective support. We could subscribe arbitrarily to either one and be able to predict θ's behavior equally well. In fact, we could subscribe to infinitely many other exotic descriptions, such as "The thermostat gets suicidal whenever it thinks the temperature drops to freezing; it believes that it's freezing whenever the read-out registers 64°; and it believes that it might succeed in killing itself if it can turn the furnace on, which might cause the house to burn down".

This argument about the indeterminacy of belief and desire can be extended yet further to an argument about the indeterminacy of rationality. For θ's behavior can be understood equally well by ascribing to it either (53) conjoined with (PS) *or* (53′) conjoined with (PS′).

(53′) The belief that the temperature has just fallen to 174°, the desire to maintain the temperature at 175°, and the belief that turning the furnace on would *prevent* the temperature from rising to 175°.

(PS′) PRACTICAL SYLLOGISM, NON-STANDARD VERSION
    S believes that state-of-affairs P obtains.
    S desires that state-of-affairs Q obtain.
    S believes that action A, under condition P, would guarantee that Q *not* obtain.
    Therefore, ceteris paribus, S performs A.

Charity advocates generally insist that beliefs are mostly true and that belief-systems are mostly rational. If belief is understood as whatever plays a certain functional role in belief-desire psychology, however, then we can see from (53′) and (PS′) that such insistence is ill-founded. Neither Verity nor Rationality is empirically licensed.

One might object to (53′, PS′) on the grounds that, though they jointly *predict* θ's behavior, they don't *explain* it or render it intelligible. But what does intelligibility amount to? This is a vexed question in the philosophy of science. Operating within the empiricist strictures of this project, however, we must cash it out in terms of prediction, retrodiction, and observation. Thus, quantum theory may or may not "explain" quantum phenomena in the sense of making it intelligible to a human being whose normal perceptual experience is limited to macro-sized events and who has been acculturated by the various deterministic ideas of Greek fate, Christian predestinationism, Newtonian physics, etc.; but surely quantum theory explains quantum phenomena in the sense that it is empirically adequate, giving precise and accurate statistical predictions. If a phenomenon is unintelligible in some human sense, yet rigorously obeys precise laws, then that is a reason for questioning not the adequacy of the laws but the adequacy of our own intelligence. What I am suggesting, then, is that if a theory achieves complete empirical success in a given domain, then that theory may be the only one we need for that domain.

Short of such a hardline attitude, there's a further reason for saying that the ascription of (PS′) renders intelligible θ's "actions": assuming (PS′) in the background, the question "Why did θ activate the furnace when it did?" can by answered by saying "Because it wanted to keep the temperature at 75°, and it happened to believe that turning the furnace on would keep the temperature from rising above 75°." This fits perfectly the deductive-nomological model of explanation. (To deny that we have a DN explanation here, on the grounds that DN explanations require true premises whereas my explanation is premised on falsehoods, begs the question.) Of course you might press further and ask why θ operates according to the strange rule (PS′) in the first place, but the situation is entirely analogous to what happens in ordinary psychological explanation. If I ask "Why did S do so-and-so?" and you answer with an elliptical explanation, one that relies on the sane Practical Syllogism (PS), then I could demand to know why S operates according to (PS). But such a demand changes the topic, for it no longer seeks an explanation for S's behavior, it now wants an explanation for S's mental processes. Furthermore, I see no reason to think that explaining why one system operates according to (PS) might be any easier than explaining why another operates according to (PS′).

I conclude that the intelligibility argument for Charity, and proposed variations on it, are unacceptable.

3.4 Some Implications

Now you might object that thermostats do not really constitute intentional systems. We might speak metaphorically, saying that they "think" and "want", but this is merely loose talk. Of course I agree that thermostats do not enjoy such qualitative mental lives as we do. Nonetheless I believe that our consideration of thermostats can serve an instructive purpose. To begin with, our ascription of mentality to thermostats, even if it is merely metaphorical, indicates our conviction that thermostats possess structures analogous to those of real minds (for without analogical resemblance metaphor is meaningless). I would go even further and argue that ascriptions like (57) are literally true, or at least as true as any ascription of mentality can be. They are not creative literary tropes but are the *most natural*, most mundane, most straightforward ways to describe the facts of the matter. The alternative to *my* way of describing the read-out – "it says that the temperature is 10° higher than it actually is" – might be "it displays numerals which correspond in *our* language to a number that is 10° higher than the temperature actually is"; this is worse than inelegant, it's pathological.

Note that, under this view, *all* systems are intentional. The behavior of an object that is stationary relative to its immediate environment, for example a rock, can be thought of as operating under the desire "I want to just sit back and enjoy the scenery", the belief "If I don't do anything then I'll just sit back and enjoy the scenery", and (PS). Similarly the moon could be thought of as having the desire "I want to comply with the laws of motion" and the belief "If I orbit the earth, I will comply with the laws of motion".

Yet we ordinarily refuse to regard inanimate objects as intentional systems (although ancients and other animists have no hesitation in doing so!). Indeed, Western tradition, rooted in anthropocentric religion, also refuses to regard lower animals as possessing intentional states. Resistance to the idea that thermostats can think and want, I believe, derives from conceiving of thought and desire as necessarily bound up with the ability to grow and learn, the ability to feel, and being a complex animal. But to bind these disparities together is as mistaken as thinking that only the feathered can fly. Another reason for ascriptional stinginess, I suggest, is pragmatic. The belief-desire theory of behavior, as applied to human beings, is the simplest one available that is also successfully predictive. Therefore human beings are regarded without hesitation as intentional systems. In contrast, the belief-desire theory of behavior as applied to inanimate objects like the moon is more complex than mechanistic theories. Indeed, the belief-desire explanation of lunar behavior in the previous paragraph makes explicit reference to the laws of mechanics, and thus contains the laws of mechanics as a component. Thus, it generally makes no practical sense to use intentionalist theory when a simpler mechanist theory is at hand.[8] Finally, the belief-desire theory is sometimes applied to things like cows and computers, and sometimes withheld. Perhaps it is withheld by individuals who assume that cow behavior can in principle be predicted by mechanist theories (even though no such theories currently exist), and perhaps it is applied by individuals who would reject such a possibility. Other factors, however, include the moral status that one is willing to extend to cows, and the level of intimacy or affection that one feels for cows.

If this be correct, then thermostats really do have beliefs and desires as much as any person does. It's just that it's almost always pointless to talk

---

[8]   Interestingly, however, physics professors frequently use intentional (and masculinist) idioms in describing the behavior of inanimate objects ("when this guy here is positively charged, he wants to move away from that guy there").

about such beliefs and desires because it is more practical to talk mechanistically. (Note: we say that thermostats can *sense* the temperature.) Likewise for dogs, cats, and horses. When I say that a dog knows where it buried its bone, I am not speaking metaphorically – I literally mean something to the effect that the dog has true warranted belief. It's true by hypothesis, it counts as a belief given its functional role in successful belief-desire explanations, and it is warranted insofar as the dog's beliefs are based on reliable memory, perception, and whatnot.

Yet there is a powerful tradition opposing what I have just said, according to which infrahuman animals lack beliefs because they lack language [a motif in Davidson, e.g. (2001)]. This position would find support if belief P were identified with the disposition to assert P. But of course the dispositional analysis – although operationally useful insofar as we rely so much on what others say in order to know what others think – is unacceptable.

Nonetheless, I think there *is* a connection between belief and language, and furthermore that language is *necessary* for belief. Instead of saying with the traditionalist that X requires language in order for X to have beliefs, however, I would propose that some interpreting subject S requires language in order for X (either the same as S or different) to be ascribed beliefs. This is not to say:

(59) X has belief $P \equiv$ there is some S who ascribes to X the belief that P.

This formulation expresses a kind of relativism, for if two subjects S_1 and S_2 respectively ascribe to X beliefs P and $\neg$P, then X would believe both P and $\neg$P; and furthermore, if S_1 and S_2 were bright enough, they would both recognize that X believed both P and $\neg$P. Now while it is possible for one to hold contradictory beliefs, such does not follow from there simply being contradictory interpretations available. Therefore it would be better to say:

(60) S thinks "X has belief P" $\equiv$ S ascribes to X belief P.

Because our recognition that someone ascribes a given belief to X does not require us to ascribe the same belief, my approach, already methodologically solipsistic, is subjectivist. However, the subjectivism of (60) – more precisely, the kind of subjectivism that one is committed to in holding that attitude-conditions like (60) displace truth-conditional characterizations of belief – does not entail relativism in the form of (59).

Thus, dogs have beliefs because we say dogs have beliefs, and we say dogs have beliefs because dog-beliefs form part of a calculus that *we* have constructed for dealing with dog behavior. It follows that the beliefs of X are not *contents* of X; regarding mental states, or at least ascriptions of mental state, content-container dualism is mistaken. Finally, since there is no more to beliefs than belief ascriptions, beliefs depend on verbalizing subjects – their existence does require the existence of language, though not in the way that tradition imagines.

To summarize, if belief is identified by its role in belief-desire psychology then a number of noteworthy theses ensue. First, it is perfectly intelligible to ascribe mostly false beliefs to an intentional system, or even entirely false beliefs; thus the principle of charity is wrong. Second, animals have beliefs, contrary to the Christo-Cartesian traditions of Western society. Third, it sometimes makes sense to ascribe beliefs to inanimate beings; thus the beliefs of animists, surprisingly, enjoy justification. And fourth, the indeterminacy of belief-ascription, as exemplified by the likes of (53–55) and even (53′), suggests a kind of irrealism about belief which may in turn be expressed by (60) and by the slogan that rejects container-content dualism as a metaphor of the mind.

As indicated at the outset, my functional-holistic interpretationist views are provisional; the preceding paragraph is one big hypothetical. What's more important is that regardless of whether we accept interpretationism or not, determining the soundness of a detailed theory of structural and lexical meaning is clearly a difficult matter that will require a great deal of integration into our assumptions about the beliefs and desires of other language-users. This is work that attitudinal and TC semantics equally have yet to do, and no failure on my part makes attitudinal semantics any worse off than TC theory.

3.5   "Contents" and "Containers"

Philosophers frequently take mental and linguistic *content* as their undefined starting point. What can they mean? It seems to me that if x is literally a content then, analytically, x must be inside some container y. So if x is mental content then the mind must be a container, and if x is linguistic content then words must be containers. But minds are not relevant containers, for either a mind is just a nervous system, in which case its contents are neurons and such, or they are not things at all, and are to be understood adverbially or syncategorematically. Likewise words are not relevant containers, for either a word is just an acoustic blast, or a psychological correlate thereof, or a theoretical abstraction. I can only conclude that standard talk about content may be intended figuratively, although I am not sure, and I can only regret that those who use the term rarely if ever explain it.

"Propositional content", I gather, is a wordy way of saying "proposition", another rarely defined term.[9] I take it that the content of a belief, like a platonic proposition, is an entity that multiple believers can stand in appropriate relation to. In other words, I take it that serious talk of content commits one to a theory of beliefs as relations to independent objects – what I call CONTAINER-CONTENT DUALISM in the study of the mind.

Loose use of the entrenched terminology is fine so long as we remember that speakers do not contain objects, speeches do not contain objects, and under absolutely no circumstance do two separate speakers contain the same object. The doctrine of container-content dualism, however, is one I reject, for such reasons as suggested in Chapters 5 and 8.8.1, Bach (1997), and Perry (1979), which also puts me in the same camp as Quine and Gauker (2003). Gauker, for instance, wishes "to set aside ... the question 'What *is* a belief?' and focus on the question 'What are we doing when we *attribute* a belief?' " (p. 219); for his "account of the attribution of beliefs and desires is already an account of the nature of beliefs and desires" (p. 271).

Aside from rejecting container-content dualism, Gauker challenges functional-holistic interpretationism. He makes a powerful case, but I am afraid that the alternative he proposes is not convincing. It's worth evaluating, though, both because it is interesting in its own right and because it might be seen as threatening to my own approach.

According to Gauker, to attribute belief P, to S, is to assert P, on S's behalf (p. 221). This makes speech explanatorily prior to thought, which reverses my own explanatory strategy [as does Quine (1987: 88)]. There is something appealing about this, perhaps because of Gauker's examples, but I just cannot get it to work out. "On behalf of" cannot mean *for the benefit of*, as Gauker admits. It means *in place of*, says Gauker, but obviously this is not intended literally: being in the same place as you, for instance being in the same restaurant, does not make my every assertion into an ascription of your beliefs.

To assert on behalf of, I can only surmise, means to assert as one's agent. But what does it mean for you to speak as S's agent? It cannot mean that you speak as S commissions or instructs, for you may ascribe beliefs to babies even though babies do not give instructions. It cannot mean that you speak as S desires, for that would be circular, belief and desire being the

---

[9]   The frustration here is due not to semantic vacuity but to excess of possible readings. Is a proposition supposed to be a platonic object, a sentence meaning, an "object" of belief, a bearer of truth-value, a truth-condition, some combination, or what? Because these characterizations do not always come together even within the regnant paradigm, it is irresponsible to use the word without elaboration.

analysanda at issue. It cannot mean that you speak as S would if S could, for that is so hypothetical as to allow anything at all. (Smith would ace the test if Smith could, but it is precisely because Smith can't that we do not ascribe knowledge to Smith.) How about tying agency to responsibility, then? After all, if you appoint X as your agent authorized to make investments, and if X invests badly, then *you* take the loss; X's action, when performed within the agentive scope, has the same moral and legal consequence as your own. Well, ascribing belief P to S does not make S responsible for having said P, nor does it even amount to the claim that S is responsible for having said P. I say that Galileo believed the earth moves, but I know full well, and do not purport otherwise, that Galileo went out of his way to avoid responsibility for asserting that the earth moves.

I conclude that Gauker's provocative account, where it appears to conflict with my project, is unconvincing.

Chapter 4

OBJECTIONS AND REPLIES

I maintain two related yet distinct theses, the first being that truth-conditionalism is untenable. Needless to say, my opening salvo against truth-conditionalism (Chap. 2) will remain, for many, unconvincing. I must say more, even though space limitations prevent my addressing every possible concern. I must at least acknowledge some rationales for truth-conditionalism and say a word about how they fail. This I do in Sections 1–7.

My second thesis is that attitudinal semantics holds promise (Chap. 3). Against it critics have raised, or could raise, a number of objections. These objections, if sound, would end my project before it even started. Fortunately for me, however, they are variously question-begging or otherwise defective, as I explain in Sections 8–14.

My two theses, though distinct, offer aid and comfort to each other in that the acceptability of either one will give the other greater prima facie plausibility. This dialectic unfolds in Part Two.

1.   The Determination Argument

The best motivation for truth-conditionalism that I've seen can be found in Stalnaker (1970: 381), Lycan (1984: 18), (2004: §2), and Bar-on et al. (1999). Whether a sentence is true or false depends in part on how the world is, and in part on what the sentence means; truth-value is a function of meaning and the world. But if there is such a function f: (meaning of P, world) → {T, F} then there must be a function g: (meaning of P) → ((world) → {T, F}). And to say this is to say that the meaning of P is a pairing of world-conditions with truth-values, i.e. the meaning of P is a set of truth-conditions.

The Determination Argument is vulnerable in many ways, however. First, it offers no grounds for granting the premise, that truth-value is a function of just meaning and the world; it offers no grounds for thinking that truth-value is a *functional* value at all. Indeed, the evidence of context-effects indicates otherwise. And this not only appears to refute formal truth-conditional semantics, as recognized by TC pragmatists, it neutralizes the Determination Argument for any kind of truth-conditionalism (Chap. 2).

Second, the present form of the Determination Argument relies on the intuition that sentences bear truth-value, which is doubtful. Many deny to sentences truth-value, holding it only for statements or only for structural descriptions. This observation by itself does not cut against TC semantics broadly construed, for the Determination Argument can be recast in terms of a function to truth-value from world plus meaning *plus context of utterance* [though see Part II and Baker & Hacker (1984: 201)]. However, debates over the fundamental and ultimate bearers of truth illustrate the danger of relying on folk intuition [cf. Reimer (2005)]. Perhaps only acts of judging have truth-value, strictly speaking; perhaps only a person's complete state of being does; perhaps only abstract propositions do. In any event, perhaps neither sentences nor statements nor any other linguistic entities stand in a relationship to truth suitable for possessing truth-conditions.

Third, the Determination Argument arguably relies on some notion of objective, absolute, and substantive truth. But perhaps the correct theory of truth is coherentist, pragmatist, minimalist, eliminativist, or other [e.g. Horwich (1990), Rorty (1991: Chap. 8)]. To clarify, I am not arguing here that this is actually so, only that TC semantics requires more defense than is usually acknowledged.

Fourth, the Determination Argument relies on the concept WORLD and perhaps even POSSIBLE WORLD. The latter poses a number of philosophical puzzles, and this makes the greater part of the TC enterprise suspect. But even the former concept, because it includes that of the universal set, is paradoxical from the point of view of formal semantics (Grim 1991). This means that no formalists, be they Davidsonian or Montagovian, can consistently appeal to the Determination Argument presented here.

Fifth, the Determination Argument, even if successful, would establish only an abstract relation between truth-conditions and meaning. It would remain possible for that relationship to be one of contingent and material conditionality. In other words, nominal TC semantics does not automatically yield genuine TC semantics (Chap. 2.3.5).

To summarize, the Determination Argument holds that, since the truth-value of a sentence is a function of what the sentence means and what the world is like, the meaning of a statement is its truth-conditions. I have identified several weak spots in the argument, the most important being that it begs the question. The conclusion is a fairly trivial extension of the premise, but the premise, be it couched in terms of determination, function, or exclusive dependence, is overly simplistic: nature is full of complex, indeterminate relations far more than it is of explanatorily real functions readily discerned by human intuition. In addition, other worries independently render the Determination Argument inconclusive at best. My aim in this section has not been to refute the argument, only to defuse it, to point out that it is very far from compelling. These considerations make room for seriously pursuing alternatives to truth-conditionalism.

2. The Covariance Argument

Meaning and truth-conditions, it is intuitively clear, always covary. This claim can be broken into two. On the one hand, it says that any difference in meaning clearly entails a difference in truth-conditions. But this is just false: necessary truths differ in meaning, yet they are true under all possible conditions; various interrogatives differ in meaning, yet they appear to be neither true nor false under any condition; if asked, most speakers of English would say that "The butcher chased the pig" differs in meaning from "The butcher chased the piggy-wiggy," yet they share precisely the same truth-conditions. This is not to say that ordinary judgments are right on these matters but rather to insist that if we did go by ordinary intuitions then we would have to *reject* strong TC semantics.[1]

But what about weak TC semantics, the thesis that any difference in truth-conditions entails a difference in meaning? It is *trivially* correct, according to Higginbotham (2006), but this cannot be right, because of indexicals. My utterance of "My aunt and niece are named Riye" is true while yours is false, yet the sentence-meaning of my utterance is the same as yours. In reply, Higginbotham might deny my claim, equating meaning with "content" rather than "character". Alternatively he might admit my claim, but dismiss it for taking his own too literally: for on any *charitable* construal of TC semantics, the meaning of a sentence determines truth-conditions *conditions*. The former option strikes me as a mistake, though some follow it, while the second option strikes me as the best one for truth-conditionalists, although it requires additional working out. Either way, the

---

[1] It's worth noting that judgments are far from uniform. Although "pig" and "piggy-wiggy" differ in meaning according to most judgments, they do not differ according to many TC semanticists; although declaratives might possess objectivist truth-conditions according to most judgments, they do not do so according to the attitudinal semanticist. Thus, when I speak of judgments and intuitions in the text, I speak of those which I think are the most common.

weak TC slogan calls for discussion and justification; even if it were true, it is not trivial and clear, and so the Covariance Argument fails.

Indexicals are not the only problem. In practice, translation often changes truth-conditions. For instance, "the French word for London is *Paris*" (Ionesco); and similarly, where the English Bible contains the word "dove", Polynesian versions of the Bible refer to a different kind of gentle bird, one found in Polynesia (Fawcett 2003).[2] Another sort of example can be found in the philosophical literature: given the German statement (1), which is supposed to illustrate the non-triviality of T-sentences, a TC-preserving translation gives (2) whereas a meaning-preserving translation gives (3).

(1) "Snow is white" ist wahr auf Englisch genau wenn der Schnee weiß ist.
(2) "Snow is white" is true in English iff snow is white.
(3) "Der Schnee ist weiß" is true in German iff snow is white.

Of course the critic may easily rationalize such truth-divergent translations: normally truth-conditions *are* preserved, and the exceptions are always explicable for pragmatic reasons. On the other hand, the covariance intuition itself can be rationalized away (p. 236). In the absence of a lot more work, the Covariance Argument is hardly compelling.

There's another reason for doubting that a difference in truth-conditions entails a difference in meaning, one that applies to both weak and strong TC semantics. Putnam's Twin Earth scenario supposedly offers a dilemma: either (i) meaning is not in the head or (ii) meaning does not determine truth-conditions. Although Putnam himself opts for (i), option (ii) remains as a viable alternative. Thus it is by no means obvious that sameness in meaning entails sameness in truth-conditions.

Personally, I do not share Putnam's Twin Earth intuitions [like very many; see Machery et al. (2004)]. And so, I would grant, it is hard to find a genuinely convincing case where truth-conditions change without a change in meaning. But this in itself is hardly impressive, for my work can be taken as an

---

[2]   For another example, Hawaiian has no word specifically for salamanders, though it does have "mo'o", usually translated as *lizard*. Hawaiian attributions of our salamander-beliefs and lizard-beliefs alike will tend to use "mo'o", and the English words "salamander" and "lizard" will both tend to translate as Hawaiian "mo'o". Conversely, anglophone attributions of Hawaiian mo'o-beliefs will use sometimes "lizard", sometimes "salamander", and sometimes "lizards/salamanders". The important point to notice is that translations of texts match attributions of beliefs – a direct fall-out of attitudinal semantics, which effectively identifies meaning in terms of belief-ascription.

extended argument that such intuition is unreliable. Aside from the fact that intuition is highly variable, and is easily contaminated by theory (p. 14), the liar paradox demonstratively proves that objectivist truth, and hence objectivist truth-conditions, are incoherent. Therefore ordinary judgments about truth-conditions are unreliable. Moreover, my belief-theoretic treatments of pejoratives, ambiguity, and quotation – problems that have been recalcitrant within the framework of TC semantics – lend inference-to-the-best-explanation support for attitudinal semantics. And if attitudinal semantics is correct, it follows again that intuitions about truth-conditions are unsound. To repeat, *this* is not an argument that certain intuitions about truth-conditions are in fact mistaken (the rest of the book is); this is an argument that intuitions about truth-conditions are *unreliable* and cannot, by themselves, justify either accepting TC semantics or repudiating attitudinal semantics.

3.   The Cognitive Argument

To understand the meaning of a statement is to understand what conditions would have to hold for it to be true; hence, the meaning of a statement is its truth-conditions. This claim can be represented by the inference from (4) to (5), where the equivalence relation is analytic or nomic rather than material.

(4) S knows or grasps the meaning of $P \equiv S$ knows or grasps the truth-conditions of P.
(5) Therefore the meaning of $P =$ the truth-conditions of P.

This argument, in carrying us from epistemic to ontic truth-conditionalism, assumes exactly what I have been denying all along. It begs the question. And as if that is not enough, I reject the inference from (4) to (5). It is a tempting inference to make, I admit, but nonetheless it is not justified.

In the first place, the Cognitive Argument reminds me of the following identity fallacy.

(6) $a = b$.
(7) Therefore, S believes that $Fa \equiv S$ believes that Fb, where either belief is de dicto.

The chief difference between the identity fallacy and the Cognitive Argument is directional: what counts as premise for the one counts as conclusion for the other. But just as the identity fallacy – whose invalidity is somehow *remarkable* (at least for those smitten by referentialism) – does not really establish an inferential connection between real-world identity (6) and cognitive equivalence

(7), so too the Cognitive Argument, despite its initial plausibility, does not establish an inference between real-world identity (5) and cognitive equivalence (4). Therefore the inference is suspect to start off with.

Granted, there is a further difference between the Cognitive Argument and the identity fallacy. The former, in (4), refers to the attitude of knowing, while the latter, in (7), refers to believing. This difference, however, does not matter to my argument. For one thing, the identity fallacy could easily be reformulated in terms of knowing and it would retain its essential characteristics: it would remain invalid, and its invalidity would remain somehow remarkable. For another thing, the Cognitive Argument could easily be reformulated in non-factive terms, for example "to think that the meaning of P is such-and-such is to think that the truth-conditions of P are such-and-such". Indeed, if we are to understand the original formulation of the Cognitive Argument in a non-question-begging way, we must construe the verb "know" non-factively and therefore akin to "believe". The only motivation for using "know" rather than "believe" in (4) is grammatical: whenever the direct object is a noun phrase rather than an embedded clause, "know" is permissible while "believe" is not. What's more, the usual factive presupposition of knowledge disappears in conditional contexts. Therefore, even without reformulations or reconstruals, there are no interesting consequences arising out of the difference in attitudes between the Cognitive Argument (4) and the identity fallacy (7).

My suspicion of the Cognitive Argument is backed by my rejection of container-content dualism. If Chapters 3.3.5 and 8.8.1 are right, we cannot read logical form off from grammatical form: just as the logical form of "the average unicorn" is not a singular term "a", the logical form of "S believes that P" is not "aRb". It is a mistake to view belief ascriptions as representing belief *contents* inside of a subject's belief *box*, for a belief is a holistic state of a subject. As a result, even if I were willing to accept premise (4), suitably modified to treat mood, indexicality, ambiguity, pejoratives, and so forth, I would not grant the move from (4) to (5).

The Cognitive Argument is also undermined by the failure of the following sort of case.

(8) S believes the king of France is bald $\equiv$ S believes the male monarch of France is bald.

(9) Therefore the current king of France = the current male monarch of France.

Statement (8) seems to be true. If S is aware of France's political structure, then the left-hand and right-hand sides are both false because S doesn't believe there is a king or monarch of France for whom the question of baldness arises; hence the equivalence holds. If S ignorantly believes that France has a king, and that he is bald, then surely S believes that the male monarch of France is bald. Hence (8) is true in general for any S. But (9) is either false or without truth-value, depending on your view of presuppositions. Unless you think of (9) as a meta-linguistic claim to the effect that "the king of France" and "the male monarch of France" co-refer or are synonymous, then (9) will seem defective in a way that (8) does not. Since (9) is not intended as a meta-linguistic claim, I conclude that it is either false or without truth-value. Since the premise can be true while the conclusion is not true, the argument is invalid. The consequence is remarkable. The presupposition example proves that the pattern behind the Cognitive Argument is fallacious. Therefore, regardless of whether the TC thesis (5) is correct or not, it is not supported by premise (4) alone.

Finally, the liar paradox offers a counterexample to the inference pattern behind the Cognitive Argument. As I discuss in Chapter 8.8, to believe (10) is to believe "(10) is true", i.e. (11); hence (12) holds.

(10) (10) is false.
(11) (10) is true.
(12) S grasps or thinks that (10) is false $\equiv$ S grasps or thinks that (10) is true.

But if (12) holds and if the Cognitive Argument is valid then it follows that (13) is true.

(13) The proposition "(10) is false" = the proposition "(10) is true".

Since (13) is inconsistent, we have another reductio against the validity of the Cognitive Argument.

To sum up, I have given a variety of reasons for rejecting the Cognitive Argument for TC semantics, and if any one of them is good then the Cognitive Argument as an objection against attitudinal semantics fails. While these reasons strike me as persuasive, I recognize that others will remain unconvinced. But I needn't actually demonstrate that the Cognitive Argument is invalid; all that matters is that I point out that it is tendentious, as I have done. Anyone who wishes to use the Cognitive Argument now has the burden of justifying the inference in question.

4. Dogmatism

It's just axiomatic that meaning involves truth-conditions. On the face of it, this claim appeals to some sort of foundationalism. The problem with the empiricist version of foundationalism is that we cannot perceive that meaning involves truth-conditions, at least not by any of the usual sensory modes. Meaning and truth-conditions do not have looks, sounds, smells, or tastes. The problem with the rationalist version of foundationalism is that it is methodologically out of bounds, and for good reason. For one thing, the a priori judgments of rationalist intuition, being analytic as they are, do not necessarily apply to anything of real interest. It may be "true" by definition, for instance, that parallel lines never meet and that God necessarily exists, but such verbal "truths" have no self-certifying bearing on reality. Besides that, we cannot intuit a connection between meaning and truth-conditions in any theory-independent way, if at all, and such judgments, being subjective and variable, are unreliable and hence epistemically worthless. Anyone who wants to identify meaning and truth-conditions, therefore, must appeal to more than his or her own dubious intuition.

The dogmatic attitude is widespread. It is explicit in Lewis (1970: 169), Cresswell (1985: 145), Cann (1993: 1), and referee reports, it is documented in Jacquette (2003: 4), and it is at least implied by McDowell (1998: 319) and Lycan (1984: 18), for whom truth-conditionalism is "truistic...the merest platitude" and "not merely theoretical." It is also implicit in Davidson (1967: 24) and again in (1984: xiv), which asserts that a "clear virtue" of truth-theoretic semantics is that it assigns truth-conditions to sentences without indicating why this is supposed to be a virtue. An especially egregious case appears in McGinn (1982):

> [a] I do not think we can rest content with a pure cognitive role theory, discarding reference and truth entirely. [b] For any adequate theory of language should address itself to relations between words and the world, [c] since such relations are clearly (to say the least) a very important feature of language: [d] we cannot just choose to ignore semantic relations in our theory of the workings of language. [e] Furthermore, there seems good reason to suppose that reference and meaning are not independent properties of expressions: [f] the meaning of a sentence surely determines its truth-conditions, and [g] one who did not know the truth-conditions of a sentence would not fully grasp its meaning. [219]

This passage begins with statement (a) that, strictly speaking, is about McGinn's personal convictions. But in the given context – a philosophy book, not an autobiography – we easily recognize the implied thesis: the assertion of referentialist, TC semantics. The remainder of the passage purports to give a whole sequence of sound arguments in favor of this thesis, as evinced by the use of "for", "since", and "good reason". Unfortunately, clause (b), despite the argumentative "for", merely repeats the thesis (adding the normative "should"). Clause (c) merely repeats it again (adding that it's *clearly important*). Clause (d), in case we haven't gotten the message, tells us that we either should or must adopt TC theory ("cannot" is probably intended normatively, but possibly as a limitation on what is possible). Clause (e) seems to announce that clause (f) is actually going to give a *reason* in favor of TC semantics; but then (f) just repeats the thesis in question (adding "surely"). Up until the last clause, the entire passage consists of nothing but naked assertion. Clause (g), finally, asserts epistemic truth-conditionalism, which does indeed entail the generic truth-conditionalism of (a), but only by begging the question. What McGinn says is so embarrassing that it makes one wonder about his real motivations. (To clarify, I am taking exception to McGinn's *argument*; his *position* is not now at issue.)

At its worst, the Dogmatic Objection carries with it the force, sometimes unspoken but sometimes freely acknowledged in conversation, that "*Nothing you say can convince me otherwise.*" It saddens me to report that this is the single most common objection that I get to attitudinal semantics (and philosophers tend to offend more on this score than other cognitive scientists, perhaps because they tend to be more committed to TC semantics in the first place). This is not to deny that the truth-conditionalist might be correct: my task in this section is not to argue that attitudinal semantics is right and TC semantics is wrong, merely to show that the putative arguments against attitudinal semantics do not really work, and that the Dogmatic Objection in particular does not itself count as either argument or evidence against attitudinal semantics.

Dogmatism is hardly limited to realist philosophy of language. It also occurs in realist philosophy of science [Fine (1986: 116) observes that realists, like the religious, make a "profound leap of faith"] and in realist philosophy of mind. Responding to the latter, Paul Churchland writes:

> The initial plausibility of this rather radical view [eliminative materialism] is low for almost everyone, since it denies deeply entrenched assumptions. That is at best a question-begging complaint, of course, since those assumptions are precisely what is at issue. [1988: 47]

Likewise, the ideology that meaning axiomatically involves truth-conditions begs precisely the question that is under dispute, and does not count as a valid objection against attitudinal semantics.

5.   A Transcendental Argument

Relative to the popularity of TC semantics there is astonishingly little argumentation for it, much of the literature consisting of appeals to unshared intuitions, brute stipulations, and begging the question. For instance, consider this reasoning:

It's not the case that "the Queen of England is sitting" is true iff she is standing on a table, and furthermore we know as much. Similarly, it's not the case that "Chase Manhattan is a bank" is true iff Chase Manhattan is both a house of finance and the lip of a river, and furthermore we know as much. Thus we often have negative knowledge, knowledge that a proposed truth-condition is incorrect, even though we virtually never command positive knowledge, knowledge that a proposed truth-condition is correct. But negative knowledge isn't possible where there's no positive knowledge. Denying truth-conditionalism presupposes truth-conditionalism.

It's true that negative knowledge can make positive knowledge sharper. If I start off knowing (a) that a certain Jan Doe is among my 30 students in a classroom, and if I learn (b) that a given student is not Jan Doe, then this negative knowledge, combined with my initial knowledge, entails the positive knowledge (c) that Jan Doe is among the other 29 students. However, negative knowledge does not entail positive knowledge by itself. The inference to (c) relies partly on (a), which itself is positive knowledge. For instance, if you know that your father is not Santa Claus, this does not entitle you to infer that someone else is, unless you furthermore assume that Santa Claus exists. Likewise, if you know that some condition Q is not P's truth-condition, you are not committed to something other than Q being P's truth-condition unless you also assume that P has *some* truth-condition, which begs the question.

In short, I can recognize that an object is not an apple without assuming that it is some other kind of fruit. I can recognize that the meaning of a statement is not a particular truth-condition, and rationally argue as much, without committing myself to its being some other truth-condition.

6.   The Success Argument

If we gave up TC semantics, we wouldn't be able to explain our success in the world. The Success Argument is criticized, successfully in my view, by Laudan (1984), Fine (1986: Chap. 7), Latour (1987), Horwich (1990: §§11 & 13), Devitt (1991: §6.6), Rorty (1991), and Field (2001: 80–81). Arthur Fine argues that the Success Argument begs the question at issue, asking "need we take good explanatory hypotheses as true?" (p. 115). Fine goes on to observe that working scientists are not necessarily realists:

If we examine the two twentieth century giants among physical theories, relativity and the quantum theory, we find a living refutation of the realist's claim that only his view of science explains progress ... Einstein's early positivism and his methodological debt to Mach (and Hume) leap right out of the pages of the 1905 paper on special relativity ... in the 1916 general relativity paper as well, where Einstein [writes that his verificationist argument] ... "takes away from space and time the last remnants of physical objectivity". [122]

Similar remarks are said to apply to the leaders of quantum theory, Heisenberg and Schroedinger and Bohr (p. 124).[3]

I regard the replies of Fine, Horwich, and others as sufficient. In addition, I wish to float a reply of my own, based on the following example. Sam says: "Millions of farmers believe that by fertilizing their crops they will reap larger harvests than they otherwise would, and it's because their beliefs are *true* that they *do* reap large harvests. Reference to truth is necessary if we are to explain why agents systematically succeed in securing what they want."

Before examining the *content* of Sam's argument, I want to consider whether her holding it can be explained without reference to the external world. We evaluate Sam and her belief in the following way. (a) Sam believes that farmers believe that fertilizing crops results in larger harvests. (b) Sam believes that farmers act on their beliefs, and that they get larger harvests. (c) Sam believes that "fertilizing crops results in larger harvests" is true. We thus conclude that Sam's beliefs fit tidily together; they are not only compatible with each other, but they rationally support each other. In particular, Sam's belief (c) seems irresistible given Sam's beliefs (a, b). So we can see why Sam insists that "fertilizing crops results in larger harvests" is *true*. However, and here's the key point, we can see why Sam says what she does without ourselves having any beliefs one way or another about the real nature of crops and harvests. We can explain Sam's beliefs without reference to truth. And what we say about Sam, of course, can also be said about us by any third party.

Although we may ordinarily square our beliefs about success and about other people's beliefs by reference to truth, a little reflection of the sort just exercised reveals that the truth – i.e. our convictions about the truth – is

---

[3] Fine's description of science, incidentally, throws into question his metaphysical quietism. Fine suggests that we can eliminate the realism-antirealism problem by simply not talking about it (i.e. we should recognize that we don't need a solution, that it's a non-problem) – because, after all, scientists don't need to commit to one side or the other. But if Fine is right about his history, scientists do in fact make (anti)realist assumptions, and these assumptions do in fact matter. See Fine §§7.2, 7.3, 8.4, and especially p. 132.

entirely internal. In other words, just as "Sam believes that crops need fertilizer" does not entail that crops need fertilizer, "We believe that P is true" does not entail that P is true (though for *us* to assert one and deny the other would be unpragmatical).

You might object that if my argument is any good, then it would destroy not only TC semantics but also physics, biology, geology, and so forth. For if we can explain the reports of natural scientists in terms of their beliefs – which need to be explained anyhow – rather than in terms of natural phenomena directly, why not rest content with doing so? Why not conclude that gravity doesn't exist – that it's merely understandable why we believe that gravity exists?

These rhetorical questions insinuate that the denial of scientific realism is absurd. But such an assumption disrespects the fact that scientific realism is controversial. Its rejection by instrumentalists and other non-realists [e.g. van Fraassen (1986), Fine (1986)] is well known. If a thesis is disputed then, right or wrong, it cannot be taken as absurd (p. 17). In addition to this one dialectical point there is another: you cannot criticize my rejection of TC semantics by appeal to scientific realism, for scientific realism is simply the assertion of TC semantics within a particularly interesting domain. Thus, the Success Argument amounts to question-begging. Finally, I should point out that for us to give up our beliefs about gravity would be akin to Sam's giving up beliefs about agriculture. We can see from our privileged point of view that Sam's beliefs, though not necessarily grounded in any correspondence relation to reality, are rational. By analogy, we can conclude that it is rational to retain our own beliefs even if they are not justified by any correspondence relation.

A particularized version of the Success Argument runs as follows: Without semantic realism, communication would be impossible; but communication is obviously not impossible; therefore solipsistic semantics cannot be true [e.g. Frege (1918: 300), Fodor (1987)]. But this argument equivocates in its use of "communication". If communication be understood merely as the use of language for (apparent) coordination, then the existence of communication does not necessitate the existence of TC content. Consider, for instance, a thermostat and furnace that operate only above freezing. Whenever the temperature drops close to 0° Celsius, the thermostat signals to the furnace that it's time to turn on, and the furnace obliges. The signal *could* be construed as possessing intentional content, but the effective cooperation of thermostat and furnace for their continuing ability to operate could just as well be construed in causal terms. On the other hand, if genuine communication be the transmission of intentional content, as truth-conditionally understood, then it is not obvious that genuine communication actually obtains. There doesn't seem to be any empirical reason for insisting that it does, and to assume that it does is to beg the question against attitudinal semantics.

Another version of the Success Argument traces back to Putnam. Since this version has enjoyed considerable influence, I'd like to briefly review it. Putnam claims – though Schopenhauer and other pessimists may differ – that "*every* philosophical position yields roughly the following story:"

(a) People act (in general) in such a way that their goals will be obtained . . . *if* their beliefs are true.
(b) Many beliefs (of the kinds I mentioned, and of other relevant kinds) *are* true.
(c) So, as a consequence of (a) and (b), people have a tendency to attain certain kinds of goals. [1978: 101]

These statements are then used in an abductive argument: premises (a, b) are taken as the best route to (c), and (c) is taken as indisputable; therefore (a, b) are true.

But this strikes me as a very bad argument, for (a–c) are either vacuous or unlikely. They're unlikely if they're taken to entail that I act so that my goals will be obtained whenever my beliefs are true; for as an adolescent my overriding goal was to live forever. I dreaded death, I wanted to be immortal, and I thought about this several times a day. I wanted to live forever, I aimed for it, and I researched cloning, cryogenic preservation, and brain transplantation. But in no sense could any true beliefs have enabled me to get what I wanted. Other examples come readily to mind: the slave in chains wants to go free, and has this as a goal; but this will not happen, even if the slave's beliefs are entirely true; the insanely jealous cuckold wants reassurance, and may act with the goal of finding out that the spouse is faithful; but the cuckold will not get it, especially given that the cuckold's tentative beliefs are true; contestants in games and pageants aim for victory, but by design only a small fraction will prevail.

In reply, Putnam might emphasize that (a) applies "in general", that (b) refers to beliefs "of the kind mentioned", and that (c) reports a mere "tendency" to attain "certain kinds of" goals. The relevant kinds of goals, I suppose, are to be understood somehow in relation to the relevant kinds of beliefs, which in turn are characterized by Putnam as follows:

Most people do have [mostly] true beliefs about where they live, what the neighborhood looks like, how to get from one place to another, etc. [1978: 101]

The problem is that this characterization is so vague as to be useless. In the first place, we don't know how to quantify beliefs (Chap. 3.3.2). Saint Augustine, let us suppose, believed that (i) politically he lived in Hippo, (ii) spiritually he lived below heaven, (iii) astronomically he lived in the center of the universe, (iv) religiously he lived in the only culture that mattered, and perhaps that (v) geographically he lived in North Africa, depending on whether his flat-earth conception (let us suppose) of Africa bears sufficient resemblance to our own plate-tectonic conception of Africa for us to say that Augustine really had beliefs about Africa. Under this accounting, therefore, Augustine held one or two true beliefs about where he lived (i, v), and three or four false beliefs (ii–v). Other accountings will return different figures of course, but the point is made: in the absence of a calculus for individuating and quantifying beliefs, Putnam's claim that beliefs about one's residence are mostly true is untenable.

Furthermore, I do not know what "etc." in Putnam's context is supposed to suggest. If it is supposed to include beliefs about immortality, which are exceedingly *common* – billions of people through history have spent inordinate time praying and thinking about how to achieve salvation of the immortal soul – then the argument looks wrong. If "etc." is supposed to include beliefs about one's spouse's faithfulness, which are exceedingly *important* – untold numbers of people through history have killed or been killed because of adultery – then the argument looks wrong. If it is supposed to include beliefs about how to escape from slavery – an institution found in more cultures than not – then the argument looks wrong. In short, I do not see any way to render Putnam's argument sound unless we define the relevant kinds of beliefs and goals as whichever beliefs and goals make (a–c) true. But to do this is to make the argument vacuous.

There conceivably is a kernel idea behind Putnam's argument that can be salvaged without implying unwarranted panglossianism (though I don't know what that might be). Yet then the argument would still fail to address my opening reply to the Success Argument. Even if I concluded that people tend to attain their goals, it would be open to a third party to explain my belief without reference to an external reality.

7.   The Paradigm Argument

TC semantics is an active research program with a pedigree. This is where the most progress has been made, by far – progress in identifying problems, in setting standards for assessing solutions, and sometimes even in reaching solutions that satisfy those standards. *Such successes pose a powerful prima facie case for TC semantics. There is an established research paradigm, it continues to advance, and there's no call for revolution.* Or so it is alleged.

The Paradigm Argument, in judging TC work by TC criteria, in part begs the question. Some of the most important TC criteria of success are widely rejected by non-TC semanticists. Specifically, TC standards of objectivity and precision are mocked by those who think that homophonic axioms such as "*horse* denotes the set of all horses" are not only uninformative to those who speak no English, they are uninformative to those who do, at best. (At worst, it is indefensible to match a vague concept with anything so precise as a set, be it a simple set as in extensional semantics or a set of sets as in intensional semantics.) Also, the criterion of compositionality does not impress those who emphasize the imagination's acting without algorithm in constantly novel environments; there is no more constancy of intention in, say, smacking the word "red" against a noun than there is in smacking your hand against some object (you do it sometimes to applaud, sometimes to kill a mosquito, sometimes to play pattycake ...); cf. Chapter 7.2 and Johnson (1987). To strike a Wittgensteinian note, words are like tools in a toolbox: though they follow general principles, they can be wielded for an open-ended number of purposes, rendering any exact account hopeless.

The body of TC semantics, like the highly articulated and elaborate theology of the medieval theist, is therefore impressive only to those who are already converted and to those who are beguiled by the arcane. But let's suppose otherwise. Let's suppose that TC semantics deserves credit for achieving objectively recognizable successes. Does this make the TC paradigm superior to its rivals?

It does, if it could be shown that disparities in success are due to disparities in intellectual merits. However, intellectual merit drops out of the picture as long as alternative explanations for recognized success are available. And indeed there is at least one explanation: the institutional robustness of truth-conditionalism, compared to its rivals, means that over the years far more personnel-hours have been devoted to developing truth-conditionalism than to all of its rivals combined. For suppose that Quinean behaviorism (say) held the potential for explaining ten times as much as truth-conditionalism; then, all else being equal, we would still expect truth-conditionalism to enjoy a record of greater success, simply because truth-conditionalists outnumber Quineans by more than ten to one.

In short, sociological reasons alone predict that a traditionally regnant paradigm will enjoy more success than its rivals. First off, it's because regnant programs, by definition, have the greatest numbers of partisans working at research centers with the most grant money, the brightest students, and so forth; hence they will show the most results. Second, it's because the results obtained by the various research programs tend to be judged according to the standards of most of the workers in the field; and most of the workers in the field, especially the most influential ones serving as gatekeepers, again by definition, belong to the regnant paradigm. [For anti-mentalist bias in the politics of academic hiring, see Kusch (1995).]

But that's not all. Whereas the development of formal TC semantics depends on formal logic, the development of mentalist semantics relies upon psychology, which is intrinsically more complex. Mentalist semantics, as Bezuidenhout says of TC pragmatics,

> calls for a general account of our inferential abilities, of how our memories are organized and retrieved, of how we are able to integrate action and belief, and of much more besides. In other words, it calls for a full story of human agency. [2002: 127]

I conclude that the Paradigm Argument is not sound. Invoking a record of comparative success alone, without regard to the intrinsic unruliness of a subject matter or to comparative social advantages, covers an appeal to tradition and naked power and more.

8.   Compatibility?

Perhaps attitudinal analyses and TC analyses are both correct. One compromise position goes like this: "Granted, attitudinal semantics succeeds in places where TC semantics fails. But this doesn't mean that TC semantics is wrong; it just means that TC semantics is incomplete. The correct theory of meaning is a two-factor theory that admits both attitudinal and TC analyses independently." Another version of compromise admits both attitudinal and TC analyses, but regards one as derivative of the other. Since "S thinks" occurs in a given attitudinal analysis on both sides of the equivalence sign, for instance, perhaps they can be cancelled out, leaving an unfettered TC analysis.

I've already cautioned against such maneuvering in my rebuttal to the Cognitive Argument (§3). Attitudinal equivalences do not amount to TC equivalences, at least not straightforwardly, else (14) would entail (14′) or (14″):

(14) (∀S: S speaks Latin)
     S thinks "cogito ergo sum" ≡ S thinks that S thinks and therefore exists.
(14′) (∀S: S speaks Latin)
     cogito ergo sum ≡ S thinks and therefore exists.

(14″) (∀S: S speaks Latin) "cogito ergo sum" is true ≡ S thinks and therefore exists.

And even if either attitudinal or TC semantics did reduce to the other, that would be a reason for taking the more fundamental theory as the genuinely explanatory one.

This leaves the independence version of the compatibility theory, a compromise that runs against its own Coordination Problem (p. 32). If attitude-conditions and truth-conditions are independent, what is to prevent (15) and (16) from both holding?

(15) "They sailed to the land where the bong-tree grows" is true in Learish ≡ They sailed to the land where the coconut grows.

(16) For any proficient speaker of Learish S, it is analytic that: S thinks "they sailed to the land where the bong-tree grows" ≡ S thinks that the owl and the pussycat wed.

Another difficulty is the MOTIVATION PROBLEM. The compatibility theorist agrees that my general framework, which governs language paradoxical, ambiguous, pejorative, moral, generic, epistemic, and so forth, is correct as far as it goes. But if this single-factor theory is empirically adequate for addressing linguistic meaning, there doesn't seem to be any *point* in supplementing it with a superfluous factor.

9.   The Irrelevance Objection

Attitudinal semantics changes the topic. According to this view, TC semantics has one subject matter while attitudinal semantics has another. Consider for example my analysis of the knowledge predicate, in response to the Gettier problem.

(17) S thinks "X knows that P" ≡ S thinks that:
(a) P; (b) X believes that P; (c) X has (what S regards as) justification for P.

Critics object that this analysis is not about either knowledge or the meaning of "know"; rather, it concerns *beliefs about* knowledge and the predicate "know". This is a different matter altogether, and it leaves untouched what is of real interest to the TC semanticist. (Incidentally, this position implicitly rejects the Cognitive Argument ascribed to truth-conditionalists in Section 3. If the inference there from (4) to (5) were valid, then claims about beliefs concerning knowledge would logically amount to claims about knowledge directly. The critic cannot have it both ways: the critic must give up at least one, the Cognitive Argument or the Irrelevance Objection.)

In reply to the Irrelevance Objection I can take either one of two different positions. On the one hand, I could accept the charge that I have changed the topic, but then I could point out that changing the topic does not necessarily make the two theories incommensurable; it is what always and inevitably happens whenever there's *any* scientific or philosophical progress. For example, we could think of Newtonian and Einsteinian physics as dealing with distinct subject matters: the former with space, time, and absolute motion; the latter with space-time and relativistic motion. Nonetheless it remains fruitful to ask, "Which theory presents a better model of reality? Which theory is existentially instantiated?" Likewise, even supposing that TC and attitudinal semantics be really about two different matters – the former involving word-world relations, the latter involving word-interpreter relations – the question remains open, "Which theory best explains linguistic phenomena?" It could turn out that each theory applies to a separate aspect of language and are compatible, or it could turn out that TC semantics by itself gives a complete and adequate account of meaning. But it could also turn out that attitudinal semantics by itself is sufficient, and that TC semantics is either self-contradictory or at best just spinning wheels. In conclusion, then, the supposition that attitudinal semantics changes the topic does not by itself undermine my claim that attitudinal semantics ought to replace TC semantics.

Alternatively we might insist that attitudinal and TC semantics are really dedicated to explaining the same thing, meaning. Granted, my analysis (17) does not talk about the meaning of "know" in isolation, but it does talk about the meaning of "know" in a *syncategorematic* fashion. Analysis (17) is just as much about the meaning of "know" as Russell's Theory of Descriptions (18) is about the meaning of "the."

(18) The F is G $\equiv \exists x$ (Fx & $\forall y$ [Fy $\rightarrow$ x = y] & Gx).

Although the left-hand side of (18) does not consist of just the definite article by itself, (18) nonetheless provides a partial analysis – whether right or wrong – of the meaning of "the" (it gives a full analysis of the definite article as used in singular grammatical subjects). Likewise, although the left-hand side of (17) is not just the proposition "X knows that P" by itself, (17) does in fact provide an analysis – whether right or wrong – of the meaning of "X knows that P" and what we mean by knowledge.

Now it doesn't matter to me whether we take the first option (admit the change of topic while denying its significance) or the second (deny the change of topic). In fact, so far as I can see, the difference between the two is merely verbal. If you agree that these two options substantively amount to the same thing, then you can take them as two different formulations of a single reply to the Irrelevance Objection. Otherwise either by itself will serve.

10.   The Regress Objection

Attitudinal semantics initiates a vicious regress. This view begins by observing that the analytical framework (19) is itself meaningful.

(19) S thinks $\Phi \equiv$ S thinks that P.

But now the analysis of the meaning of (19) requires a higher-order biconditional (20), one where the entire biconditional (19) is embedded as the object of belief in the left-hand analysandum, and where the right-hand analysans gets filled out in whatever complicated manner that is suitable:

(20) S thinks $(19) \equiv$ S thinks that...

That is to say:

(20′) S thinks "S thinks $\Phi \equiv$ S thinks that P" $\equiv$ S thinks that...

The analysis of analysis (20/20′), in turn, requires subordinating (20) to a yet more complicated belief-theoretic biconditional (21), ad infinitum.

(21) S thinks $(20) \equiv$ S thinks that...
(22) S thinks $(21) \equiv$ S thinks that...
(23) S thinks $(22) \equiv$ S thinks that...

No doubt, infinite regress is in the offing here. However, such regress is by no means vicious; it does not undermine attitudinal semantics. The reason is that we need to recognize the distinction between *understanding* (the meaning of) Φ, and *analysing* (the meaning of) Φ. The understanding of Φ is that which takes place in the subject who believes or otherwise entertains Φ; understanding Φ happens whether or not anyone ever turns linguist or philosopher, and whether or not anyone ever arrives at an explicit theory of meaning; understanding Φ does not call for any lexical resources beyond the vocabulary that occurs in Φ itself. In contrast, an analysis of meaning is a kind of description of understanding which takes a third-person perspective; in English this description takes place by means of the words "S", "thinks that", "if and only if", etc. It follows that if we were to analyze all the statements that we ourselves understood, doing so exhaustively and in detail, we would admittedly never end. The reason is that each new analysis would create another statement that we understood, one that was heretofore unanalyzed and therefore requiring a new analysis, which in turn would create another statement that we understood. The result is that we can never explicitly give a complete semantics for ourselves.

This conclusion, however, does not constitute any objection to attitudinal semantics. It is perfectly compatible with the epistemological and metaphysical maxims articulated in Chapter 1.2 and with what we know about meaning. For one, it does not contradict the idea that every expression in English has meaning; as we have already seen, a limitation on the available analyses of meaning does not limit the number of existing meanings. Moreover, it does not contradict the possibility that the totality of meanings for some object language can be analyzed; for if the analyses of language L_1 are conducted in L_2, then it would be possible for L_1 to be completely analyzed. Finally, even if a language has an unbounded number of expressions, each requiring a distinct analysis, then even though it will remain beyond the capacities of us finite beings to explicitly generate each analysis, there is the possibility of finitely schematizing those untold pairings of expression and meaning.

11.   The Self-Refutation Objection

Attitudinal semantics "commits cognitive suicide" [e.g. Baker (1987: Chap. 7) and Stove (1991: Chap. 4)]. The idea here is that if my theory is correct then sentences lack truth-conditions, in which case no statement is true or false. But if no statement is true or false then "attitudinal semantics is correct" cannot be true.

By the same token, of course, "attitudinal semantics is incorrect" could not be true either. Therefore, by temporarily assuming the truth of attitudinal semantics, the Self-Refutation Objection does not really acquire the means to dispute attitudinal semantics. But all of this assumes that the critic's basic strategy is valid, which it's not. The claim that P is not objectivistically true or false is compatible with the facts that P can legitimately be believed or doubted, asserted or denied, endorsed or rejected, and even *called* "true" or "false", and that there are rational grounds for choosing between a pro attitude and a con attitude, grounds that involve something other than objectivist truth.[4] Moreover, whether my theory be right or wrong, there is nothing self-contradictory about saying that utterances are meaningful, that

---

[4] Defining rationality is a project that would lead us from semantics to epistemology. Although extremely interesting and important, it lies beyond the scope of the present work.

meaningfulness does not involve truth or falsity, that objectivist truth does not exist, and that the utterance "Meaningfulness does not involve truth or falsity" is nonetheless true (as attitudinally construed). As Arthur Fine writes in a different context,

> The fact that scientific practice involves serious monopole talk ... does not even begin to address the issue of realism. For what realism is after is a very particular interpretation of that practice. [1986: 139]

Likewise, the fact that ordinary and scientific practices involve truth talk does not really address the issue of truth-conditionalism.

The Self-Refutation Objection is analogous to a criticism sometimes made against eliminative materialism. This criticism, reports Paul Churchland, runs as follows. Eliminative materialism claims "the familiar mental states do not really exist. But that statement is meaningful ... only if it is the expression of a certain *belief*, and an *intention* to communicate, and a *knowledge* of the language ... But if the statement is true, then no such mental states exist, and the statement is therefore a meaningless string of marks or noises, and cannot be true". But this begs the question and, for those who cannot see it as such, Churchland offers an analogously fallacious argument proving vitalism.

> My learned friend has stated that there is no such thing as vital spirit. But this statement is incoherent. For if it is true, then my friend does not have vital spirit, and must therefore be *dead*. But if he is dead, then his statement is just a string of noises, devoid of meaning or truth. Evidently, the assumption that antivitalism is true entails that it cannot be true! [1988: 48]

Just as the vitalist illegitimately assumes that the appropriate utterance of a justifiable, meaningful sentence presupposes the existence of vital spirit, the Self-Refutation Objection illegitimately assumes that the appropriate utterance of a justifiable, meaningful sentence presupposes the existence of objectivist truth-conditions. [For additional arguments that charge the Self-Refutation Objection with question-begging, see Devitt (1991: §6.2) and Rosenberg (1991).]

12. Skeptic Anxieties

In divorcing reference from meaning, attitudinal semantics denies the possibility of making assertions about reality; in rejecting objective truth, it makes objective truth unknowable; its arguments either assume or entail sweeping skepticism. There is a whole cluster of concerns here.

(i) While the Argument from Ignorance does hold that speakers lack knowledge of the truth-conditions of their statements, it does not cite possibilities of error due to dreams, demons, or deranged scientists, it does not draw a meta-induction over our history of scientific failures, it does not broach the sad fact that *veritas magna, vita brevis*, and it does not point at the tendencies toward fallacy in human cognition or the built-in biases of science as a social institution. (I do the latter in rebutting the Paradigm Argument, not in setting forth my affirmative arguments.) In short, my argument does not assume global skepticism. The limited skepticism that it does build upon, that speakers do not know truth-conditions, is not a blind postulate. It is premised on the argumentation of Chapter 2, that speakers can know the total world-condition and still not know whether a statement is true.

(ii) Nor do my arguments commit us to skepticism as a conclusion: "the meaning of a statement is not its truth-conditions, hence statements have no truth-conditions, hence statements are never true, hence statements never express true beliefs, hence true beliefs do not exist, hence knowledge does not exist, hence global skepticism is true". Aside from defeating itself, this cute argument is invalid almost every step of the way, and my position is not committed to it.

(iii) The argument fails chiefly because the truth-conditionalist's charge of skepticism is founded on a truth-conditionalist's understanding of what truth and hence knowledge are, which begs the question. Just as a truth-conditionalist can talk, prima facie without contradiction, about attitudes, so too an attitudinal semanticist can talk, prima facie without contradiction, about truth. The difference resides entirely in how belief and truth are understood: truth-conditionally or objectivistically in the former case, attitude-conditionally or internally in the latter.

The truth-conditional way is unacceptable because its conception of truth is self-contradictory, as demonstrated by the liar paradox. To be sure, despite the concerted attack on the liar paradox and the failure to find an objectivist solution, many will insist, as an article of faith, that objectivist truth is coherent. But even if it were, would we have any reason to say that it applied to anything? Many concepts are internally consistent but nonetheless inapplicable. What reason is there for saying that statements are objectively either true or false?

The reasons fall into two classes. At the high level we have theorizing from semantics, psychology, and epistemology – for example "P is obviously meaningful; to be meaningful, P must for various reasons have truth-conditions; and by having truth-conditions and being in the world, P is objectively either true or false." To show that this sort of reason does not stand up is the burden of this book.

At the low end we have direct intuitions – for example "I am right-handed" is simply, indubitably, and objectively true, "Pigs fly" is plainly false. Of course intuitions are notoriously unreliable and must be treated with care. Intuitively, after all, we stand on an unmoving earth; intuitively, there is a mysterious duality of mind and matter (at least such is the intuition pervasive in Judeo-Christian, Plato-Cartesian cultures); intuitively for Aristotle and Aquinas the world is full of objective meaning and purpose; intuitively for some materialists, the world is a speck of dust in a vast cosmos mostly void of life and matter, and on this speck of dust all is sound and fury. The point is that intuitions, *by themselves*, carry little if any epistemic authority, especially if they purport to distinguish objective and subjective nature.

Still, I recognize the need to explain how all intuitions – be they true or false – come about and persist (p. 15). In the case of truth, I would suggest it is easy to think that a sentence is true if it is mentally associated, but not exactly correlated, with a class of statements that are true; that it is easy to confuse a statement, an object of utterance, with a stating, an act of utterance; and it is easy to confuse a stating with a concurrent belief-state. The result is that it may be perfectly rational, for casual purposes, to assert that a given statement is either true or not true. But this does not mean that sentences or even utterances are technically bearers of truth-value.

13.　Attitude Objections

To explain meaning in terms of belief is illegitimate. Belief and the other attitudes introduce either circularity or mystery. It's illegitimate, for instance, to explain meaning in terms of belief because both are intensional.

This view is unconvincing. To be sure, Davidsonian semantics (purportedly) explains meaning while strictly adhering to extensionalism. However, Davidson regards meaning itself as a genuinely extensional phenomenon, in which case he is explaining the extensional in terms of the extensional; and if this is legitimate, then it's arguably legitimate to explain the intensional in terms of the intensional. Granting for the sake of argument that the extensional is understood better than the intensional, extensional explanations may be preferred whenever possible. But this observation does nothing to undermine my claim that some intensional explanations of intensional phenomena are more satisfying than some extensional explanations. If the critic wants to attack attitudinal semantics, it has to be for something more than the fact that it attempts to explain the intensional via the intensional.

Few semantic paradigms, in fact, escape intensionality. Grice's analysis of meaning is based on intentions (in the ordinary sense of the word), which are certainly intensional; Montague's analysis of meaning is based on possible worlds, and hence is intensional. Whether right or wrong, these theories are certainly neither predictively nor explanatorily empty. And Davidson himself writes, "My way of trying to give an account of language and meaning makes essential use of such concepts as those of belief and intention, and I do not believe it is possible to reduce these notions to anything more scientific or behavioristic" (1976: 175; see also 1990: 310). Thus attitudinal semantics, insofar as it invokes belief, is comparable to Davidsonian TC semantics.[5]

Moreover, I might point out that Davidsonians and Montagovians alike make explanatory use of truth; thus, in addition to their intensionalism, all TC semanticists explain the intentional (in the technical Brentano sense) in terms of at least one intentional notion. Therefore, given my freedom from the intentional, my use of the intensional does not in itself make my program any worse off than truth-conditional theories are.

But, the belief critic might persist, our understanding of belief and the other attitudes is worse off than our understanding of truth is, and this makes attitudinal semantics worse than TC semantics. Now I agree that the absence of a decent belief theory represents a shortcoming for attitudinal semantics. However, in this respect attitudinal semantics actually fares better than TC semantics. To begin with, TC semantics relies on *truth*. Although we might *seem* to know a lot more about truth than about belief, we also know from the liar paradox that the generally available conceptions of truth are either self-contradictory or otherwise unfit for service in a semantic theory. Accounts of belief, in contrast – whether ultimately right or not – so far remain viable (even if imprecise and speculative). Because incompleteness is preferable to inconsistency, attitudinal semantics is preferable to TC semantics.

Even if I am mistaken in what I've just said, most versions of TC semantics are vulnerable in their reliance on the notion of reference, which is at least just as problematic as that of belief. First, there are paradoxes

---

[5]   Needless to say, there is an important difference between these two approaches in the exact role that belief takes: in attitudinal semantics, explicit reference to belief appears in the analytic biconditional, plus possibly in the empirical justification for arriving at particular analytic biconditionals; in TC semantics, reference to belief appears *only* in the empirical justification, and not in the biconditionals themselves. However, the fact that belief appears in the Davidsonian theorizing at all means that if belief is a self-contradictory, confusing, or otherwise illegitimate theoretical notion, then Davidsonian semantics is just as unacceptable as attitudinal semantics.

that appear to be as damning for reference as the Liar is for truth, such as Berry's. Though this is not a claim that I can pursue here, its significance should not be underestimated or forgotten. Second, even without paradoxes proving that the concept of reference is inconsistent, reference has yet to be successfully understood by any naturalistic theory. Causal theories remain open to the problem of misrepresentation while both they and teleological theories fall to the problem of arbitrariness, as admitted by both friend and foe [cf. Devitt (1996: 161), Wagner (1996)]. Perhaps these problems can be solved; but until they are, referentialist semantics is living on a promissory note just as much as my own approach is.

Finally, the very nature of theoretical semantics demands a certain circularity. For semantics, due to its subject matter, requires that the analysandum be a linguistic expression; and any theorizing by its nature requires that the analysans be formulated by a linguistic expression. Therefore an expression is always analyzed by an expression, and this potential circularity becomes especially acute when we realize that in a complete semantics *every* expression occurs as analysandum. This means that no matter which expressions get used as analysans, all of them must appear eventually as analysandum. As a result, my belief-theoretic approach to meaning is circular in the sense that analyses of belief-sentences themselves use the notion of belief. But of course this is analogous to TC semantics, in which analyses of sentences containing the truth predicate themselves explicitly use the notion of truth.

In summary, attitudinal semantics is incomparably better off than realist semantics, given the Liar and Berry paradoxes. And even if these paradoxes were somehow magically solved, the other considerations show that attitudinal semantics is at least no worse off than its rival. More concretely, I deny that by invoking belief-attribution in the analysis of knowledge (p. 107) and of pejoratives, ambiguity, quotation, and truth, the attitudinal approach ends up trying to explain the comparatively simple by means of the comparatively complex. Whereas the problems raised by knowledge, pejoratives, ambiguity, quotation, and truth remain recalcitrant within the TC framework, new and interesting things can be said about them within the attitudinal framework. These, to me, look like successful cases of "explaining the intensional in terms of the intensional", even though (as I am the first to insist) my accounts do not begin to offer the last word.

14.   The Ho-hum Objection

Attitudinal semantics doesn't say anything new. Attitudinal semantics, or something like it, is already embraced by the prevailing theories of meaning, at least implicitly. This objection is contradicted by the recurrence and stridency of the Dogmatic and Irrelevance Objections, among others. And even were that not so, I believe my project would be worthwhile.

To start with, if attitudinal claims are in fact correct then they deserve to be made explicit. Granted, some writers do acknowledge the thesis that meaning somehow depends on and is relative to interpreting subjects. Cresswell (1983: 68) states, "There is strictly no such thing as what a picture represents, there is only what a beholder takes it to represent," while Davidson is well known for his interpretationism, instrumentalism, and rejection of correspondence truth. He says, warming the cockles of my heart:

> The only direct manifestations of language are utterances and inscriptions, and it is we who imbue them with significance. So language is at best an abstraction, and cannot be a medium through which we take in the world nor an intermediary between us and the world. [1999: 668]

Most notably, Davidson repeatedly adverts to the construction "someone holds Φ true", which resembles my own "S thinks Φ".

However, such insight strikes me as more absent than not in the truth-conditional literature. Even with Cresswell and Davidson, I question the depth and seriousness of any affinity between TC semantics and attitudinalism. It appears to me, for instance, that Davidson effectively negates his earlier observation when he comes to "the conclusion that we cannot explain how language works without invoking an ontology and assigning objects to singular terms" (1999: 669). Because of the principle of charity (which I undertake to refute in Chapter 3.3), Davidson infers from "S thinks that P" to P; moreover, an utterance has certain truth-conditions only if the speaker intends it to be interpreted as having those truth-conditions (1990: 310).

Thus, Davidson relates S's having the right intentions to S's utterance *actually having* truth-conditions, not to its just being *thought* to have truth-conditions. In fact, by far most philosophers of language repudiate mentalism as I use the term. Objectivism also shows up, for instance, in the eagerness of the philosophical community to follow the Putnam-Kripke-Burge intuitions about wide content.[6] Even writers who insist on the sufficiency of narrow content for the purposes of the empirical sciences typically accept the existence of wide content [e.g. Fodor (1987)].

Genuine mentalism can be found in cognitive semantics and CRS (Chap. 1.3). However, these are both neglected in the canonical literature. In a survey of textbooks for philosophy of language, I discovered that

---

[6] For criticisms reflecting the opponent viewpoint, see Unger (1983), Cummins (1991), Katz (1996), Segal (2000), Machery et al. (2004).

Lycan (1999) devotes only four pages to CRS; Devitt & Sterelny (1999) devote more than ten times as much to truth-conditional referentialism as to CRS and structuralism combined; Stainton (1996) and Miller (1998) neither mention CRS nor cite any of its literature; and not one of these textbooks reports results from cognitive semantics. Out of six anthologies for philosophy of language (Garfield & Kiteley 1991, Harnish 1994, Ludlow 1997, Baghramian 1998, Nye 1998, and Martinich 2001), there are scores of articles by Frege, Tarski, Davidson, and other truth-conditionalists and only two that marginally represent either CRS or cognitive semantics. In a survey of reference works, I discovered the following. The *Routledge Encyclopedia of Philosophy* (Craig 1998) has articles on TC semantics and CRS but not cognitive semantics. The *Blackwell Companion to Philosophy* (Bunnin & Tsui-James 2003) covers TC semantics but neither CRS nor cognitive semantics. Blackwell's *Companion to the Philosophy of Language* (Hale & Wright 1997) includes several chapters on truth-conditions, truth, and reference, but only a few pages on CRS, buried in articles on analyticity and holism, and nothing on cognitive semantics. The *Concise Encyclopedia of Philosophy of Language* (Lamarque 1997) includes entire units on truth, reference, logic, and formal semantics, but appears to contain nothing on CRS. Of its roughly 150 articles, it has just one related to cognitive semantics, namely "Family Resemblance". It is untenable, therefore, to claim that my pushing for cognitive semantics is superfluous.

Although my work is, by design, compatible with other work in cognitive semantics, and even assuming it be compatible with Cresswellian and Davidsonian semantics, such compatibility does not amount to identity. Even if my attitudinal framework be old hat, as the Ho-hum Objection alleges, my specific work makes new contributions to understanding pejoratives, ambiguity, quotation, the liar paradox, and so on. To these I now turn.

PART II CASE STUDIES

Chapter 5

HATE SPEECH

What is the meaning of pejorative terms such as "kraut", "jap", and "nigger"? For illustrative purposes I will refer time and again to statement (1):

(1) Nietzsche was a kraut.

The small body of literature on the topic is primarily truth-conditional. According to the Simple Conjunction Theory, (1) is equivalent to "Nietzsche was German, and Germans are despicable"; it is therefore false. According to the Indexical Conjunction Theory, (1) is equivalent to "Nietzsche was German, and I despise Germans"; its truth-value varies from speaker to speaker. According to the Bracket Theory, pejoration is a pragmatic feature independent of semantics, and (1) is semantically equivalent to just "Nietzsche was German"; it is true. According to the Stereotype Theory, (1) is equivalent to "Nietzsche was a stereotypical German", whose truth-value is vague. According to Disquotational Semantics, (1) is true if and only if Nietzsche was a kraut, and it is not the job of semantics to tell us whether Nietzsche was a kraut. According to the Multi-proposition Theory, (1) is equivalent to <Nietzsche was German, Germans are despicable>; it is partly true and partly false. According to available Non-proposition Theories, (1) rests on a false presupposition; it is neither true nor false.

In contrast to the foregoing accounts, I shall suggest that (1) is neither true nor false because it functions *expressively*, and I shall offer a way of understanding expressive language. Instead of identifying the meaning of a statement with the conditions under which it is *true*, I propose to identify the meaning of a statement with the conditions under which it is *thought* to be true, is believed, is hoped, is feared, or is otherwise *held*. If I am correct,

121

pejorative language serves as evidence against truth-conditional semantics and for mentalist semantics.[1]

The topic is relevant as more than a test case for semantic theory, for it has legal consequences. The criminality of group libel, by means of pejoratives, is established in Canadian and European law, it is advocated by a number of jurists [e.g. Hartman (1992)], and it somewhat appears in the US Supreme Court's Beauharnais vs. Illinois, 1952 (Greenawalt 1996: 60). Assuming the traditional principle that libel requires falsehood, such jurisprudence is wrong-headed according to my semantic analysis.

I proceed by cataloging truth-conditional analyses of the pejorative and some objections to them, arriving in the end at my own analyses, both semantic (§8) and socio-pragmatic (§9).

1.   The Disquotational Theory

According to Donald Davidson (1967), an adequate theory of meaning will specify the truth-conditions for every declarative sentence by entailing the appropriate homophonic T-sentences. Applying this conception to (1) we get:

(2)   "Nietzsche was a kraut" is true ≡ Nietzsche was a kraut.

However, disquotational T-sentences are uninformative. For those who already understand the word "kraut", knowing (2) is unnecessary; for those who do not, knowing (2) is insufficient. Of course, this sort of complaint has been made before. The problem of the pejorative, however, adds new urgency. For T-sentence (2) is worse than merely uninformative; it expresses ethnic hostility. Rather than ascribing (2) to others, as I am doing, Davidsonians must assert (2), or at least they must assert axioms that entail (2) such as "*kraut* denotes krauts", which are themselves offensive.

Davidson may reply that the object- and meta-languages need not match, in which case "Nietzsche was a kraut" would be mentioned on the left-hand side while the rest of the T-sentence would be cast in some foreign language, say German or Japanese. To make this move, however, is to give up (homophonic) disquotational semantics! It moreover invites its own objections. First, decamping to a foreign language should not be necessary; surely a speaker of English can be told the meaning of (1). Second, appealing to German or Japanese is not sufficient. For it is doubtful that German

---

[1]   For conceptual-role treatments of the pejorative, see Dummett (1973: 432) and Brandom (2000: 69).

speakers would have vocabulary for denigrating themselves, or that Japanese speakers would institutionalize pejorative terminology against people they have had comparatively little contact with, aside from one notable alliance. Translations of (1) would have to be paraphrastic, and it is not clear how they would go. Something meatier is called for.

2. The Conjunction Theory

A.J. Stenner (1981) offers two versions of what I shall call the Conjunction Theory. The simple version analyzes (1) by means of (a):

(a) Nietzsche was a German; moreover, it is appropriate to speak of Germans as krauts.

The indexical, doxastic version analyzes (1) by means of (b):

(b) Nietzsche was a German; moreover, *I believe* it is appropriate to speak of Germans as krauts.

Appeal to "appropriate speech" is evasive; more importantly, the word "kraut" appears in the analysans, which makes both accounts circular. However, the spirit behind (a) and (b) might be preserved by (a') and (b').

(a') Nietzsche was a German, and Germans are despicable.
(b') Nietzsche was a German, and I believe Germans are despicable.

In (a'), the first conjunct is true and the second is false, making the conjunction as a whole false. In (b'), the conjunction is true or false depending on who the speaker is. In either case, the meaning of (1) is collectively specified by a conjunction of truth-conditions.

Along the same line, Simon Blackburn (1984: 148) effectively analyzes (1) as "Nietzsche was a German and on that account he is a fit object for derision." This amounts to three conditions: (i) that Nietzsche be German, (ii) that Nietzsche deserve derision, and (iii) that the one account for the other, i.e. that Germans generically deserve derision. Condition (ii) follows from (i) and (iii), and is redundant. Conditions (i) and (iii) make Blackburn's account a variant of Stenner's Conjunction Theory.

The Conjunction Theory, however, is easily refuted, for it entails that (3) amounts to (3a) or (3b).

(3) All krauts are krauts.
(3a) ∀x (If x is German and Germans are despicable then x is German and Germans are despicable).

(3b) ∀x (If x is German and I believe Germans are despicable then x is German and I believe Germans are despicable).

Whereas (3) is loaded, (3a) and (3b) express neutral tautologies. Since the meaning of (3) is not the same as that of (3a) or (3b), the Conjunction Theory is untenable.

The Conjunction Theory also fails to deal with negation. If (1) is equivalent to (a') or (b') then (¬1) should be equivalent to (¬a) or (¬b).

(¬1) Nietzsche was not a kraut.

(¬a) ¬(Nietzsche was a German and Germans are despicable), that is either Nietzsche was not German or Germans are not despicable.

(¬b) ¬(Nietzsche was a German and I believe Germans are despicable), that is either Nietzsche was not German or I do not believe Germans are despicable.

Since Germans as a class are not despicable, (¬a) is true; and since I believe as much, (¬b) – as spoken by me – is true. Yet (¬1), if it has truth-value at all, is false.

One might object that (¬1) is really true. But to do this is to confuse the ordinary negation (¬1) with the metalinguistic negation (4):

(4) Nietzsche was not a "kraut" [... he was a *German*].

Statements (¬1, 4) are distinct. In the first place, metalinguistic negation typically exhibits both a special intonation and a special stress pattern. In the second place, to metalinguistically negate a proposition P is not to claim that P is false, as can be seen in the following exchange.

A: It's cold in here.
B: It's not "cold" – it's *freezing*!

Although "It's freezing" entails "It's cold", B's statement is not self-contradictory. This is because B's denial does not negate the truth of A's statement, it negates the implication that A's statement is an adequate representation of the most relevant facts.[2]

My argument that metalinguistic negation is distinct from ordinary negation, together with the observation that negation (¬1) expresses the

---

2   See Horn (1989: Chap. 6). My argument against the Conjunction Theory does not assume that negation's ambiguity is lexical or structural, for the alternative poses its own difficulties for truth-conditionalism [Chap. 6 and also Atlas (1978, 1989)].

latter, is meant to convince you that ($\neg$1), if truth-valued at all, is false. This contradicts the Conjunction Theory because ($\neg$a) and ($\neg$b) are true. But even if I am mistaken, we can still see that ($\neg$1) and ($\neg$a/$\neg$b) mean different things to us. Quite simply, ($\neg$1) is offensive while ($\neg$a, $\neg$b) are not.

3. The Stereotype Theory

It has been suggested that pejoratives apply to those and only those who conform to suitable stereotype (personal communications from Alistair Isaac, Steven Todd, and Evan Dukofsky). Under this view, "Hitler was a kraut" would be true because Hitler was authoritarian, an Aryan supremacist, and bent on conquest, while "Einstein was a kraut" would be false.

In order to develop this approach, I shall consider the following stereotypical features of Asians in America:

(A) inscrutable; sinister; "clever", meaning smart but only imitatively so; deferential and law-abiding; industrious and enterprising; asexual (the men) and yet carnal (the women); bad at driving, . . .

According to the Simple Stereotype Theory,

(5) X is a gook $\equiv$ X exhibits features (A).

However, stereotype (A) is mixed: some of it is flattering, some denigrating, and some cuts both ways. One might very well satisfy (A) without on balance ever being viewed derisively, and such a person would not be called "gook". Since "gook" is pejorative, the Simple Stereotype Theory is better revised as the Negative Stereotype Theory:

(6) X is a gook $\equiv$ X exhibits some weighted balance of the negative features in (A).

But even when the negative elements of (A) happen to be satisfied by those of European or African descent, no one would call them a gook except metaphorically. Accordingly the Heritage Negative Stereotype Theory holds:

(7) X is a gook $\equiv$ X is East Asian [or Vietnamese, depending on dialect] and X exhibits some weighted balance of the negative features in (A).

This whole approach is motivated by the comedian Chris Rock's reported comment, "I love black people, but I hate niggers." The claim is that "nigger" refers only to those individuals who conform to the negative features of the black stereotype, "kraut" refers only to those who conform to the negative features of the German stereotype, and so forth.

According to any version of the Stereotype Theory, calling me a kraut should denigrate me alone, not others. But pejoratives do not function this way. They are *slurs*, denigrating everyone in some designated class.

Stereotype-theorists might try to explain slurs by Gricean principles. If speaker S says that Nietzsche was a negatively stereotypical German then S pointedly *invokes* the idea that most or even all Germans fit some particular mold, and this may suggest, without entailing, that S personally *subscribes* to it, in which case S presumably dislikes Germans generically. Thus pejoration may be an implicature.

While I grant that pejoratives may sometimes be used without casting aspersions on a whole class, I think such purported uses are more often disingenuous than not. Indeed, Chris Rock's statement strikes me as notable precisely because he seems to be doing something new with an old word. In pulling devaluation apart from racial reference in the way he does, Chris Rock strikes me as attempting to *reform* the word "nigger" rather than using it according to its traditional meaning. In some speech, "I don't hate blacks, I just hate niggers" is offensive sophistry.

The Stereotype Theory faces other objections as well. For one, it entails that calling me a kraut would not necessarily be offensive to me; it would be like calling me warlike or rigid, in which case if I happened to be proud of being warlike and rigid, I would happily embrace being called a kraut. Since targets typically do not embrace pejorative labels even when they happen to satisfy a stereotype, the theory is mistaken. For another thing, the features of a stereotype are not necessary for an epithet to apply. A manager might say, "you're fired, you lazy gook!", even though laziness runs counter to the Asian stereotype. The term "gook" is applied by those who despise Asians for any reason. Finally, the features of a stereotype are not sufficient for an epithet to apply. Unless you prejudicially lump Asians together in a denigrated class, you could easily agree that particular Asians are inscrutable, sinister, and whatnot, while rejecting the proposition "they are gooks".

In reply to the last point, the stereotype theorist might hold that, since it is part of any stereotype that the members of a specified group are "all alike",

(8) X is a gook ≡ (i) X is Asian, (ii) X exhibits some weighted balance of the negative features in (A), and (iii) Asians generally exhibit the negative features in (A).

But condition (ii) follows from (i, iii) and is superfluous. The result is just a twist on the Simple Conjunction Theory, which has already been rejected.

4. The Non-Proposition Nonsense Theory

Patrick Grim (1981) holds that (putative) pejorative statements are neither true nor false because they fail to express propositions, and they fail to express propositions because they are "gibberish" or meaningless. Let's consider these two claims in turn.

4.1 Non-Propositionality

Grim argues that if we accept (1) then we are committed to ethnocentric or racist claims; and if we accept the negation of (1) we are committed to ethno-racist claims. Since we are not committed to ethno-racism, neither (1) nor its negation is true, hence (1) is neither true nor false.[3]

This argument, however, is unconvincing. To begin with, the case for linking truth to ethics is undermined by the following moral dilemma. Suppose that I have no choice but to testify in court; by asserting P, "I saw him at the scene of the crime that night", I uphold procedural justice though I contribute to the conviction of the defendant, whom I know for a fact to be innocent; whereas by denying P I save the defendant though I commit perjury. Since assertion P and denial ¬P are both unethical, then by Grim's reasoning "I did not see him then, there" lacks truth-value, and thus is not perjury after all! But this I take to be a reductio. Considerations of morality do not render my words null and void.[4]

Grim's argument is further unacceptable because the bare *truth* of (1) cannot commit anyone to racism; being true is a state, and states are not causes. At best, the *assertion* of (1) – an event – commits the speaker to racism. If no one asserts (1), then arguably (1) is true without being the object of commitment. Supposing that no one was racist, (1) would be true but unassertable.

In reply, Grim writes:

> One mark against [true] "unassertables", and against any theory which carries them, is the fact that they conflict with a standard ideal of rational discourse. The ideal, or paradigm, or stereotype of rational discourse is one in which holding a theory involves a willingness to assert and defend a set of claims and their entailments ... "Unassertables" are, after all, something of an intellectual embarrassment, and a rival theory which avoids them is to that extent to be preferred. [294]

---

[3] Truth and morality are also intertwined in Chinese philosophy; see Nisbett (2003: 167).
[4] Many deny the possibility of moral dilemmas, to which I reply in Saka (2000).

To the contrary, the "ideal of rational discourse" does not demand the willingness to assert all sentences that one regards, implicitly or explicitly, as true. My claim is supported by any number of considerations.

(i) Supposing that "P" is true, "P and P and P" is also true. Yet it is irrational to assert redundant conjunctions, and downright impossible to assert infinitely long conjunctions. The necessary unassertability of infinite conjunctions does not by itself deprive them of truth-value, nor even does the practical unassertability of lengthy finite conjunctions. What this shows is that there can be rational considerations apart from truth-value – considerations for instance involving the limited resources of human agents – for making a statement effectively unassertable.

(ii) The statement "Congress is bicameral" is true, but it is irrational to say it to foreigners who do not speak English. It is irrational, that is, if your aim is to impart a civics lesson; if your aim is to test your audience's comprehension of English, or to convey friendliness or solidarity by just chattering, "Congress is bicameral" may be perfectly assertable. Likewise, asserting "Nietzsche was a kraut" may be true yet either rational or irrational. If you want to express disdain for Germans, it is rational; otherwise not.

(iii) Rational discourse takes place in society, and its aims and manner are modulated by societal concerns. Although it may be true for someone to tell another, "You have the ugliest mug I ever have seen", it would be rare for this statement to be called for, relevant, or required by the ideals of rational discourse. With its combined irrelevance and offensiveness, it may even be morally prohibited. Likewise pejorative statements might be true yet unassertable for reasons of prudence, protocol, or common decency.

(iv) When Napoleon said, "L'etat, c'est moi", he used a sentence to make an arguably true statement. Despite its truth, *I* cannot use the same sentence to make a true statement. I can assert the proposition expressed by Napoleon's statement, namely that Napoleon was sovereign; but I cannot truthfully repeat Napoleon's utterance itself. To use the indexical "moi", a certain relation must normally hold between the speaker and the intended referent, namely identity. Likewise, to use a pejorative term, perhaps a certain relation must hold between the speaker and the referent, namely the possession of the attitude of contempt. In short, indexicals give a further reason for saying that some sentences cannot be used by everyone to make true statements.

Now I am not arguing that pejoratives are redundant or pointless, that their assertion requires infinite resources, that they contain covert indexicals, or that they are unassertable for any of the other reasons just listed. Rather, I am simply pointing out that there exists a wide variety of "true unassertables", and that so long as reasons can be given for why they are true but unassertable, they are not particularly problematic. To this class it is easy to add pejoratives (one might argue): example (1) is true because Nietzsche was German, and (1) is unassertable by me because I do not disdain Germans as a class.

4.2   Nonsense

In explaining how pejorative sentences can be neither true nor false, Grim writes that they are "gibberish", or meaningless. For if (1) is neither true nor false, then (1) is not true, and if (1) is not true and yet meaningful then we have (¬1), i.e. "Nietzsche was not a kraut", which is unacceptable. Thus Grim treats pejoratives as meaningless. Unfortunately no available notion of meaninglessness, I shall argue, can explain the pejorative.

Lexical meaninglessness is exemplified by "jklsdf", compositional meaninglessness by "dog fox brown quick the". Obviously pejorative terms do not fall into these categories; indeed, it is precisely because pejorative terms are meaningful, in the ordinary lexico-syntactic sense of "meaningful", that they are offensive. Rather, in calling pejorative statements gibberish, Grim is comparing them to category mistakes like (9) and "perhaps" to statements that rest on false presuppositions like (10) and (11):

   (9) Green ideas sleep furiously.
   (10) Nixon stopped smoking grass.
   (11) Nixon did not stop smoking grass.

These cases are quite different, and neither one resembles pejoratives very well.

   (i) CATEGORY MISTAKES. My general critique of category mistakes appears elsewhere (Saka 1998a: Chap. 3.2). In a nutshell, category mistakes, understood in the traditional way as in (12), do not exist. The anomaly of "green idea" is, rather, to be understood as in (13).

   (12) "Green ideas" is meaningless because ideas are necessarily not
        green.
   (13) One's motivation for saying "green ideas" is normally unintelligible
        (except where one speaks figuratively), because ideas are obviously
        not green.

From this perspective (9) is truth-valued because it is straightforwardly false. But if category mistakes are truth-valued and if pejoratives are relevantly like category mistakes then pejoratives are truth-valued.

Furthermore, category mistakes purportedly arise from "mismatches" between subject and predicate. But if the predicate fails to match the subject in (1) – or better yet, in "all krauts are krauts" – then it is hard to see how the predicate can match *any* subject; and if the predicate does not match *any* subject, then the problem is that the predicate is *intrinsically* meaningless. In that case, pejoratives do not involve category mistakes at all!

(ii) PRESUPPOSITIONS. According to the semantic presupposition view, pejorative statements are neither true nor false because they rest on a false presupposition. Just as (10) and (11) are said to lack truth-value because both presuppose that Nixon once smoked grass, "Nietzsche was a kraut" and its negation are said to lack truth-value because both presuppose that Germans are despicable.

However, there is a difference between pejorative statements and statements that make false presuppositions: some pejoratives possess greater epistemic value than others.

(14a) Nietzsche was a kraut.
(14b) Nietzsche was not a kraut.
(15a) Sartre was not a kraut.
(15b) Sartre was a kraut.

While these are all unassertable by me, I can recognize that the (a) statements contain *something* of value that the (b)'s lack, regardless of whether it is called truth or not. This distinction is totally missed by the semantic presupposition view.

More fundamentally, the very existence of semantic presupposition is now largely repudiated [e.g. Levinson (1983: §4.4)]. Given that President Nixon surely never started smoking grass, he can't have stopped. "Nixon never stopped smoking grass" is true, albeit in ordinary contexts misleading. While this leaves pragmatic varieties of presupposition as potentially real features of language (to be addressed in §6), the semantic variety invoked here is untenable.

One reason for denying semantic presuppositions can be seen by viewing the prototypical case of presupposition, existence presupposition.

(16) The (present) king of France is bald.

Frege (1892), Strawson (1950), and many others hold (16) to be neither true nor false, as it presupposes that there is a particular king of France now in existence. However, it is a mistake to think that existence presupposition is encoded in the linguistic meaning of (16). For if it were, it would either be lexical (and therefore not able to generalize, except accidentally, across "queen", "czar", and all other nouns); or it would be structural, a consequence of the particular subject-predicate grammar involved. Yet the latter can't be true, as it's easy to find examples sharing the same structure while lacking any existence presupposition. Examples include, aside from fictive discourse, definitional characterizations (17, 18); appropriately embedded clauses (19); cases of cancelled implicature (20); negative existential statements (21); and even positive existentials, insofar as you agree that (22B) does not presuppose the very same thing that it asserts.

(17) The unicorn is a one-horned horse.
(18) The king of France is a Gallic monarch.
(19) You are wrong to say that the king of France is bald.
(20) The king of France is not bald, for the king of France does not exist.
(21) The fountain of youth does not exist.
(22) A: The queen of England is not bald, for the queen of England does not exist.
     B: The queen of England does too exist!

In short, existence presupposition is not a strictly linguistic phenomenon, and it's certainly not a lexical phenomenon. Therefore pejorative lexemes cannot be understood in the same way as ordinary terms that do not refer.

To summarize: I myself accept the non-propositionality thesis. However, it is thus far neither supported nor explained. If (1) be neither true nor false, it is not because it is meaningless, or because its assertion and denial are both immoral, or because it commits a category mistake, or because it rests on a false semantic presupposition.

5.   The Non-Proposition No-Reference Theory

According to Kriste Taylor (1981), "The niggers in this town will benefit from improvements in medicine" is neither true nor false because it fails to express a complete proposition; and it fails to express a complete proposition because pejorative terms do not refer or denote. (In denying that pejorative terms denote or contribute to truth-conditions, while acknowledging that pejorative terms are meaningful, Taylor may seem to hold that meaning is at least partly separate from truth-conditions. She works, however, within a Strawsonian framework and I take her, like Grim, as holding a kind of three-valued or supervalued truth-conditionalism: if Germans were despicable then (1) would be true iff Nietzsche was German; otherwise (1) lacks truth-conditions.)

Since speakers certainly use pejoratives with the intention of referring, Taylor recognizes that her case rests on the distinction between intended and successful reference:

> We know that when this individual says "niggers and broads", he *means* to refer to or *intends* to refer to the blacks and women in the town. But just as in the example of one intending to refer to their cat by the use of the expression "my dog", we can go on to ask whether or not one *succeeds* in referring to blacks and women and cats by the use of the expressions "nigger", "broad", and "dog". [313]

Unfortunately Taylor neglects to specify the conditions under which actual reference goes beyond mere intent. One would have thought that reference consists in a suitably recognized intention to refer (Grice 1957). Surely if David Duke, the Ku Klux Klanner in the Louisiana state legislature, uses the word "nigger" with the intention of referring to blacks, and if you recognize this intention, then he has successfully referred.

Granted, one or more distinctions can be drawn between attributive and referential uses (Donnellan 1966), between linguistic and speaker meaning (Grice 1968), and between correct and incorrect reference, and in each case the one may fail where the other succeeds. But then we need to know, if we are to judge whether pejoratives successfully and strictly and conventionally denote, *how* such denotation might diverge from reference otherwise construed. So far as I can see, there are only four possibilities.

(i) PERFORMANCE ERROR. Taylor compares pejorative reference failure to the case where someone refers to her very own cat as a dog. Although she does not explain why anyone would do this (is it a joke? secret code? dementia?), let's suppose that it is some kind of slip of the tongue, and not a confusion about either the nature of the beast or the conventions of language. The relevance of this performance error, however, is lost to me. When David Duke refers to "niggers", he does so not because of inattention, neural misfiring, or other momentary lapse. He does so consistently, deliberately, and unapologetically.

(ii) LINGUISTIC INCOMPETENCE. A certain child defines one horsepower as the energy it takes to drag a horse 500 feet, another describes an obtuse angle as an "obscene angle", and in Japan the sign on a trashbin says "please waste". In these cases (correct) reference fails because the speaker does not fully know English; or to put it another way, the speaker's idiolect does not relevantly match that of the audience. But again, the use of pejoratives is not of this kind. David Duke knows full well the conventional meaning of "nigger", and it is precisely because he knows it that he chooses to use it.

In reply, Taylor flatly denies that there is any convention by which "nigger" refers:

> One could not secure reference to any individuals by the use of this expression because there is a linguistic convention – an agreed upon practice – that prohibits successful reference by the use of this expression. [314]

Unfortunately, this is an instance of wishful thinking. In fact there *is* a linguistic convention for the use of pejoratives: if no convention existed for their reference, predication, or other signifying function, they would never exist. Taylor would not have written a paper on the topic, and even if she had then her discussion of "broad" and "nigger" would have been pointless and incomprehensible.

Taylor perseveres:

> [a] even if it were true that a certain group of speakers regarded it as an acceptable practice to refer to women as "broads" and blacks as "niggers", [b] other speakers of the language might have a moral obligation to work at changing the "customs" and practices of the other speakers. [315]

Skipping over the egregious blindness to facts implied by the subjunctivity of clause (a), let's grant, for the sake of argument, moral obligation (b). Still, it does not alter the relevant facts of the matter, namely that speakers *do* use pejoratives, they do use them to intend to refer, they do use them to secure audience recognition of the intended reference, and in so doing they do use conventional regularities of language.

(iii) FACTUAL IGNORANCE. If the man in the corner is holding water then "the man in the corner with the martini" fails to denote. In this case, correct reference fails because the words express attributive content that is not satisfied on the given occasion. So if pejoratives fail to refer for the same reason, pejoratives must express attributive content that is unsatisfied. But this line of thinking threatens to return us to the Conjunction Theory. That aside, David Duke's problem is not simply that he is uninformed. Though he may subscribe to ignorant theories of heredity or theology as part of his racist worldview, they are not necessary. It is possible for two individuals to share the same background factual beliefs but differ in their values and emotional outlook, in which case the one may actively use pejoratives while the other does not.

(iv) COMMUNICATIVE LIES AND FIGURATIVE LANGUAGE. If you know that a man is holding a martini glass full of water, you may nonetheless refer to him as "the man holding the martini". You may do so because you believe that your audience assumes the martini glass is full of martini, in which case using the accurate description would only be confusing, and you may deliberately use an inaccurate phrase even when you believe your audience is knowledgeable, simply because the truth is too wordy. [To say "martini" when you mean "martini glass containing a martini-looking substance" saves minor effort that can be cost-effective given that the production and interpretation of figurative language – metaphor, metonymy, hyperbole, and much else – is as spontaneous and effortless as that of literal language; see Gibbs (1994).] Such deliberate inaccuracy for the sake of saving on explanation is routine, except among pedants. But such use is, strictly speaking, *false*, not neither-true-nor-false. Besides, David Duke's use of "nigger" is not an example of loose language. In using it he does not see himself as waxing poetical or as saying something that is technically false in order to strike a greater communicative success.

In conclusion, pejorative use is not a result of performance error, broken English, simple ignorance, or figurative language. Taylor is mistaken in claiming that pejoratives distinctively do not denote.

The mistake comes out even more when you consider that Taylor focuses on cases where the pejorative term occurs as part of a definite description in subject position. But as (1) shows, pejoratives may also occur as predicates. How would Taylor deal with such constructions? On the one hand, she might say that pejoratives fail to function only in subject position; as predicates they work fine. But to deny truth-value to some pejorative statements on grounds of offensiveness while accepting that others have truth-value is inconsistent.

On the other hand, Taylor could revise her theory, so that pejoratives fail not only as subjects but as predicates. But if she wants to deny that (1) is truth-valued, she should say the same thing about other constructions with non-denoting predicates. Not only would (23) lack truth-value, so would (24).

(23) The present king of France is bald.
(24) Louis XIV is the present king of France.

This of course is just plain wrong; (24) is straightforwardly false on anyone's account.

6.   The Bracket Theory

As an alternative to his own Conjunction Theory, Stenner prefers what I shall call the Bracket Theory, which holds (25), or better (25′):

(25) Nietzsche was a kraut $\equiv$ Nietzsche was a German. [I believe it is appropriate to speak of Germans as krauts.]

(25') Nietzsche was a kraut ≡ Nietzsche was a German. [I believe Germans are despicable.]

Here the brackets

> indicate what is suggested but not stated by the original. Bracketed material then is not construed as expressing part of the truth-conditions of the original. On this analysis [1] comes out true after all. [304]

The Bracket Theory is also held by Frege [see Copp (2001: 15)], it is impressively developed by Copp (2001), and it is floated by Blackburn (1984: 148), though Blackburn questions whether there can be any facts of the matter to distinguish it from the Conjunction Theory.

Since bracketed material does not add to truth-conditions, (25) is truth-conditionally equivalent to (TC), which is at best incomplete as an analysis of pejorative meaning.

(TC) Nietzsche was a kraut ≡ Nietzsche was a German.

Because Stenner claims that there are two kinds of meaning, "stated" and "suggested", or truth-conditional and non-truth-conditional, or semantic and pragmatic (in one special sense of these terms), perhaps his theory can be cast in the form of two separate biconditionals, with the semantic component specified by (TC). As for how to specify the pragmatic component, Stenner drops a number of hints. Unfortunately, none pan out.

(i) PARALINGUISTIC ANALOGY. Like Frege, Stenner compares vocabulary choice to "tone of voice or a look" (p. 303). Blackburn likewise compares pejorative terms to derisive intonation, while Altman (1994: 141) compares pejorative meaning to that of spitting at someone. However, there is an important difference between pejorative language and its purported analogues. Pejorative terms, like obscene terms, are matters of linguistic convention, varying from place to place. For example, American "fanny" refers to the buttocks, and the usage is precious, jocular, or euphemistic, whereas British "fanny" refers to the vagina, and the usage is vulgar or obscene. The significance of nasty glares and spitting, in contrast, is neither linguistic nor conventional; these appear to be cross-cultural universals (Ekman & Davidson 1994, Flynn 1977). Consequently, if Stenner's similes are to be helpful then we must be given guidance on the *respects* in which one thing resembles another. Here we have none except the naked claim that pejorative meaning, like tones, looks, spit, is non-truth-conditional – though of course non-truth-conditionality is what we wanted to understand in the first place!

(ii) SHARED VALUES. Stenner's use of brackets recalls Grice (1967) and subsequently Bach & Harnish (1979). In these works, bracketed material is "common ground" or "mutual knowledge" and it stands outside the scope of operators such as negation, just as we want (§2). Pejorative communication, however, may take place without speaker and audience sharing derogatory assumptions about the intended targets; indeed, speakers may use pejorative terms in successful communication without either implying or thinking that their audience shares derogatory assumptions.

(iii) IMPLICATURE. Stenner's distinction between the stated and the suggested recalls Grice's (1967) distinction between the said and the indicated in his lectures on conversational and conventional implicature. But pejorative meaning is not the result of conversational implicature, for otherwise it would be rationally inferable from truth-conditional component (TC), in which case "kraut" and "German" would be equally pejorative. Nor is calling pejorative meaning the result of conventional implicature helpful, for that simply bandies a label without explanation. Indeed, as Bach (1999: 335) writes, "to the extent that putative conventional implicatures really are implicatures, they are not conventional, and to the extent that they are conventional they are not implicatures."

(iv) FELICITY-CONDITIONS. Stenner's reference to what is "appropriate" recalls Austin (1962) and his discussion of felicity-conditions. Felicity-conditions come close to being performance-conditions, those conditions necessary and sufficient for the performance of a speech act (such as stating, ordering, promising). Performance-conditions, however, fail to capture pejorative meaning, for one can succeed in making pejorative statements without feeling contempt just as one can make promises without intending to carry them through. Performances do not require sincerity, yet conditions of sincerity are somehow part of meaning.

Austin realizes this and speaks at length of sincerity-conditions and much else. But he leaves felicity undefined. If felicity subsumes truth, hence if felicity-conditions include truth-conditions, then the felicity-conditions of (1) would incorporate the truth-conditions specified in (TC):

(26) "Nietzsche was a kraut" is felicitous ≡ (a) Nietzsche was German and (b) Germans are despicable.

But if we accept this then (TC) would seem to serve no purpose. Alternatively, if felicity and truth are coordinate virtues, so that (TC) and something like (27) are both required for semantic analysis, then I have no inkling at all of what the felicity is supposed to be.

(27) "Nietzsche was a kraut" is felicitous ≡ Germans are despicable.

One could stipulate that felicity is appropriate assertability in all manners except for truth. But this not only relies on an unexplained notion of what is appropriate, it is ad hoc and it destroys whatever unity there is that would make felicity a single quality.

(v) UTTERANCE-CONDITIONS. Blackburn suggests that "The convention would be that you only put beliefs about Germans using that overtone (or the derisory word) if you have the contemptuous attitude" (p. 149). I take it that "putting a belief" amounts to making an assertion or uttering a declarative, in which case Blackburn's suggestion is that:

(28) If S asserts/utters "Nietzsche was a kraut" then S despises Germans.

Of course this analysis too falls to the sincerity problem. Speakers may say (1), without actually despising Germans, for speakers may lie or otherwise dissemble. Consequently it is better to hold (29) or Copp's (29'):

(29) If S sincerely asserts/utters "Nietzsche was a kraut" then S despises Germans.
(29') It is a convention that if S says "Nietzsche was a kraut" then S despises Germans.

While I applaud the direction this is heading, it falls short of a biconditional "if and only if," and making it into one, as below, would be a mistake because one may despise Germans without ever referring to Nietzsche at all.

(30) S sincerely utters "Nietzsche was a kraut" $\equiv$ S despises Germans.

Nor does it suffice to revise (30) as:

(31) S sincerely utters "Nietzsche was a kraut" $\equiv$ S despises Nietzsche.

For this fails to capture the fact that it is never appropriate to call any particular person a kraut unless it is appropriate to speak of Germans in general as krauts. Nor does combining the analysans clauses from (30) and (31) work either.

(32) S sincerely utters "Nietzsche was a kraut" $\equiv$ S despises Nietzsche and Germans.

For if S sincerely said "Nietzsche is a kraut philosopher", and no more, then the left-hand side would be false while the right-hand side would be true.

Instead of speaking of S's linguistic behavior we might formulate the pragmatic component in mental terms:

(33) S believes that Nietzsche was a kraut $\equiv$ S believes Germans are despicable.

Yet this is still false because S may be under the impression that Nietzsche was Italian. The right-hand side of the pragmatic component must somehow incorporate the information given in (TC), p. 135:

(34) S believes that Nietzsche was a kraut $\equiv$ (a) S believes Nietzsche was German and (b) S believes Germans are despicable.

This analysis makes the truth-conditional clause (TC) superfluous and eliminable. By positing (34), we have been led into a wholly non-truth-conditional framework, indeed we have been led into attitudinal semantics.

To summarize, the Bracket Theory has two aspects. As a negative claim that truth-conditions are insufficient for representing the full meaning of pejoratives, it is correct. As a positive claim about what non-truth-conditional meaning consists in, it is clearly erroneous where it is clear at all.

7.   The Multi-Proposition Theory

Inspired by phenomena sometimes regarded as conventional implicature, Bach (1994: §4) suggests that we surrender the "insidious assumption" that every declarative sentence expresses exactly one proposition [see too Wilson & Sperber (1993)]. Neale (1999) quotes Frege to the same effect – "it may well happen that we have more simple propositions than sentences" – and he applies the idea to pejoratives. The proposal seems to be:

(35) "Nietzsche was a kraut" expresses the sequence of propositions <Nietzsche was German, Germans are despicable>.

If both elements of the sequence were true, or if both were false, (1) would be categorically true or false. Because the elements differ in truth-value, however, one hesitates in judging the value of (1). In some contexts, the first element is most salient or relevant, in others it is the second, and in still others the two elements share equal or indeterminate priority.

In claiming that multiple propositions are ordered, Neale should specify the ordering relation but does not. Since this part is obscure to me, I would prefer appealing to a *set* of propositions rather than a *sequence*. Either way, however, the Multi-proposition Theory elegantly captures our basic intuitions regarding pejoratives while avoiding, I would add, the troubles that beset the Conjunction, Non-proposition, and Bracket theories.

Yet challenges from Chapters 1 and 2 recur. First, what is a proposition? Since the Multi-proposition Theory precludes the standard nominalist strategy of identifying propositions with sentences, statements, or utterances, the problem of platonism threatens. Second, if knowledge of meaning is knowledge of truth-conditions, then it would seem that to know the meaning of (1) is to know that it expresses a set, ordered or otherwise; but Conjunction Theorists, among others, do not know that (1) expresses a set.

Even if the Multi-proposition Theory be accepted, one might wonder whether it is genuinely truth-conditional. Already TC semantics appears to be dying a death of a thousand wounds, and multi-propositionalism arguably delivers the coup de grace: "Granted, truth is mysterious, being prone to paradox. At the very least, we want to say that the meaning of the Liar sentence is not the same as its truth-conditions. Also, obviously, we want to restrict truth-conditionalism to declaratives. Even in that case, knowledge of meaning is not the *same* as knowledge of truth-conditions, but only entails it. And given vagueness, we want to say that to know the meaning of a statement is not completely to know the conditions under which it is true, but rather some imprecise subset thereof. Of course, context matters, so what I'm really talking about is *conditions on* truth-conditions. Then too, keeping in mind the Multiple Proposition Theory of pejoratives, let's say that knowledge of meaning is knowledge of a *set* of conditions on partial truth-conditions. So my considered opinion is that to know the meaning of a sentence is to know at least something of the set of sets of truth-condition conditions, plus other things, so long as the sentence is both declarative and well behaved. But I'm open minded, so I admit that further twists might be called for. See? Meaning is truth-condition!"

My doubts about the truth-conditionality of multi-propositionalism are fanned by Neale's exposition. First, Neale admirably speaks of words as providing instructions that generate propositions, which implies that propositions are mental constructs, a story that precludes TC semantics if the Coordination Problem truly rules out duplex semantics (p. 32). Second, Neale repeatedly subordinates truth-values to judgments:

an utterance is judged true (false) if and only if some contextually weighted number of the propositions it expresses are judged true (false). [58]

Because such a mentalist account renders objectivist truth-conditionalism superfluous, I would like to turn to forthright subjectivism.

8.   The Attitudinal Theory

We have looked at several theories of the pejorative. The Disquotational, Conjunction, and Stereotype Theories identify the meaning of
a pejorative statement with classical truth-conditions. Available non-
proposition theories identify pejorative meaning with three-valued or supervalued truth-conditions. The Bracket Theory identifies pejorative meaning
with truth-conditions plus something extra, and for the Multi-proposition
Theory this something extra is more truth-conditions. None of these theories, I
have argued, is adequate, except insofar as they get transformed into a wholly
non-truth-conditional semantics. It is to such semantics that we now turn.

According to attitudinal semantics – what some would call pragmatics –
meaning is not antiseptic, impersonal, abstract, objective. Sometimes we
speak as if it is, as when we ask for the meaning of "the brain is wider than
the sky" (Emily Dickinson). But this is elliptical for "what does it mean *to
you?*", "what did it mean *to the author?*", "what does it mean *to the typical
speaker of present English?*", "what does it mean *to a knowledgeable and
sensitive literary scholar?*", and so forth. Furthermore, meaning is not a
thing, it is an embodied event, and to specify it we must explicitly situate it
against its rich background.

For these reasons, among others, I propose a fundamental shift in the
very subject matter of linguistics. Instead of taking propositions like (1) as
our object of inquiry, I propose to take facts like (1′):

(1′) As a member of the anglophone community, S thinks "Nietzsche
    was a kraut".

Instead of seeking the truth-conditions of (1), I seek the truth-conditions of
(1′), which I call the attitude-conditions of (1). In particular, I propose:

(ψ) For any member S of the anglophone community, S thinks "Nietzsche
    was a kraut" $\equiv$ (a) S thinks that Nietzsche was German and (b) S
    disdains Germans as a class.

Now I would like to try to convey what this does and does not claim. To
begin with, (ψ) does not purport to tell us everything about the meaning
of (1). It says nothing about the nature of the anglophone community, for
instance its wars against Germany, it says nothing about the genealogy of
"kraut", which derives from "sauerkraut", it says nothing about metalinguistic uses of "kraut". These are matters for other branches of theorizing
that, combined with (ψ), are hypothesized to account for all speech facts.

Second, an anglophone is not just *any* speaker of English. Analysis (ψ) is not falsified simply because a surprising number of my students do not know the word "kraut". In saying that S ranges over anglophone subjects, I mean that S ranges over those subjects whose linguistic competence extends to (1).

Also, I am not committed to the exact word choices in (ψ). For instance, "disdain" might be replaced by "deride", "deprecate", "despise", "revile", "scorn", "scoff at", or "have contempt for". Nor do I mean to suggest that disdain is exclusive of thought: it may very well be a kind of thought, or imply a kind of thought. Further, the vagueness of "German" – citizen of Germany, German-speaking inhabitant of Austro-Germany, anyone of German ancestry, etc. – need not necessarily match the vagueness of "kraut"; each word, after all, has its own history. What I do claim is that the analysis of pejoratives takes the *form* of (ψ).

Note that the ascription of contempt in clause (ψb) stands outside the scope of the propositional attitude in (ψa). For if the propositional attitude took wide scope, as in (36), then negated pejorative statements would have to be analyzed as in ($\neg$36).

(36) S thinks "Nietzsche was a kraut" $\equiv$ S thinks that
     (a) Nietzsche was German and (b) S disdains Germans as a class.
($\neg$36) S thinks "Nietzsche was not a kraut" $\equiv$ S thinks that not both
     (a) Nietzsche was German and (b) S disdains Germans as a class.

If this were the case then (37), together with some commonplace postulates regarding belief, would entail (38):

(37) S does not disdain Germans as a class.
(38) S thinks "Nietzsche was not a kraut."

But (37) does not ordinarily entail (38). Therefore analysis (ψ) is preferred over (36). (Analysis (36) might be desirable if, lacking a separate theory of metalinguistic negation, we *wanted* to show that (37) implies (38). However, since metalinguistic negation can apply to all sorts of statements, not just pejoratives, metalinguistic negation must have its own account.)

Finally, the contempt is directed not just at Nietzsche but at Germans generically; (39) would be a mistake.

(39) S thinks "Nietzsche was a kraut" $\equiv$ (a) S thinks that Nietzsche was German and (b) S disdains Nietzsche.

On the one hand, specific reference to Nietzsche is not necessary in the contempt clause (b). For in the usual case (ψb) will suffice to indicate, via implicature, that S also holds contempt for Nietzsche in particular, though this implicature can be cancelled, as when a bigot tells someone:

(40) You're the only kraut I like and respect.

On the other hand, reference to Germans as a class is necessary. Suppose that you sincerely respect Germans in general, but you cannot stand one Bruner, to use one of my ancestral names. Then you would not be likely to think of Bruner as a "kraut". (You might *call* her a kraut if you wanted to make her think that you despised her entire people. However, your choice of words would be deceptive. The attitudinal analysis applies to your *thoughts*.) Furthermore, an expression like "that kraut Bruner" is, aside from extrinsic offensiveness to those who object to ethnic slurs, intrinsically insulting not only to Bruner but to all Germans. In short, the analysis of "kraut" must refer to Germans generically as a disdained class.

Which is why the left-handed compliment (40) is nonetheless offensive. Furthermore, its offensiveness goes beyond saying "I dislike Germans in general, but you are an exception." For in order to believe that a pejorative applies to someone, one must have not only contempt for a certain class but also access to conventionally established pejorative terminology; one must belong to a linguistic community in which pejoratives exist. Since the conventionalization of contempt relies, like all convention, on societally recognized norms, every pejorative utterance is proof not only of the speaker's contempt, but proof that such contempt prevails in society at large. This is why pejoratives make powerful insults, why repeated exposures to pejoratives can create feelings of alienation, inferiority, and self-hatred, and indeed why a single pejorative utterance evokes measurable bias in overhearers (Greenberg & Pyszczynski 1985, Kirkland et al. 1987, Simon & Greenberg 1996).

So: is (1) true, false, or neither? One possible view is that the truth-evaluable content of (1) is given by the sum of the cognitive contents (ψa) and (ψb). Since the content of (ψb) is affective and non-propositional, the cognitive content of the whole amounts to just (ψa); hence (1) is true. Another possible view identifies the truth of (1) with the correctness of (1'), and the correctness of (1') with that of (ψa) & (ψb). In this case, some will hold that it is never correct for anyone to disdain Germans as a class and hence (1) is false. Others will hold that if S has personally suffered at the hands of genocidal Germans then prejudicial disdain on the part of S may be legitimate and therefore, in that sense, correct. On this view the truth-value of (1) is indexical.

Alternatively, my own preference, one may say that there is no such thing as the *proposition* or *belief* expressed by "Nietzsche was a kraut", there is only the *attitude-complex* involving (a) the pure belief that Nietzsche was German and (b) a cognitive-affective attitude toward Germans. We might say that (a), as a pure belief, is true or false, while the attitude-complex is not. S's belief-complex encompasses *something* of value, namely the true belief (a), but it also encompasses something deleterious, namely ethnic hostility (b). In this case, the mental state reported in (1') is neither true nor false as a whole.

It is also possible that the concept lexicalized in English as "truth" is too indeterminate to yield a clear answer to the question of (1)'s truth-value. While this indeterminacy is contradicted by those theories that predict a robust truth-value (or robust lack of truth-value) for every statement, it fits comfortably with attitudinal semantics.

In conclusion, my analysis captures that which is right with the others. Like disquotational semantics, attitudinal semantics attempts to offer biconditional analyses that can be abstracted from orthogonal facts of etymology, sociology, pragmatics, and so forth. In order for the various theories to interface, however, they must possess common vocabulary, which I locate in the form of "S", the speaker/subject. Like the Conjunction and Bracket Theories, my analysis discerns in pejoratives a complex of two components, the cognitive and the affective. Finally, representing a sort of compromise between the Indexical Theory on the one hand, which sees (1) as true-for-S if S disdains Germans and false-for-S otherwise, and truth-conditional Non-proposition Theories on the other hand, which sees (1) as categorically neither true nor false, my analysis sees (1) as "true-for-S" if S disdains Germans and otherwise as probably neither true for S nor false for S.

9. Extensions & Elaborations

My analysis of "kraut" is incomplete as an account of the pejorative for a number of reasons. For one thing, it fails to give an idea of the extensive range of pejorative lexemes and constructions. It is important for me to rectify this if I am to show that the pejorative is not just an exceptional feature of language that can safely be ignored by truth-conditional semantics. For another thing, the account so far fails to distinguish among different kinds and intensity of pejoration. The facts of such variation, I shall need to explain, can be addressed by socio-pragmatic analyses that function in parallel to my framework.

As for range, pejoratives run along lines involving ethnicity and race (41); sex, marital status, and gender (42); sexual orientation (43); morals

(44); politics (45); religion (46); health and age (47); substance abuse (48); and popularity (49).

    (41) gringo, wetback, honky, nigger, coon, limey, frog, kraut, Polack, Spic, dago, wog, wop, kike, hebe, hymie, Yid, Injun, gook, Jap, Nip, Chinaman, Chink, slant-eye, towel-head, sand nigger [White House term for Arab, Matsuda (1989: 2334)], Canuck, Yank, redneck, cracker, boy [in reference to adult]

    (42) broad, chick, wench, dame, skirt, girl [in reference to adult]; spinster; sissy, wuss

    (43) bugger, dyke, fag(got), fairy, fruit, pansy, queen, queer, sod; perv; breeder

    (44) bimbo, floozy, harlot, slut, strumpet, whore; prig, prude

    (45) Commie, pinko, Nazi, fascist

    (46) Bible-thumper, Christ-killer, heathen, heretic, infidel, papist

    (47) four-eyes, crip; geezer, punk

    (48) druggie, freak, hophead, lush, wino

    (49) nerd, geek, dweeb; loser

    (50) bum, prole; goon, pig; snitch, stool-pigeon

There are also pejoratives for the mentally aberrant, including the insane (51), the inane (52), the uninformed (53), and the naive or inexperienced (54).

    (51) lunatic, psychotic, sociopath, nut, deranged, bonkers

    (52) idiot, imbecile, moron, dolt, dingbat, doofus, buffoon, cretin [from "Christian"]

    (53) ignoramus, dunce, numskull, airhead, blockhead, chowderhead, birdbrain

    (54) fool, rube, clodhopper, nincompoop

Further pejoratives come from proper names (55), others refer to animals (56) and primitives (57).

    (55) Jezebel, Judas, Benedict Arnold, Quisling, Hitler, Stalin, martinet

    (56) dog, hog, pig, swine, cow, rat, toad, snake, worm, beast

    (57) barbarian, savage, brute, troglodyte, Neanderthal

Finally, there are terms for mean, nasty, inconsiderate people, terms both vulgar (59) and otherwise (60).

    (59) bastard, SOB, bitch, cunt, prick, asshole, shithead

    (60) creep, jerk, twerp, twit, punk

Needless to say, these listings are not meant to be comprehensive; nor do the categories carry any deep linguistic significance (though they are socially and cognitively significant inasmuch as they indicate the sorts of referent for which people have found it desirable to deploy pejorative terms, and the sorts of referent which commonly gives rise to metaphor). One point they do illustrate, however, insofar as I expect my every reader to have used at least one of these terms, is that pejoratives are used by everyone from every demographic.

Pejoratives can be generated by systematic principles, and they can sometimes be used in various non-pejorative and quasi-pejorative ways, which I now itemize along with other remarks.

(i) Some of these words are ambiguous between technical and everyday senses. For instance, "moron" is clinically defined as any adult with a mental age between 7 and 12, while it is vernacularly defined as anyone who is very stupid. Again, "Nazi" has a technical sense ("member of the German National Socialist Party") and a colloquial sense ("right-wing/authoritarian/totalitarian power-monger"). In general it is only the colloquial or vernacular sense that is pejorative by convention.

(ii) Terms of abuse are sometimes used among friends, and this calls for explanation. Flynn (1977: 82) suggests that friendly abuse is a means of expressing emotionally charged feelings without the threat of appearing sentimental. This raises a puzzle, however: where the ploy is transparent, the speaker will appear just as sentimental as if more honest vocabulary were used; and where the ploy is opaque, "friendly abuse" will appear as genuinely hostile. Flynn also suggests, more convincingly, that friendly abuse is a means of testing and reinforcing an intimate relationship (p. 84). Like sexual sadomasochism, it serves to signify that no behavior between two parties is forbidden. Regardless of the correct explanation, "friendly" verbal teasing, like "friendly" punching and pinching, is to be explained by non-linguistic theory, and is not the responsibility of semantics.

(iii) Blacks sometimes use the word "nigger". The foregoing reflections in (ii) might apply here too, although there's another possibility as well. Perhaps such pejorative remarks are sometimes meant to signal camaraderie: "*you* are derogated by society for being black, and obviously I am black, therefore *I* am derogated by society, so let's stick together". In this case, instead of claiming that all speakers of English who use "nigger" do so to express contempt, with respect to this one lexeme we can divide the anglophone population into two sociolects.

(61) For black speakers of English S, S thinks "X is a nigger" ≡ (a) S thinks that X is black and (b) S feels camaraderie toward X.

(62) For non-black speakers of English S, S thinks "X is a nigger" ≡ (a)
     S thinks that X is black and (b) S disdains blacks as a class.

The existence of such a racially based dialect difference, of course, does
not preclude black and white speakers from understanding the doxastic and
emotive attitudes expressed by the others. Thus the truth of (61), if it be
true, does not undercut the pejoration in the white use of the word "nigger",
or in all uses by blacks.

(iv) Pejorative labels are also used non-pejoratively by homosexuals who
call themselves "queer". This is an instance of *appropriation* by which some
victim group attempts to change the conventional meaning of some term.
From a semantic point of view, such political appropriation works rather as
scientific appropriation does: just as scientific usage of "star" inhibits the
lay public from using "star" to refer to planets, so the homosexual use of
"queer" inhibits the straight public from using "queer" to express contempt.

The importance of appropriation for socio-political change merits a closer
look at the case of "queer". As a speculative etymology I offer the following.

(a) In the beginning, everyone who uses "queer" does so disparagingly.
    The lexically conventionalized association between homosexuality
    and contempt encourages the average citizen to unthinkingly develop
    a negative attitude toward gays. (This is not to suggest that language
    is the only factor, or the most important.)
(b) Some gays, in a deliberate act of reform, or perhaps out of sarcasm,
    begin to use "queer" non-disparagingly. By changing the meaning
    of the word, they themselves come to feel its sting a little less than
    they otherwise would.
(c) After stage (b), "queer" is variously used in pejorative, neutral, and
    prideful ways. As a result, the average citizen is not sure what
    connotations to associate with the word, and hence it loses some of
    its pejoration.
(d) As gays and non-gays both come to see "queer" as non-pejorative,
    even enemies of homosexuality lose the ability to use the word as an
    instrument of assault. They may still disdain homosexuals as a class,
    but they will view the word "queer" as being as neutral as the word
    "lesbian".

Supposing that something like this is correct, could blacks appropriate the
term "nigger", divesting it of pejoration? Possibly, but it's important to
keep certain differences in mind. Race and ethnicity are more visible than
sexual preference. Not only are they more visible, but they have always

been a greater source of xenophobia. Moreover, in our society race is widely regarded as somehow essential to a person's identity, whereas sexual preference is widely seen as a behavioral overlay. Finally, the history of slavery in America creates a stigma that dies hard given the superstitious practice of blaming the victim.

To return to the main point, pejoratives can be appropriated for non-pejorative use, perhaps depriving them in the long run of any conventional pejoration. Nonetheless the terms in (41–60) are, to a greater or lesser extent, still pejorative.

(v) Suppose Sam asserts:

(63) Xavier really likes Spics.
(64) I really like Spics.

Unlike (63), (64) conveys an air of inconsistency. On my account, (63) is analyzed as:

(65) Sam thinks "Xavier really likes Spics" ≡ (a) Sam thinks Xavier likes Hispanics and (b) Sam disdains Hispanics.

Since there is no conflict between clauses (a) and (b), Sam's belief is coherent. In contrast, (64) is analyzed as:

(66) Sam thinks "Sam really likes Spics" ≡ (a) Sam thinks Sam likes Hispanics and (b) Sam disdains Hispanics.

Given that Sam knows his own likes, (a) and (b) contradict each other. Either Sam's beliefs are very confused, or Sam does not really believe that he "likes Spics".

Nonetheless there *is* a reading of (64) that makes it sincere and coherent. Suppose that Jake says "I wish the Spics would stay out of our neighborhood" and Sam replies "Hey – I really like Spics!" In this echoic use, Sam is momentarily taking Jake's perspective.

(67) Sam thinks "Sam really likes Spics" ≡ (a) Sam thinks Sam likes Hispanics and (b) Jake disdains Hispanics.

This derives from the general scheme by replacing S not with the speaker but with someone whose point of view the speaker is adopting, in this case S's interlocutor. Sam himself does not disdain Hispanics, but he takes the perspective of someone who does, either as a show of solidarity; for the sake of argument; or as a kind of performance error, where the lexical access of "Hispanic" is primed by the recency of "Spic".

(vi) Sometimes pejoratives may be used in innocence. Evan Mecham, governor of Arizona until he was impeached, once referred to black children as "pickaninnies." In the face of public outrage, Mecham defended the term, saying that it was not contemptuous or offensive. He may have spoken in honest ignorance of conventional English – I myself had never heard the term, so I can easily believe that Mecham may have once heard the word without understanding its full nature. In short, plenty of idiolectal differences are to be expected with regard to (41–60).

Given some of his other public statements, though, I think it's more likely that Mecham was indeed speaking contemptuously or at least condescendingly. This is not to say that Mecham was deliberately undermining his career by making racist statements in public. Rather, contempt and condescension, like arrogance, can be held and expressed by someone who is not aware of it.

Both of these cases, the innocent use and the unconscious use, differ from the disingenuous use.

(68) What's wrong with saying that kikes are smart? By "kike", I just mean Jews, and Jews are smart, aren't they?

Any normal adult who says (68) knows perfectly well that "kike" is conventionally a term of abuse, and that by stipulating an idiosyncratic meaning in place of the customary he or she is maliciously playing on words (and this aside from prejudice in the claim that Jews are especially smart).

(vii) Pejoratives vary a good deal in their intensity. For example, "Chinaman" is less offensive than "Chink", and "kraut" is less offensive than "nigger". A part of the reason for this variation in intensity has to do with the circumstances that have created and continue to sustain the existence of pejoratives. The derogatory force that attaches to "kraut" stems from the two wars between Germany and the English-speaking countries. ("Krauts" are not just German, but in the prototypical case are German soldiers fighting against the Allies.) The derogatory force that attaches to "nigger", in contrast, is rooted in a history of slavery, Jim Crow laws, lynchings, continued discrimination including state-endorsed racial profiling, and innate xenophobic prejudice. Thus, to classify everything in (41-60) as pejorative is not to say that they are all equally offensive.

(viii) Pejoratives also differ in kind. A *slur*, I now define, is any term that intrinsically signifies contempt for an entire class, as the racist and sexist pejoratives do. *Particularistic* pejoratives, in contrast, do not. For instance, "Alphonsa is a jerk" is better analyzed not as (69) but as (70).

(69) S thinks "Alphonsa is a jerk" ≡ (a) S thinks Alphonsa is menacingly insensitive and (b) S generically disdains the menacingly insensitive.

(70) S thinks "Alphonsa is a jerk" ≡ (a) S thinks Alphonsa is menacingly insensitive and (b) S disdains Alphonsa.

If you were a sadist then you might be pleased at the existence of thoughtless and insensitive people in the world who thereby do harmful things; and if you were generally oblivious yourself then you might not have any attitudes one way or the other toward the harmfully inconsiderate. In either case you would not generically disdain jerks. But if for some reason you took a disliking to Alphonsa, and thought of her as negligently unaware, you may easily call her a jerk, and judge her as such.

So "jerk" is not a slur. It is, however, pejorative, for its analysis must refer to contempt, disdain, hostility, blameworthiness, or the like.

Flynn seems to be grappling toward the same distinction:

> "You are a stupid fool!" is an insult which refers to the supposed lack of judgment or ability of a particular individual. "You dumb nigger!" insinuates that the object is dumb because he is a black person, rather than because of his uniquely individual capacities. [1977: 55]

This explanation is misleading. The words "stupid" and "nigger," as types, are each applied to many people; the utterances "You're stupid" and "You nigger," as tokens, are each directed against a single individual. The difference between particularistic pejoratives and slurs does not lie in their denotative functions but in the affective attitude of the speaker toward an individual versus toward a class of individuals.

(ix) Not all pejoratives refer to people. For example, "hovel" means something like "miserable, impoverished dwelling." "Impoverished" is a necessary component. If you find a very expensive, spacious mansion miserable (say, it is too drafty or too impersonal or decorated in bad taste), it would still not be a hovel. "Miserable" too is a necessary component; two speakers who argue whether x is a hovel make as little sense as two speakers who argue whether x is good. An utterance of "x is a hovel" expresses something about the speaker's internal state and is not a report about objective reality.

(x) Pejoratives are not limited to nouns, nor even to lexical items. Pejoration can be conveyed by adjectives, verbs, and tone. According to playwright David Mamet,

One of the things I learned when I studied acting is that the content of what is being said is rarely carried by [the denotation or even] the connotation of the words. It is carried by the rhythm of the speech and the posture of the speaker and a lot of other things [e.g. context, gaze, facial expression?]. [1995: 53]

Although he overstates the case, paralinguistic cues are significant, their exact significance varying from culture to culture. Flynn (1977: 9) reports that tone is used for insult by the Yoruba more than it is used by Westerners, and I conjecture that the importance of paralinguistic cues within a culture is a function of literacy. Since tone is not represented in writing, literates tend to assume that tone is not part of what is said. The more widely this assumption is shared, the more nearly it becomes true.

(xi) Pejoration can also be conveyed compositionally, where the message is not in any one element (be it lexical or phonological), but in the construction. For instance:

(71) John called Mary a Republican, and then *she* insulted *him*. [Lakoff]
(72) (71) somehow suggests that "Republican" functions as a term of abuse.

To understand why (72) is true, consider the logical form, as it, were of (71).

(73) S believes that (a) John called Mary a Republican at time t_1, and (b) *she* insulted *him* at subsequent t_2.

From S's belief in clause (b) we can infer that S believes that John insulted Mary at some time prior to t_2. [Demonstrating the grounds for this inference would entail giving a theory of contrastive stress, which would take me too far afield from the theory of pejoratives; cf. Ladd (1996).] If clause (a) represents S's only belief regarding John's actions toward Mary prior to t_2, or the most salient such belief, it follows that S believes that John's calling Mary a Republican constitutes an insult, in which case S believes that Republicans are generically contemptible. Thus, (72) is a loose way of saying:

(74) (71) implicates that S disdains Republicans as a class.

Of course much more can be said about compositional pejoratives, but enough has been sketched here, I think, to indicate the usefulness of the attitudinal framework.

(xii) Proper names, not linguistically pejorative, can nonetheless be used to disparage. If you refer to an Asian as Charlie Chan without reason to think that the referent is in fact so named, the implicature is that you regard all Asians as indistinguishable and interchangeable, which in turn implies that you regard Asians as second-class persons. Similar remarks apply to "Abdul", "Pedro", and "Sambo". The same kind of disrespect is conveyed in deliberate mispronunciations ("A-rab"). Again, it's instructive to note the difference in pejoration based on socio-historical background: whereas calling someone "Sambo" conveys a hint of threat, calling someone "Mac" conveys, at most, minor disrespect.

(xiii) Pejorative statements make negative evaluations, but other kinds of evaluation are possible too. These include expressions of euphemism [see Allan & Burridge (1991)]; terms of endearment such as "baby, darling, sweetheart"; honorifics, which in English are mostly limited to vocatives like "ma'm, sir, Your Excellency" but are much more systematic in some other languages; and moral and esthetic judgment. (A range of evaluatives from positive to negative can be seen in Bertrand Russell's paradigm "I am firm, you are stubborn, they are pig-headed".)

(xiv) The attitudinal framework applies to explaining not only evaluatives but to all cases where two terms, sharing the same reference, are accompanied by distinct senses or conceptualizations. This includes register and examples like "corpse/cadaver/carcass". While these terms all refer to dead bodies, their differences in meaning might be captured by differences in attitude or perspective.

(75) S thinks "X is a corpse" ≡ S thinks that X is a dead body, and S thinks of X as a former person, an object fit for funerary treatment.

(76) S thinks "X is a carcass" ≡ S thinks that X is a dead body, and S thinks of X as an object fit for the butcher or wild carnivore.

(77) S thinks "X is a cadaver" ≡ S thinks that X is a dead body, and S thinks of X as an object fit for autopsy or scientific dissection.

(78) S thinks "X is the Morning Star" ≡ S thinks that X is Venus, and S thinks of X as appearing in the morning.

(79) S thinks "X is the Evening Star" ≡ S thinks that X is Venus, and S thinks of X as appearing in the evening.

The attitudinal theory, because it possesses the intensional resources of belief and mind, provides a framework for the representation of linguistic intensionality.

(xv) The separation of the belief and contempt attitudes captures the intuition of Stenner, Blackburn, and ethical non-cognitivists that evaluatives possess two kinds of meaning (truth-conditional on the one hand and pragmatic, expressive, emotive, or prescriptive on the other). But is this a good thing? Do we really want to postulate an either/or mechanism that neatly assigns every word or statement into exclusive classes, the evaluative and the purely descriptive, the pejorative and the non-pejorative? Or is it better to suppose, since statements run the gamut in their degree and kind of offensiveness, that semantic representations ought to employ something other than the thinking/disdaining dichotomy that I have used?

There is experimental evidence that stereotypes consist of separate factual and evaluative components [e.g. Kirby & Gardner (1973)]. In addition I think that some kind of emotive content must be a conventional part of some words and not others, e.g. "nigger" versus "black". Those who use slurs do not simply have different beliefs about the world from those who do not. For what could those different beliefs consist in? If they are factual of the sort listed in (80), they would not in themselves suffice to cause anyone to use pejorative terminology.

(80) Blacks are in the minority.

Blacks have traditionally faced prejudice. If they are accompanied by value judgments –

(81) Anyone in the minority deserves contempt. Tradition is a good thing.

– then we have evidence that "nigger", but not "black", is conventionally associated with a value judgment on the part of the speaker.

A similar case can be made for the other words on the list (41-60). For example, imagine two nurses at a home for the feeble, A and B. Nurse A, who views the patients matter-of-factly, knows that the patients are stupid, and can tell you which ones can't even dress themselves, but does not hold it against them. Nurse B, in contrast, frownfully wonders how such imbeciles could ever come to exist. Which nurse uses the word "dolt"? The answer is clear. Even if professionalism prevents nurse B from ever addressing a patient as a dolt, even if a sense of shame keeps B from ever referring in public to a patient as a dolt, B still thinks of the patients as dolts, and it may come out either in private conversation or in anger. Nurse A, however, hardly makes use of the concept "dolt", and even in the loss of temper A is not likely to think of the word or to invoke it. What this example is meant to show is that "dolt" cannot simply mean "very very stupid". Both nurses recognize that their patients are very very stupid, but only one of them employs the pejorative. This is because only one of them has a contemptuous attitude.

By insisting on a semantic category of pejorative terms, I do not mean to bulldoze the facts. I have acknowledged the importance of context, explaining that pejorative terms can be used non-pejoratively in (ii) horse-play, (iii) in-group situations, (iv) political protest, (v) shows of solidarity, for the sake of argument, as a performance error, and (vi) ignorance. Conversely, the "Republican" example shows that non-pejoratives can be used pejoratively. My discussion of "kraut" and "nigger" (vii) is meant to show that the proposed analysis is compatible with the fact that pejorative intensity comes in grades, while my discussion of "jerk" (viii) points out that not all pejoratives are slurs. I have also tried to emphasize that pejoratives are not a freak aspect of language, that they themselves are wide-ranging lexically (41-60), compositionally (xi), and figuratively (xii), and that they may be related to euphemism, terms of endearment, honorifics, and moral vocabulary (xiii), and to register and intensionality (xiv). In conclusion, the phenomena are much richer than the simple biconditional (ψ) conveys by itself, they are consistent with (ψ), and they nicely interface with (ψ) insofar as socio-contextual facts and (ψ) both refer to speaker-subjects.

Chapter 6

AMBIGUITY

It is widely assumed that all ambiguity is either syntactic or lexical; that syntactic ambiguity can be represented by means of brackets; that lexical ambiguity can be represented by subscripts; and that ambiguity poses no principled difficulties for semantic theory in general, or for truth-theoretic semantics in particular. Such assumptions are more often than not implicit, however; for although the topic of ambiguity is commonly raised in the analytic literature, it is usually acknowledged only so as to be dismissed. It receives nothing like the attention of, say, indexicality. (Formal semanticists, who typically use predicate logic, do spill much ink on quantifier scope. But *internal* to logic there is no issue of ambiguity, as every sentence in logic is supposed to be univocal, while *externally* the exact relation between the sentences of logic and those of linguistics is largely left unspoken.)

Yet there is much to be said about ambiguity, far more than I can say here. Ambiguity can be found in languages both artificial and natural, in affixes, words, sentences, extended discourse, and also in silence, in art and images (Atlas 1989: Chap. 1), in live actions and states of affairs (Schick 2003: Chap. 1), and in clues and evidence. Ambiguity is not always linguistic, and even where it is linguistic it is not always syntactic or lexical. In every case, however, ambiguity seems to involve multiple interpretations or multiple meanings. To mention multiplicity, in turn, is to imply some kind of combination of elements, either conjunction or disjunction. Thus, colloquial formulations of ambiguity include "Φ might mean P *and* might mean Q (and maybe R ...)", "Φ does mean P *and* does mean Q", "Φ might mean P *or* Q", "Φ does mean P *or* Q". Now my question is this: how are such claims to be represented by semantic theory? This is what I call the *representation problem*. It is distinct from what I call the

155

resolution problem, and it finds modality (*"might* mean") both unclear and unnecessary.[1]

My concern is with the representation problem. I shall argue that, of all the truth-theoretic representational formats that suggest themselves, and of all those suggested in the literature, none is adequate. Disjunctive truth-conditional treatments of ambiguity are examined and rejected in Section 1; conjunctive truth-conditions, in Sections 2 and 3 (including simple, token-relative, propositional, disquotational, and subscripted truth-conditions). Section 4 addresses the *identification problem*: how can we tell whether an expression is, or is not, ambiguous? The answer carries surprising consequences for TC semantics! Finally, Section 5 explains how ambiguity, as distinct from generality and analytical indeterminacy, can be either disjunctively or conjunctively represented by a non-truth-conditional, mentalist semantics. Throughout, I shall focus on the ambiguity of just declarative sentences, although my framework is intended to ramify to other expressions more generally.

1.   Disjunctive Truth-Conditions

Pretend, for the sake of simplicity, that "x is a bank" is just two-ways ambiguous. (I'm using "x" to stand for any singular term you care to choose, though you are also free to think of it as a proper name.) Assuming an extensional truth-conditional format, there are two candidates for representing ambiguity by means of disjunction:

(1) WIDE-SCOPE DISJUNCTION
    x is a bank ≡ x is a [certain kind of] financial institution *or*
    x is a bank ≡ x is a [certain kind of] slope.
(2) NARROW-SCOPE DISJUNCTION
    x is a bank ≡ (x is a financial institution or x is a slope).

Disjunction (1) would be true even if "bank" univocally meant just 'financial institution', and it would be true even if "bank" univocally meant 'slope'. Asserting (1) implicates that we as analysts don't know which meaning uniquely belongs to "bank", which is different from saying that "bank" has two different meanings. Therefore wide-scope disjunction is not the correct format for representing ambiguity.

---

[1]   The vast bulk of the literature on ambiguity comes from computer science and is devoted to the distinct topic of ambiguity resolution. See Gorfein (1989, 2002), Hirst (1992), Schutze (1997), Stevenson (2002), van Deemter & Peters (1996).

The problem with (2) is that it does not really claim that the word "bank" is ambiguous; it shows only that "bank" is *general*, that it labels a single concept whose denotation ranges over two different kinds of object, just as the definition below makes no claim about ambiguity:

(3) x is an uncle of y ≡
    x is a brother of one of y's parents or x is a brother-in-law of one of y's parents.

This disjunction view of generality appears to be rejected by Atlas, who correctly observes that "game" does not mean 'chess or baseball or pick-up-sticks...' (1989: §2.3). But the fact that generality is generally not due to disjunction fails to establish that generality *never* involves disjunction. What I would like to do is to present some examples to show that generality *can* involve disjunction, and therefore that if narrow-scope disjunctive truth-conditions are to be used, they must be reserved for representing some cases of generality rather than ambiguity.

First, consider "parent". Although "mother" and "father" are sometimes defined as 'female parent' and 'male parent', it would accord better with the facts of developmental psychology to take 'mother' and 'father' as primitives and to define "parent" disjunctively as 'mother or father' (Wierzbicka 1972: 37–47). In other words, since children acquire the words "mother" and "father" before the word "parent," it is plausible to suppose that their concept 'parent' is more complex than the concepts 'mother' and 'father', a complexity that can be naturally captured in terms of disjunction. In reply one might observe that the juvenile concept behind "parent" differs from the mature concept, and that the juvenile concept, being disjunctive, is not general but rather ambiguous. But if this were the case then children would interpret "Where are your parents?" as meaning either 'Where are your fathers?' or 'Where are your mothers?' Instead they rightfully understand the question as meaning 'Where are your x's, where x is a mother or father?' Indeed, the mature concept 'parent' too may be disjunctive, given the comparative frequencies of "parent", "mother" and "father" in adult speech.

Another example is "uncle", which definition (3) represents disjunctively. Granted, one could eliminate the disjunction and still get the truth-conditions to come out nearly right, but such a move would be a mistake.

(4) x is an uncle of y ≡ x is a brother-in-law of one of y's parents.

If x is a brother of your father, then x is your uncle, and is indeed normally the brother-in-law of your mother. But if your father died during your conception, and if your mother barely knew your father and never met his family, then arguably x remains your uncle (whether you are aware of it or not) though x is no brother-in-law to your mother (no matter how casually one defines kinship relations). More important, biconditional (4) gets wrong the *reason* that x is y's uncle: it is in virtue of x's relation to the father and not x's relation to the mother. To be sure, a non-disjunctive biconditional might be couched in terms of 'first-degree lateral relation', but it remains to be seen that this concept is itself non-disjunctive.

Finally, there are technical terms like Chomsky's "governing category":

(5) x is a governing category of y ≡
     x is a governor of y, and x is a minimal NP or S that contains y.

The disjunction "NP or S" might very well one day receive a unified characterization, but in contemporary theories of syntax it remains a disjunction. Of course, independent of our ability to characterize something, speakers surely devise covert, ineffable categorizations; that is, perhaps expert syntacticians possess an atomic concept 'NP-or-S' in the language of thought which underpins the disjunctive concept 'NP or S' in natural language. However, such a supposition is utterly implausible for novice syntacticians; and semantic theory must be able to represent the speech of neophytes as well as of experts.

To summarize, then, disjunctive truth-conditions are incapable of representing ambiguity: wide-scope disjunction reflects uncertainty regarding the analysis of univocal expressions while narrow-scope disjunction represents generality.

2.   Conjunctive Truth-Conditions

It is natural to say that an ambiguous expression has more than one meaning. For instance, the sentence "x is a bank" means that x is a certain financial institution *and* it means that x is a certain slope. Needless to say, this idea cannot be rendered by narrow-scope conjunctive truth-conditions:

(6) NARROW-SCOPE CONJUNCTION
     x is a bank ≡ x is both a financial institution and a slope.

Alternatively, ambiguity might be represented by either WIDE-SCOPE CONJUNCTION or a listing of multiple T-sentences:[2]

---

[2]   Examples (7) and (8) are T-sentences, recall, because they are abbreviations for:

   (7′) "x is a bank" is true ≡ x is a financial institution.
   (8′) "x is a bank" is true ≡ x is a slope.

(7) x is a bank $\equiv$ x is a financial institution [and]
(8) x is a bank $\equiv$ x is a slope.

The problem, as first emphasized by Katherine Parsons in 1973, is that T-sentences (7) and (8) mistakenly entail (9).

(9) x is a slope $\equiv$ x is a financial institution.

Defenders of wide-scope conjunction might insist that the left-hand side of (7) says something about banks in the financial sense, and it occurs in a true biconditional, and that the left-hand side of (8) says something about banks in the topographical sense, and *it* occurs in a true biconditional. Because they contain distinct tokens, they are able to have different meanings, the consequence being that the conjunction of (10) and (11) together says all that needs to be said about the meaning of "x is a bank". According to this TOKEN VERSION of the (wide-scope) conjunction theory, it would be more perspicuous to render plain (7) and (8) as existential quantifications:

(10) Some tokens of "x is a bank" are true $\equiv$ x is a financial institution.
(11) Some tokens of "x is a bank" are true $\equiv$ x is a slope.

This move fails to work, however, for in some cases of ambiguity two readings of one token are equally in effect at the same time. As one example, consider the pun in the old slogan for Morton salt:

(12) When it rains, it pours.

According to token conjunctive truth-conditionalism:

(13) Token (12) is true $\equiv$ when it rains, it rains hard.
(14) Token (12) is true $\equiv$ when it rains [and is humid], Morton's salt dispenses easily.

Together these entail that:

(15) When it rains, it rains hard $\equiv$ when it rains, Morton's salt dispenses easily.

However, the proverbial left-hand side, whether or not construed metaphorically, is a false exaggeration, while the right-hand side is presumably true.

It may be said that although the Morton company *played* on meaning (13), it seriously intended only (14). As a result, despite lurking in the consciousness of the audience, (13) is not asserted and is unavailable for the inference to (15). However, sometimes punning genuinely invokes multiple meanings, as does my paper "Quotation Matters". Does the title mean to refer to issues relating to quotation, or refer to the kinds of material that get quoted, or assert that quotation is relevant – and if the latter, does it mean that the study of quotation is important, or does it mean that quotation marks are grammatically required? While denying the last reading, I would say that the others were all simultaneously meant.

There is also simultaneous meaning in some commissions of the fallacy of equivocation. Suppose that we have an argument with premises A, B, and conclusion C, and suppose that its formal validity hinges on recurring term t. We could say (i) that t means one thing in A, switches meaning in B, and reverts back in C. Alternatively we could say (ii) that t holds constant meaning, but that premise B is false. Which would the proponent of such an argument say? Adherents of (i) would never regard the argument valid; adherents of (ii) would never regard the argument sound. Because sincere proponents of equivocal arguments regard their arguments as valid and sound, explanations (i) and (ii) ought to be dropped in favor of (iii): that a single token of t possesses two meanings, one that licenses the acceptability of B and one that licenses inference in the given argument. I conclude that token conjunctive truth-conditionalism is untenable.

Nonetheless, the idea of tokens might be harnessed to formulate PROPOSITIONAL CONJUNCTIVE TRUTH-CONDITIONALISM. The first step links tokens to propositions:

> (16) Some tokens of "x is a bank" express the proposition that x is a financial institution.
> (17) Some tokens of "x is a bank" express the proposition that x is a slope.

The second step links propositions to truth-conditions:

> (18) The proposition that x is a financial institution is true $\equiv$ x is a financial institution.
> (19) The proposition that x is a slope is true $\equiv$ x is a slope.

This two-step structure keeps tokens from correlating directly with truth-conditions, thus enabling a single token to have two incompatible meanings without rendering self-contradictory the theory that describes it.

There is a problem, however, in explaining just what this theory amounts to. What does it mean "to express"? And what is a proposition? A proposition cannot be a platonic object on pain of violating naturalism. A proposition is not a set of truth-conditions or a set of possible worlds in the context of

(17), for saying that a sentence expresses a set of any sort seems to commit a category mistake (unless "express" is intended in some technical and undefined sense). A proposition, for current purposes, cannot be a sentence in a computational language of thought, as I shall argue in the next section.

To avoid reference to propositions, Davidson invokes a disquotational theory of meaning, according to which semantic axioms yield homophonic T-sentences. This approach can be developed in two ways. According to DISQUOTATIONAL CONJUNCTIONISM, the theory of meaning must separately generate (20) and (21) in order to treat both financial and topographical meanings.

(20) "x is a bank" is true ≡ x is a bank.
(21) "x is a bank" is true ≡ x is a bank.

But which is which? Does (20) give us the financial sense, or the topographical? Notice that it does no good to trace their derivations: while (20) derives from axiom (20′), and (21) from *separate* axiom (21′), the fundamental axioms themselves do nothing to distinguish the two senses at issue.

(20′) "bank" denotes banks.
(21′) "bank" denotes banks.

This reinforces my earlier conclusion, that disquotational semantics does not give truth-conditions (Chaps. 2.2.2 and 5.1).

Davidson's proposal to let ambiguity carry over from the object-language to the meta-language (1967: 30) can alternatively be understood as prescribing that (20) and (21) be collapsed into a single T-sentence. The idea of such non-conjunctive DISQUOTATIONAL PUNNING is that, since the analysandum is ambiguous and the right-hand side is ambiguous, and the two are ambiguous in just the same ways, the one T-sentence by itself succeeds in expressing two analytic equivalences.

But disquotatonalism fails in both its forms, conjunctional and punning. First, the meta-language should work for any language (except possibly itself, given the liar paradox), and ambiguous expressions in other languages generally do not translate into ambiguous expressions of English. Second, disquotationalism brings ambiguity from the object of inquiry into the inquiry itself, thereby violating a fundamental condition on adequacy for any theory whatsoever. Theories should be free from serious misunderstanding, hence free from any ambiguity that is unresolvable in its context. Regardless of whether a truth-theory entails (20) and (21), or a merger thereof, we can't evaluate it because we have no way of knowing whether the following is being entailed instead:

(22) "x is a bank", in the 'financial' sense, is true ≡ x is a bank in the 'slope' sense.

Third, there is a sense in which the left-hand and right-hand sides of (20) differ in ambiguity. The left-hand side refers to a decontextualized linguistic form having semantic equipotential. In contrast, the ambiguity potential of the right-hand side dies away once (20) is interpreted. That is to say, (20) may mean either of the following:

(23) The ink "x is a bank" expresses a true statement ≡ x is a financial institution.
(24) The ink "x is a bank" expresses a true statement ≡ x is a slope.

But these lead back to the erroneous deduction that slopes are identical to houses of finance.

3.   Conjunctive Truth-Conditions with Subscripts

We have been considering ways to express a tenable wide-scope conjunctionism. The simple version (7 & 8) falls to the "slope = house of finance" deduction, token conjunctionism falls to puns and equivocations, disquotational conjunctionism faces a nest of problems, and propositional conjunctionism as stated is at best an empty promissory note.

The "classic" way to overcome the refutation of simple conjunctionism, and also to explicate a kind of propositionalism, is proposed by Donald Davidson and urged by Brendan Gillon.[3] For Davidson, T-sentences do not, strictly speaking, use quotation names of sentences; they use *structural descriptions* or SDs, where the "structural description of an expression describes the expression as a concatenation of elements drawn from a fixed finite list (for example of words or letters)." An obvious move combines this notion of structural description as lexical specification with the standard linguistic notion of structure as syntactic constituency. Gillon takes this step; for him, SDs specify lexical elements by spelling or pronunciation, with subscripts added where necessary to distinguish homonyms, and they

---

[3]   Gillon's work essentially repeats that of Davidson (1967: 18) and Harman (1975: 177) [see also Lycan (1984: 38)]. It appears in 1990b, again in 1990a, and again in 2004, where it is billed as a classic.

specify syntactic structure by means of labeled tree diagrams or, what is equivalent, bracketing. Thus, sentence (25) has two SDs:[4]

> (25) Enraged cow injures man with ax. [newspaper headline]
> (a) [$_S$ [$_{NP}$ Enraged cow] [$_{VP}$ injures [$_{NP}$ man [$_{PP}$ with ax]]]]
> (b) [$_S$ [$_{NP}$ Enraged cow] [$_{VP}$ injures [$_{NP}$ man] [$_{PP}$ with ax]]]

This structural difference allows us to formulate a separate T-sentence for each reading: the sentence specified by (a) is true iff the man with an ax was injured by the cow, *and* the sentence specified by (b) is true iff the cow injured, with an ax, the man. Gillon's appeal to SDs could also be extended so as to handle not just the scopal ambiguities of syntactic form but quantifier-scope ambiguities and event-structure ambiguities of logical form.

The notion of an SD does more than allow for the derivation of accurate T-sentences, according to Gillon; it allows for a conceptual analysis or definition of ambiguity:

> (A) An expression is ambiguous $\equiv$ it can accommodate more than one SD.

Definition (A) is supposed to have the virtue of unifying our concepts of structural ambiguity and lexical ambiguity. However, this is an empty unification given that (A) relies upon a disjunctive conception of SDs (SD_1 differs from SD_2 if it differs either syntactically *or* lexically). This is not to deny that structural and lexical ambiguity have something in common; I simply point out that (A) does not capture whatever it is.

More importantly, Gillon's use of SDs runs up against various problems. First, Lycan (1984: 39) argues that it does not really succeed in treating structural ambiguity. Second, I shall argue that it does not succeed in treating lexical ambiguity (§3.1). Third, there are other kinds of ambiguity that it does not even purport to treat (§3.2).

3.1 Ambiguities are Unnumbered

Subscripts cannot be taken too literally; if little numbers actually appeared on words there would be no such thing as lexical ambiguity. No, Gillon presumably means for us to construe subscripts as distinguishing marks that we as analysts impose for our own convenience. There remains a difficulty, however, for there is a difference between representing lexical ambiguity by means of subscripts and representing syntactic ambiguity by means

---

[4] Here and elsewhere I clean up some of the technical errors in Gillon's account.

of brackets. Brackets depict or *specify* differences in structure – a bare modicum of syntactic training, if even that, usually suffices for revealing which structure goes with which reading. Subscripts, in contrast, do not really specify words; were they reversed, no one would be the wiser. In other words, Gillon's so-called structural descriptions *do not describe.*

Merely signaling that lexical differences are at hand is not sufficient, for otherwise subscripts would take care of structural ambiguity as well. Why bother figuring out the correct bracketing in (25) when we could equally as well say (26)?

(26a) [Enraged cow injures man with ax]$_1$
(26b) [Enraged cow injures man with ax]$_2$

Subscripts are mere gesticulations toward a theory. Just as they neither describe nor genuinely distinguish the multiple readings due to structural ambiguity, so too they fail to do the job for lexical ambiguity. The use of subscripts only labels or defers or disguises the problem and does nothing to solve it.

But there is a difference, my critics insist, for "we're usually interested in structure, though in the case of lexical items we're not." As a sociological matter, the point is well taken; indeed, it echoes my opening remark about current research apathy regarding ambiguity. As a philosophical matter, however, the point is irrelevant: because semantics is the study of sentence meaning, which is a function of a given sentence's lexical elements and their mode of combination, ignoring the elements really is comparable to ignoring their mode of combination.

If subscripts are to be used, they must stand in for substantive information regarding the identity of words. Gillon seems to realize this, for he appeals again and again to the information available in dictionaries. Bookstore dictionaries such as the *American Heritage* are our authorities, he writes [2004: 174; cp. (2004: 172), (1990a: 402)]; what's more, "standard lexicographical practice . . . guarantees that ambiguous words have distinct lexical addresses" (1990b: 180).

The problem is that lexicographical practice, the way dictionaries are in fact written, does *not* guarantee any facts about the linguist's lexicon, which is a theoretical structure of either the mind or something abstract. The two are very different kinds of thing, serving distinct functions and molded by distinct constraints: whereas dictionaries cater to the general population, descriptions of lexicons are written for specialists; whereas dictionary entries cite other words, lexicons are generally presumed to map from word entries to non-verbal objects (or processes); whereas dictionaries are ordered alphabetically, lexicons enjoy random access; whereas dictionaries typically omit obscene language, lexicons do not; and the list goes on. On general grounds, therefore, facts about dictionaries do not yield prima facie facts about lexicons, let alone do they guarantee any facts.

Additional problems emerge when we get down to the nitty-gritty of lexicographical practice, especially from the point of view of truth-theoretic service. For instance, consider the *American Heritage* entry for "bank":

(1.1) Any piled up mass, as of snow or clouds.
(1.2) A steep natural incline.
(1.3) An artificial slope.
(1.4) The slope of land adjoining a lake, river, or sea.
(1.6) Lateral tilting of an aircraft in a turn ...
(2.1) A business establishment authorized to perform financial transactions ...
(2.2) The building in which such an establishment is located.

Definitions (1.1, 1.4, 1.6) are truth-conditionally faulty because a pile of leaves is not a bank, "bank" can also refer to the side of a pond, and race-cars bank as well as aircraft. Moreover, the division into senses is unconvincing. There is no evidence, intuitive or otherwise, to suggest that 'natural incline' (1.2) and 'artificial slope' (1.3) are distinct senses or that such slopes differ from the semi-submerged slope of (1.4).[5] Additional well known criticisms of standard lexicographic practice appear in Weinreich (1964), and criticisms of using lexicography for Gillon's purpose appear in Scheffler (1979: 3–4, 11–12). Not so incidentally – because indicative of the sad state of lexicography – the *American Heritage* overlooks the piggy-bank sense.

Dropping Gillon's commitment to *lexicographical* practice in favor of a more reasonable commitment to *lexicological* principles would likewise fail to provide the substantive information we need, for theoreticians cannot agree on lexicological fundamentals. For instance, platonists and naturalists

---

[5]   In fact, I would like to make a stronger claim, that there *cannot* be the ambiguity indicated. For I propose as a principle of lexicology the following:

> If two concepts C_1, C_2 exhaustively divide a domain then C_1, C_2 cannot be distinct senses of a single lexical item or of homonymous items.

This principle allows for the existence of tautonymy, where a single word-form can have a general sense and a specific sense (e.g. "cow", 'bovine' and 'female bovine'). However, it prohibits any word from being ambiguous between 'natural embankment' and 'artificial embankment.'

are divided as to whether the lexicon is abstract or psychological, while externalists and internalists are divided as to whether narrow content exhausts meaning.

An alternative to Gillon's lexicographical approach is to suppose that subscripts individuate lexemes, or readings more generally, by reference to either external context or internal speaker/hearer state. Following up the former suggestion, we might take a clue from Davidson's treatment of indexicals, (1967: 34), and regard T-sentences (7) and (8) as abbreviations for:

(27) "x is a bank", as spoken in context C_1, is true $\equiv$ x is a financial institution.

(28) "x is a bank," as spoken in context C_2, is true $\equiv$ x is a slope.

But context-dependent T-sentences are patently implausible. As Cohen (1985: 130) observes, "Some circumstances must be possible in which neither [sense] c nor c′ prevails. Otherwise one would not be able to appreciate the inherent ambiguity of the sentence so well" [see also Parsons (1973)]. What's more, even if some non-circular context-dependent T-sentences were true, specifying them would be unrealistic.

Subscripts have also been used in the literature to signify processing paths, individuated either computationally [Field (1994: §10)] or physically:

(29) "x is a bank", as spoken when S's neurons flare up in sector 2281949, is true $\equiv$ x is a financial institution.

Putnam (1988: 80) rightfully observes that, if meaning is so individuated, meaning would not hold constant across speakers. As mentioned earlier, such a result conflicts with one of the pillars of truth-conditionalism (p. 46). More importantly in my view, if meaning reduced in the way just illustrated, it would be hard to see what purpose the truth-theory served. We could just as well skip the T-sentences and go directly to correlating linguistic expressions with the computational or physical state of the language users.

Even if, contrary to all I have said, subscripts did solve the problem of lexical ambiguity, truth-theoretic semanticists would be only part way home. The reason is that much ambiguity is neither structural nor lexical.

3.2   Ambiguities are Innumerable

As the excerpt from the *American Heritage* shows, standard lexicographic practice divides meaning into lemmas and senses (and sometimes subsenses). This is related to the distinction that lexicologists make between homonymy and polysemy. Homonymy obtains when two different words sound or look the same and have different meanings; this is lexical ambiguity. Polysemy obtains when a *single* word has two different meanings (or "senses" or "uses"). The intuition is that polysemous senses are somehow related to each other in a way in which homonymous senses are not. For example, "bank" is homonymous between 'slope' and 'financial institution' while it is polysemous among 'corporation that deals in finances', 'the physical plant where such abstract entities manifest themselves', and 'piggy bank'. Now the existence of polysemy invalidates Gillon's proposal.[6] For even when we identify the string "bank" as the word that excludes the slope sense, it still remains ambiguous among a number of senses. Thus, (30) is false because x is a bank when x is a piggy bank.

(30) "x is a bank$_1$" is true $\equiv$ x is a financial institution.

Gillon might want to deny the distinction between homonymy and polysemy. Indeed, the distinction is notoriously difficult to make.[7] For instance, native judgments on the form "ear" vary ('auditory organ' versus 'unit of corn'): some informants resolutely judge this case to be one of homonymy, some informants judge the two senses here to be polysemes, and most informants just cannot tell. The fact that such difficulty exists suggests that perhaps the homonymy/polysemy distinction is illegitimate. But in pursuing this idea, we come to the mistaken extremes that I shall call Radical Homonymy and Radical Polysemy [both positions are described in Kempson (1977: 80), Lyons (1977: 553)].

According to Radical Polysemy [cf. Quine (1960: 130)], homonymy does not exist: regardless of how many meanings are at hand, formal identity

---

[6]   This problem is anticipated by Cohen (1985). Though Cohen is cited in Gillon (1990b), his main point is simply ignored.

[7]   To distinguish between homonymy and polysemy, Kempson (1977: 82) proposes that we use the Conjunction Reduction Test of Lakoff (1970). According to Kempson's construal of this test, polysemous words permit simultaneous interpretation while homonyms do not. For example, in (i) the "platonic content" and "physical object" senses are simultaneously available, indicating that "book" is polysemous:
(i)   My book is 300 pages long and is quite incomprehensible.
In contrast, (ii) cannot mean 'my parents gave birth to me and they are uninteresting to my friend'; thus, "bore" is homonymous.
(ii)   My parents bore me and my friend.
But if Kempson is right, then most words traditionally classified as polysemous turn out to be homonymous, for instance "run":
(iii)   The car is running well and down the hill.
Since "run" cannot simultaneously mean 'to function' and 'to move fast on its own', Kempson must claim that these two senses constitute distinct lexical entries, that "run" is homonymous. I suggest that (iii) counts as a reductio against the validity of Kempson's use of the Conjunction Reduction Test.

suffices for individuating wordhood. However, this position is untenable. Even if we relativize our theory to a single language, English say – so as to prevent foreign homophones such as Basque "lai" 'vine' from counting as the same word as English "lie" – we still face the fact of morphological patterning. If "lie" 'to rest horizontally' and "lie" 'to speak falsely' were the same word, then "lie" would have a *single* past-tense form instead of the two forms "lay" and "lied".

Radical Homonymy makes the opposite mistake. It denies the existence of polysemy, claiming that whenever a single form is associated with more than one sense, then by definition there are distinct words. But if "run" 'manner of locomotion' and "run" 'to compete for elected office' were different words, we would not expect them both to take the same irregular past-tense form "ran".

At this point the Radical Homonymist might claim that the distinct denotations of "run" are subsumed under a single general sense just as tabbies and tigers are subsumed under "cat." The chief proponents of such a generality approach, Atlas (1989) and Ruhl (1989), convincingly maintain that both linguists and philosophers are far too eager to postulate polysemy. Nonetheless, surely some polysemy exists. Aside from suggestive empirical studies such as Lehrer (1974a), Lakoff (1987), and Jorgensen (1990), there is a conceptual point in favor of the existence of polysemy: in cases of ambiguity it frequently seems that one sense is basic, and that the other senses are derivative. This is the case with "run", where 'manner of locomotion' is primary while 'to compete for elected office' is secondary. If these senses represented independent words, such asymmetry would not exist; hence, the senses appear to be structured aspects of a single word.

Cases of polysemy arguably constitute one sort of figurative language, the conventionalized sort. Another kind of figurative language appears in comparatively novel uses. For example, in a restaurant a customer has just eaten a ham sandwich and one server informs another,

(31) The ham sandwich is waiting for his check. [Nunberg 1979: 149]

"Sandwich" can refer to, or can be used to refer to, either a comestible or a consumer, but this does not mean that English has two lexical items "sandwich$_1$" and "sandwich$_2$".

Of course there is a context-sensitive function f, in this case mapping from comestible to consumer, that gives us:

(31′) f(The ham sandwich) is waiting for his check.

However, the acceptability or truth of (31′) does not mean that (31′) is a structural description of (31). SDs, in the operative, syntactic sense, describe sentence structure, i.e. the parts of a sentence and their interrelations. SDs, that is, specify sequencing, hierarchical, and coindexing arrangements of words, morphemes, and syntactically induced null constituents; they do not include interpretive functions such as f.

The present example is ambiguous between its literal linguistic meaning and its non-literal speaker meaning. Now sometimes it is said that linguistic meaning, the object of semantics, is where truth-conditions lie, and that speaker meaning, the object of pragmatics, has nothing directly to do with truth [e.g. Davidson (1978)]. According to this division, (31) has only one set of truth-conditions – it is true iff there is a contextually salient masculine ham sandwich x waiting for x's check – and semantics need not worry about the ambiguity of (31). However, this line faces difficulties.

First, it is doubtful that the distinction between literal and non-literal meaning matches the distinction between truth-conditional and non-truth-conditional meaning. Although one can respond to (31) by saying (32), one could just as well respond with (33):

(32) *Literally speaking*, it is false that the ham sandwich is waiting for the check; it is the customer who is waiting.

(33) In *some* manner of speaking it is *true* that the ham sandwich is waiting for the check; it is true in the figurative, metonymic sense.

Second, the literal/non-literal dimension is independent of the various figurative/non-figurative dimensions, including that of metaphoricity. On the one hand, non-metaphoric speech includes both literal and non-literal uses. Examples of the latter include novel hyperbole, irony, metonymy, and certain other figures of speech. At the same time, metaphoric speech can be literally true when it is conventionalized. The conventionalization of figurative speech is what may give rise to polysemy and is ubiquitous [see Lakoff & Johnson (1980); an alternative explanation, in terms of learning theory, can be found in Jennings (2005)]. The status of "run$_2$," for instance, is that it is neither novel nor non-literal. Its metaphoricity explains our intuition that "run$_2$" is less basic than "run$_1$" while its existence in the American English lexicon – as opposed to British "stand" (for office) – means that for Americans "run$_2$" is as fixed a part of the language as any other literal expression. I conclude that every expression is ambiguous because it may be metaphorical, and that its metaphorical reading may require a semantic treatment just as much as its non-metaphorical reading.

The "non-literal equals non-truth-conditional" formula cannot plausibly account for deeply entrenched kinds of metonymy either. For example, type/token ambiguity applies to every concrete noun:

(34) How many books has Isaac Asimov sold?
     About 400, most of them to Doubleday.
     Millions and millions, most of them in English editions.

Another kind of systematic ambiguity turns on 'toy/fake/representation' versus 'real', as recognized by Scheffler (1979: 74) and, again, Cohen (1985).

(35) Does Junior have a rabbit?
     Yes, and she also has two teddy bears.
     No, but she has a stuffed-animal rabbit.

These are genuine cases of ambiguity, as indicated by the Contradictory Test. According to the Contradictory Test, which Gillon favors, a question is ambiguous if it allows for two truthful but contradictory replies. Since "rabbit" is surely a single lexical item, its ambiguity cannot be accounted for by Gillon's definition of ambiguity.

In summary, trying to dismiss figurative meaning does not save truth-conditional semantics. Metonymic meaning is sometimes literal and metaphoric meaning is sometimes literal and, even were they not so, non-literal meaning is sometimes truth-conditional if anything is.

In addition to indefinitely many novel metaphors and metonyms, which can be viewed as pragmatic phenomena, there are yet other kinds of pragmatic ambiguity, for instance those involving speech acts. To begin with, utterances like (36) have multiple meanings:

(36) Can you tell me the time?

On the direct reading, (36) is a yes/no question; on the indirect reading, (36) is a request. This ambiguity is neither structural nor lexical. For one thing, if the ambiguity between question and request were a strictly lexical idiosyncrasy, we would not expect to see it in other modal verbs and in other languages, which we do. For another thing, if "can" in some sense intrinsically signified a request, then in that sense we would expect it to occur in declarative or imperative sentences as well, which we do not.

Another kind of speech-act ambiguity involves use and mention, as can be seen in quotation (Chap. 7.1.3) and in negation. Whereas normal negation may be said to result from denying the content of an assertion, "external" or metalinguistic negation may be regarded as the denial of making an assertion:

(37) She's not *happy*, she's *ecstatic*.

Gillon dismisses this example, without justification, as a case of lexico-structural ambiguity (1990a: 409). Yet so far as SDs are concerned, negation appears to be univocal. On the one hand, (37) does not have multiple syntactic constituency; at least, no syntactician claims that it does. At the same time, "not" is lexically univocal, as substantiated by cross-linguistic patterns (Horn 1989: 139).

As an argument against this, I've been told that modern Greek uses "dhen" and "oxi", respectively, for ordinary and metalinguistic negation, and that this fact, that Greek has two lexically distinct kinds of negation, is evidence that English has two lexically distinct kinds of negation, even though in English they accidentally sound alike. But such reasoning is fallacious. It is like saying that Chinese, which lexically distinguishes between elder and younger brother, gives evidence that there are two English words "brother"; or that English, which lexically distinguishes between "hello" and "goodbye", gives evidence that there are two Hawaiian words "aloha". That a lexical distinction is "an option available for natural language" does not mean that it is an option taken by any particular language.

There is also what I would call componential ambiguity. At a banquet, you begin a speech:

(38) Friends – I know you too well to call you ladies and gentlemen – ... [Margalit 1983: 132]

The rules for using "lady" and "gentleman" each decomposes into two conditions, one pertaining to the speech situation and the other pertaining to the nature of the referent. Thus, you could possibly mean that you are too familiar with the audience to use formal addresses; or you could mean that you know the audience members well enough to realize that they are uncouth. This ambiguity hinges upon neither different structures nor different words, but rather upon the different factors of the meaning of a single word.

Aside from sometimes resulting from figurative speech, referential ambiguity can arise from a proper name's having more than one referent, from an overt indexical such as "it", or from an implicit indexical, as in ellipsis or when a variable ranges over a restricted quantifier domain.

(39) I'm not trying to make you look a fool, Sid. It's obvious. [Lea 1979: 90]

In this example, "it" can refer either to the proposition that I'm not trying to make you look a fool, or to the proposition that you look a fool.

Finally, pragmatic ambiguity emerges from the following sorts of vagueness.

(40) Thank you for sending me a copy of your new book; I will waste no time reading it. [Moses Hadas]
(41) Panda mating fails; veterinarian takes over. [headline]
(42) Include your children when baking cookies. [internet]

Indexicality, vagueness, and ambiguity are usually regarded as different animals, as indeed they are if ambiguity is necessarily either lexical or structural. For the truth-conditionalist, however, I shall argue that this is just not so.

4.   An Ambiguity Test

In order to determine whether indexicality is a species of ambiguity, we need a criterion for identifying ambiguity. Brendan Gillon surveys a variety of tests that have been proposed, and concludes that ultimately the only good one is the contradictory test (which goes back, it should be acknowledged, at least to the Scholastics). Gillon formulates the test thus:

> Let α be an expression. Let $\delta(\ )$ be an expression frame such that $\delta(\alpha)$ is a sentence liable to being judged with respect to a truth-value. Let s be a state of affairs. If $\delta(\alpha)$ is alternately judged true and judged not true with respect to s, then α is prima facie ambiguous. [2004: 166]

For example, let α be "sole" and let δ be "I have a ____". Then given that I have feet but no fish, $\delta(\alpha)$ is (or can be) alternately judged true and judged untrue, and "sole" is prima facie ambiguous.

Gillon's test calls for minor revisions. For instance, if the given values of α and δ are reversed then α is not ambiguous, not even prima facie so. It does not, on *first appearance*, seem ambiguous; and as a general matter, if δ and α combine to create an ambiguous sentence, there is no default reason to locate ambiguity in either δ specifically or α specifically. What Gillon *should* say is more like "α is *ceteris paribus* ambiguous": α is ambiguous all else being equal, i.e. α is ambiguous if all other potentially relevant factors are excluded, such as δ's being ambiguous. A more straightforward and accurate rendering of the contradictory test, therefore, might be: if there is some state of affairs according to which statement token P would both seem true and seem false, then it is reasonable to treat P as ambiguous (sentence types are normally not judged true or false).

Gillon justifies the contradictory test by invoking the Fregean doctrines of sense and compositionality. This may conflict with Gillon's Davidsonianism, but the conflict is inessential, for the contradictory test in fact follows from any truth-conditional theory of meaning. Here is my argument.

(a) If P has multiple truth-values under a single condition then P has distinctive sets of truth-conditions (has distinctive sets of conditions under which P would be true).

(b) If P has distinctive sets of truth-conditions then P has multiple meanings.

(c) If P has multiple meanings then P is ambiguous.

(d) If P has multiple truth-values under one condition, then P is ambiguous.

Premise (a) follows from the concept of truth-condition, (b) follows from the assumption of truth-conditional semantics, (c) holds by definition, and (d) is a logical consequence of (a-c).

Regardless of whether one accepts Gillon's test and justification thereof, or mine, it follows that at least some indexicals are ambiguous. Although any token of "me" is arguably univocal, in many cases a particular "it" or demonstrative "this" may seem to different audience members to refer to different objects, with direct consequences for judged truth-value. Indeed, a particular indexical may enjoy alternating semantic valuations from one and the same hearer over time.

Appealing to the speaker's intention, of course, does not block simultaneous judgments of truth and falsehood. First, the speaker's intention is not always authoritative. Just as a speaker can be mistaken in thinking that "the man with the martini" denotes Dean, one can be unreasonable in thinking that "this" denotes something prominent in one's own mind that is in fact obscure to everyone else. Second, if speaker's intention blocks ambiguity in the case of "this", it would do so in other cases. Ambiguity would hardly exist at all!

It may be objected that the objective context of utterance fixes the semantic values of indexicals; that if you and I disagree about the denotation of "this" then one of us is necessarily wrong; and that the contradictory test can be revised to reflect as much. I disagree, but I won't argue the point. Instead I observe that appeals to context cannot serve as a *general* response to my anti-truth-theoretic ambiguity argument because they do not apply to cases of vagueness:

(43) Parachuting is dangerous.

Where context is rich enough to resolve vagueness, it is generally rich enough to resolve lexico-syntactic ambiguities. Hence, to say that any token of "dangerous" is unambiguous in its own particular context of utterance is akin to claiming that any token of "bank", or "injures man with an ax", is unambiguous in its own context, which I take to be a reductio. Besides, an auditor of (43) may judge it to be false while in one mood and then later on, while in another mood, judge the same token to have been true. Indeed, one and the same person in one and the same situation may respond to "Is it dangerous?" with "Well, it is and it isn't". Therefore, from the truth-conditional point of view, *cases of vagueness are cases of ambiguity.*[8]

I do not for a moment suggest that vagueness and indexicality have entirely the same nature as homonymy and structural ambiguity – only that they do have this in common: that they lend variable contributions to truth-conditions. As a result, SDs – descriptions of sentence structure formulated in terms of lexically instantiated phrase markers – cannot be mapped into or onto truth-conditions, thus ruling out truth-conditional semantics. One alternative is to retreat to truth-conditional pragmatics, the view that SDs *plus context* uniquely fix truth-conditions. I believe that this view too is untenable, for the sorts of reasons given directly above. Another alternative, which I find more promising, is that of attitudinal semantics.

5.   Attitude Conditions

In Section 1 I rejected two versions of the disjunctive truth-conditionalist theory of ambiguity because wide-scope disjunction actually represents uncertainty on the part of the analyst as to which truth-condition uniquely applies to "x is a bank", while narrow-scope disjunction represents generality.

(1) WIDE-SCOPE DISJUNCTIVE TRUTH-CONDITIONS:
    (x is a bank ≡ x is a financial institution) or (x is a bank ≡ x is a slope).

---

[8]   My own view, like that of Atlas (1989, 2005), is that linguistic ambiguity is fairly rare, and that neither indexicals nor vague expressions are, per se, ambiguous. This position is open to those who reject the premise that meaning is truth-conditional.

(2) NARROW-SCOPE DISJUNCTIVE TRUTH-CONDITIONS:
   x is a bank $\equiv$ (x is a financial institution or x is a slope).

Sections 2 and 3 reject various versions of conjunctive truth-conditionalism, for example because the simple wide-scope view leads to the falsehood that slopes are identical to financial institutions. If ambiguity is to be represented by combination, either disjunction or conjunction, then we require some kind of operator for providing another level of scope.

This hypothesis is reinforced when we recall the original intuitions behind combinability, phrased in terms of meaning. Reference to meaning, or reference to psychological state, gives just the kind of added resource that we need. As a first approximation, I propose to use the operator "S ψ," where S is a subject and ψ is a propositional attitude. Combining this attitudinal operator with disjunction yields three distinct representational formats.

(44) WIDE-SCOPE DISJUNCTIVE ATTITUDE-CONDITIONS
   (S ψ Φ $\equiv$ S ψ P) or (S ψ Φ $\equiv$ S ψ Q).
(45) NARROW-SCOPE DISJUNCTIVE ATTITUDE-CONDITIONS
   S ψ Φ $\equiv$ S ψ (P or Q).
(46) MIDDLE-SCOPE DISJUNCTIVE ATTITUDE-CONDITIONS
   S ψ Φ $\equiv$ ([S ψ P] or [S ψ Q]).

I shall argue that middle-scope disjunction may be a good format for representing ambiguity; that is to say, Φ is ambiguous between P and Q iff (46) holds. The wide-scope and narrow-scope formulas express something different.

As in Section 1, wide-scope disjunction continues to express uncertainty. What's more, the difference between wide-scope and middle-scope analyses can be seen in the case where Φ is unambiguous, P is its paraphrase, Q is unrelated, S thinks Q, and S does not think Φ or, therefore, P. Then the equivalence of "S ψ Φ" to "S ψ P" is sufficient to make (44) true, despite the univocality of Φ. In contrast, the truth of "S ψ P or S ψ Q" makes (46) false, which is what we want if we are to align the truth-value of our ambiguity formula with the presence or absence of ambiguity.

Narrow-scope disjunction continues to represent generality. If you asked after the meaning of Japanese "aoi", say, then I could correctly answer, "It means blue-or-green" (which is different from saying "It means blue or it means green"). Here we have a *single thought*, and it is improper to demand of it, "Which sense was intended – BLUE or GREEN?" Although in any given case a specific intention might be possible, it is neither necessary nor even usual. It is appropriate, therefore, that for generality, disjunction be subsumed under a single ψ operator.

In contrast, the disjunction on the right-hand side of (46), exemplified here, refers to two different thoughts:

> (47) S thinks "x is a bank" $\equiv$ S thinks that x is a financial institution or S thinks that x is a slope.

The thought that x is a financial institution is separate from the thought that x is a kind of slope. They may punningly co-occur, but they need not, and this distinctness is successfully captured by the attitudinal analysis.

The attitudinal disjunction for representing ambiguity applies not only to lexical ambiguity but also polysemy, figurative ambiguity, etc.

> (48) S thinks "x is a bank" $\equiv$ S thinks that x is a financial institution or S thinks that x is a piggy bank (or...).
>
> (49) S thinks "The ham sandwich is sitting at table 20" $\equiv$ S thinks that a kind of comestible is sitting at table 20 or S thinks that the customer who ordered the ham sandwich is sitting at table 20 (or...).

By specifying modes of thinking we can distinguish among kinds of ambiguity. To focus on just literal readings, for instance, we can ask under what condition S *literally* thinks "The ham sandwich is sitting at table 20", in which case the answer is not disjunctive as it is in (49).

Careful attention to the exact value of ψ is necessary for another reason. Suppose that S knows that Jan is either making a deposit at her S&L or having a picnic next to the river, but does not know which. Then the left-hand side is true but the right-hand side is not:

> (50) S knows "Jan is at the bank" $\equiv$ S knows Jan is at S&L or S knows that Jan is at the riverside.

The biconditional likewise fails when ψ stands for "believes". However, the biconditional holds when ψ stands for "thinks" or "cognizes" or (metaphorically) "grasps". You cannot entertain or otherwise think "Jan is at the bank", as a proficient speaker of English, without entertaining or otherwise thinking at least one of its meanings. Therefore, in at least the case of ambiguity, attitudinal analyses must restrict ψ to non-epistemic and even non-doxastic attitudes.

According to the disjunctive attitudinal approach, then, ambiguity can be defined as follows.

(A′) An expression type Φ is ambiguous for S ≡ the meaning of Φ for S is correctly represented by middle-scope disjunction of form (46), as qualified above.

Alternatively attitudinal semantics may go in the direction of token conjunctionism. In the truth-conditional case, recall, token conjunctions, given the existence of equivocation, entail falsehoods such as that x is a financial institution iff x is a slope.

(10) Some tokens of "x is a bank" are true ≡ x is a financial institution.
(11) Some tokens of "x is a bank" are true ≡ x is a slope.

In contrast, mentalist conjunctions, even when contradictory, are innocuous:

(51) TOKEN CONJUNCTIVE ATTITUDE-CONDITIONS
    For some cases of S's thinking: S thinks Φ ≡ S thinks P [and]
    For some cases of S's thinking: S thinks Φ ≡ S thinks Q.

When S equivocates, there is a single particular case in which S has two different thoughts, and so S thinks P iff S thinks Q. When P factually conflicts with Q, the truth-conditionalist's "P iff Q" is a real-world contradiction, an impossibility, whereas the mentalist merely ascribes a cognitive contradiction to someone, an inconsistency internal to a set of beliefs.

The token attitudinal account generalizes; "think" can be replaced with arbitrary attitude. In this way it may seem preferable to the disjunctive attitudinal account, although it may be that ultimately the two accounts are compatible. Because they differ at least superficially, however, we have another definition of ambiguity:

(A″) An expression type Φ is ambiguous for S ≡ the meaning of Φ for S is correctly represented by token conjunction of form (51).

The latter approach somewhat resembles that of Harman (1975: 177), for whom "an expression is ambiguous if a person can sometimes treat it as having one sort of [conceptual] role and at other times treat it as having a different role." However, I prefer my own formulation because it is fully biconditional, it makes explicit the subjective character of ambiguity, and it avoids gratuitous invocations of potential ("*can*"). While these particular differences may be more stylistic than substantive, Harman also sees the conceptual role of an expression Φ as fixed by Φ's syntax and lexical make-up, and he sees lexical items as individuated by subscripts – two assumptions discredited in the previous section. There thus appears to be genuine difference between CRS and attitudinal semantics, not to mention the distinct justifications on offer.

The important point, though, is that neither disjunctive attitudes nor token conjunctive attitudes succumb to the objections raised against truth-conditionalism. To repeat, Gillon proposes that structural descriptions can save TC semantics from the problems of homonymy and structural ambiguity. However, I have argued that other kinds of ambiguity (understood truth-conditionally) remain unresolved. These include direct versus indirect construals; internal versus external negation; decompositional or sublexical ambiguity; metaphor and other figures of speech; polysemy; and indexicality and vagueness. Furthermore, Gillon's proposal does not even work for pedestrian ambiguity: there is no way for the truth-theorist to non-circuitously individuate expressions on the basis of their lexical and structural constitution.

Apart from Gillon's classic account, I have canvassed seven possible approaches to representing ambiguity within truth-conditional semantics, and I have argued that all are unsatisfactory, meaning that the existence of ambiguity in natural language is evidence in favor of attitudinal semantics as against TC semantics. Even if I be mistaken, however, I hope that I have convinced you that the problem of representing ambiguity is not trivial. There is no warrant for the current widespread practice in the literature of acknowledging the phenomenon of ambiguity only to airily dismiss it.

Chapter 7

QUOTATION AND USE-MENTION

I recognize two intersecting aspects of language: *functional* distinctions, such as that between use and mention (as technically understood), and *formal* distinctions, for example, between plain expressions and those having quotation marks. More precisely, there is one functional distinction between use and non-use and another between mention and non-mention, and there is a whole variety of formal distinctions drawn by marks of quotation: double apostrophes and single, italics, and indented displays (each carrying their own conditions of use). My cognitivist or psychologistic orientation toward language, as opposed to one that is "realist", referentialist, or platonist, avoids appeals to truth-conditions, emphasizing instead mental associations, speech-act conditions, and pragmatic factors more generally.

My approach to understanding quotation, one version of the Identity Theory, is supported in part by the fact that it fares better than its rivals. In defending it, therefore, I shall summarize other approaches to quotation and argue that they are adequate, namely the Name Theory and the Demonstrative Theory.

According to the Name Theory, quotations name their referents, where a name is a semantic atom. Tarski writes:

> Quotation-mark names may be treated like single words of a language ... the single constituents of these names ... fulfill the same function as the letters and complexes of successive letters in single words. Hence they can possess no independent meaning. [1933: 159]

In other words, the mark of quotation (typically a pair of double-apostrophes) and quoted matter (that which appears inside the quotation mark) together constitute a quotation name, an expression whose separate components – quotation mark and quoted matter – contribute no meaning to the whole.

179

This view seems incredible, and Gomez-Torrente (2001) argues that Tarski did not really mean it. Along a similar line, Quine appears to advocate the Name Theory while denying it too:

> From the standpoint of logical analysis each whole quotation must be regarded as a single word or sign, whose parts count for no more than serifs or syllables. A quotation is not a *description*, but a *hieroglyph*; it designates its object not by describing it in terms of other objects, but by picturing it. The meaning of the whole does not depend upon the meanings of the constituent words. [1940: 26]

On the one hand, Quine indicates that quotation lacks meaningful structure. On the other hand, he says that quotation is a hieroglyph, a picture, even though one property of iconic representations is that they contain significant subparts.

It's all too easy to fall into inconsistent thinking, and I believe that methodological charity – bending over backwards so as always to ascribe reasonableness and consistency – fails to treat our philosophical heroes as the humans they are. Be that as it may, and regardless of Tarski's and Quine's actual views, their legacy, as embodied in scores of textbooks in logic, treats quotations are names.

The Name Theory, however, is untenable (Saka 1998b). First the productivity problem: the quotation mark is a systematically productive device that can be applied to expressions that we have never heard quoted before, enabling us to go not only from knowing any expression to knowing its quotation but also from knowing the quotation of any expression to knowing the expression itself. Second, the simultaneity or "mixed-quotation" problem: expressions can simultaneously be used and mentioned.

(1) Quine says that quotation "... is weird".

As Davidson (1979b) observes, and Saka (1991) and Cappelen & Lepore (1997) emphasize, the material inside the quotation marks (minus the ellipsis, to be strict) is mentioned insofar as I am attributing exact words to Quine. At the same time, the words are being used insofar as they form a predicate rather than a noun phrase, singular term, or name. Third, the resemblance problem: mentioning an expression is very like using it, which is why editors generally refuse to print mentioned vulgarities. Whereas the Name Theory fails to explain why " 'fucking asshole!' " is offensive, for after all it merely refers to a piece of English, the next theories recognize that such reference works by actually containing an obscenity.

1. The Demonstrative Theory

The Demonstrative Theory is advocated by Prior (1971), Partee (1973), Davidson (1979b), Goldstein (1984), Bennett (1988), Garcia-Carpintero (1994–2005), Cappelen & Lepore (1997–2005), Simchen (1999), and Benbaji (2004–2005). The classic version, that by Donald Davidson, treats (2) as equivalent to (2'), which contains a description containing a demonstrative.

(2) "Lobster" is a word.
(2') Lobster. The expression type of which *this* is a token is a word.

Similarly, according to Bennett,

every quotation "X" means something like 'The type whose every token resembles, in respects $R_1 \ldots R_n$, *this*: X.'

Respects $R_1 \ldots R_n$, are language-relative. In English, the relevant respects for identifying tokens as types involve (for instance) top-bottom orientation ("u" versus "n"), but not ink-color. Reference to $R_1 \ldots R_n$ provides the Bennett account with descriptive content; reference to "this: X" provides it with demonstrative content.

A recent version, due to Cappelen and Lepore, is self-described as "elegant", "enormously attractive", "almost irresistible", and "ingenious" (1999b: 217–218). It treats (2) as equivalent to a complicated quantificational structure which Cappelen and Lepore simplify as (2'').

(2'') $\forall$x (x is a word if x tokens the same as *that*). Lobster

For the sake of brevity, not to mention misgivings about taking (2) as expressing a quantificational structure, I will sometimes represent the Demonstrative analysis as (2*) instead of (2'/2''). Nothing hinges on my doing so, however.[1]

(2*) Lobster. This/that is a word.

Several features of the Demonstrative account can be discerned.

(a) THE PARATACTIC THESIS: quoted matter is logically external to the quoting sentence.
(b) THE REFERENCE THESIS: quotation marks are deictic referring terms, or correspond to descriptions or quantificational structures that contain deictic referring terms.

---

[1] Objecting to my friendly rendition, as do C&L (1999a: fn 8), is impertinent.

(c) THE MARK THESIS: mentioning an expression requires using quotation marks.

(d) THE CONGRUENCE THESIS: quoting is the same as mentioning, and an explication of the one is an explication of the other.

These form a fairly tidy package. To begin with, (a) implies (b), which is to say that (a) gives at least some grounds for inferring (b). For if the quoted matter in (2) is removed from the sentence then the remaining portion, (3), will be ungrammatical unless the pair of quotation marks is understood as the grammatical subject, and hence as a referring term or a quantificational structure containing a referring term.

(3) " " is a word.

Conversely, if quotation marks are referring terms then (2) will be ungrammatical unless the quoted matter is regarded as parenthetical or extra-sentential; (b) implies (a). Furthermore, if the quoted matter is removed from (2), and if there were no quotation marks to serve as referring terms in the remaining sentence, then the remaining sentence would be ungrammatical; (a) implies (c). Given that quotation marks and acts of mentioning co-occur, accounting for one may automatically account for the other; (c) implies (d).

For some, the Demonstrative package comes apart, though it is not explained how this is possible: Read (1997) and Recanati (2001) hold (a) while rejecting (b), Goddard and Routley (1966: 21) hold (b) without (a), Caplan (2002) holds (a) and (b) without (c), and Wittgenstein (1953: §16) and Searle (1983: 187) equivocate. Nonetheless, I take it that (a) and (b) jointly make up the heart of any Demonstrative Theory, that (c) and (d) are derivative, and that (a–d) form a prototypical cluster.

1.1   Quoted Matter Belongs to the Sentence

I begin by countering an argument in favor of (quotational) parataxis and then I give positive arguments against parataxis.

(i) REBUTTING THE PARATACTICIANS. What I call the universality argument for supposing that quoted material is paratactic or extra-sentential rests on foreign words and animal sounds. We can quote foreign words and animal sounds, in fact any producible sound or image at all, even though they are not part of English; and being no part of English, they are no part of English sentences [cf. Caplan (2002: 75)]. Against this view, suppose that spark plugs manufactured in Canada are installed in cars that are otherwise completely manufactured in Detroit. We need not fancy an alternate plane of existence, wherein spark plugs really are separate from cars, to judge of a car that it is American-made. Likewise a sentence containing a foreign element, if put together by an anglophone using an anglophone matrix, can be viewed as English without pretending that on some other plane of existence the foreign term stands outside the sentence.

To put the point less allegorically, ordinary beliefs about individuating language are simply mistaken. Few non-linguists realize that a language is little more than "a dialect with an army" (that there is no *linguistic* distinction between languages and dialects), and few even have the vocabulary for referring to idiolects. I reject the whole question of language as an immaterial object ("does x belong to language L's lexicon?") and would replace it with questions of actual language users ("does x belong to speaker S's repertoire?", "for population Σ, does x belong to the repertoire of most members of Σ?", etc.). Knowing a foreign word, I can say for instance that "mahatma" means GREAT-SOULED, or knowing of a word I can say that Gandhi was called "mahatma", whatever that means. In so doing, I perform a speech act, about the language of others, entirely in my own idiolect. The fact that an anglophone can quote from another language does not make the quoted matter sentence-external.

I turn now to the case against the paratactic thesis.

(ii) THE EMPTY QUOTATION ARGUMENT. The paratactician argues that quoting a word, and saying something about it, is like pointing at an object, and saying something about it: the word quoted is no more a part of the sentence than is the object pointed to. But if this were true then we should be able to remove quoted matter from its context while maintaining well-formedness. Just as I can say "that is an apple" in the absence of an apple (I can do so grammatically if not felicitously), so too should (2) be grammatically sayable or writable in the absence of "Lobster", i.e. (3) should be just as good as (4).

(3) " " is a word.
(4) That is word.

Without context (3), like (4), will lack truth-conditions; but like (4), it should seem like a complete sentence. Yet it doesn't. Quoted matter is an integral part of any quotational sentence.

My critics have said that (3) is grammatical, but they equivocate. True, (3) is grammatical if it is taken as quoting a very small blank space, and it is also grammatical if it is taken as a case of plain mentioning, that is as a case where the pair of quotation marks, without itself being quotation-marked, is being called a word. However, the grammaticality status of (3) under *those* interpretations is irrelevant. My claim was that (3) – not when it's about white space and not when it's about quotation marks but *when it's not about anything* – is ungrammatical.

Others may reply that grammar is deceptive: a sentence can be ill-formed on its surface yet well-formed at the level of logical form, and in fact at the level of logical form (3) is admissible because its lonely quotation marks are covert referring terms. But this position – that quotation marks are both overt (visible at the level of syntactic form in [3]) and covert ([3] lacks a subject at the level of syntactic form but not at that of logical form) – strikes me as inconsistent. That aside, still there is a problem. When syntactic form deviates from logical form, it does so either as a matter of historical contingency or for a general reason. In the former case we should expect other languages to represent quotation very differently from English, namely we should expect quoted matter to be presented as external to the sentences that normally contain them. But I am not aware of any language that does this. On the other hand, if quotational syntactic form is deceptive for some general reason that applies to all languages, one would hope to have some clue as to what this reason is, or evidence that it at least exists. But again I am not aware of any.

(iii) THE SCARE-QUOTE ARGUMENT. The paratactic thesis is additionally refuted by scare quotes.

(5) Chang is a "bad" boy.
    Lee "shamelessly" flirted.
    Ishmael floated "above" the other astronaut.

According to the Demonstrative Theory, these are equivalent to:

(5') Chang is a that boy. bad
     Lee that flirted. shamelessly
     Ishmael floated that the other astronaut. above

For Demonstrative Theorists, quotation marks must be convertible to any syntactic category – in (5) they function variously as adjective, adverb, and preposition. Although English is unusually liberal in allowing words to convert, I do not know of any English lexeme that can so naturally be used as any part of speech at all, and I would be surprised if quotation marks really could. The implausibility of the case is magnified when we consider those languages having quotation marks that generally prohibit conversion. Besides, postulating conversion doesn't work in cases like:

(6) Chang wants to "call upon" Chung.

Because the quoted matter in (6) does not form a syntactic unit, no pro-noun, pro-verb, or pro-form of any kind can take its place. I conclude that quoted matter is an integral part of the sentence that it appears to be in.

The current argument may be said to fail on the grounds that it changes the topic. Our topic, so the charge goes, is metalinguistic citation as illustrated in (2), whereas the counter-examples on hand are cases of scare-quotation; indeed, the policy of some publishers is to distinguish the two cases (double quotes for the former, single quotes for the latter). However, I do not believe that I am changing the topic. First, marks of metalinguistic citation and marks of scare-quotation are typically identical, which means that there is a prima facie reason to assume that a single theory should handle both; in switching from one to the other I am not equivocating. Second, cross-linguistic patterns reinforce the prima facie appearance: in every case I know of, namely in French, German, and Japanese, metalinguistic and scare-quotation take identical forms. Third, it makes rational sense to see both metalinguistic and scare-quote uses of quotation as reflexes of a single underlying linguistic mechanism (§2).

Responding to a related problem involving "mixed" quotation (a mixture of direct and indirect discourse report), Garcia-Carpintero (2004: §2) posits an implicit "as he puts it" right before the quotation in (7).

(7) Quine says that quotation "... has an anomalous feature."

This move, however, yields a logical form that is uninterpretable:

(7′) Quine says that quotation, as he puts it, this. has an anomalous feature.

Although Garcia-Carpintero's exact idea fails, the basic idea demands attention. For one could argue instead that the quotation marks in (7), functioning as a demonstrative, combine with an implicit reference to satisfaction so as to yield (7″).

(7″) Quine says that quotation [satisfies] this [expression]. has an anomalous feature.

By extension, judicious postulations of implicit content could arguably render (5) intelligible. For instance, the flirt example might be construed as:

(5″) Lee flirted [in a manner described by] this [expression]. shamelessly

What, however, is the status of implicit content? Is (5″) supposed to give the deep structure of (5)? the truth-conditions of (5)? a paraphrase equivalent to (5) for some practical purposes? Since implicit content varies from case to case, ascribing it to the conventional meaning of quotation marks would be ad hoc and implausible. To hold, on the other hand, that implicit content is imaginatively projected based on context fails to explain how (5) can be grammatical. As suggested in my 1998b: 119, the utterance "I drive a" can combine with pointing at a Studebaker to yield the partially implicit message that I drive a Studebaker; yet this implicit content renders "I drive a" neither grammatical nor – except in charades, interrupted discourse, and false starts – the sort of expression that is ever actually uttered.

1.2   Quotation Marks do not Refer

Demonstrative Theorists insist that quotation marks are demonstratives or contain demonstratives. It is strange, then, that they neither define "demonstrative" nor refer the reader to any of the distinct accounts available in the literature.

I take it that demonstratives do more than point. Fingers point but are not demonstratives. A demonstrative is a verbal element with syntactic properties, having referential power and contrasting with names and pure descriptions. It may refer to a singular object (this, that), a plurality of objects (these, those), a manner (thus, so), a property (such), or a degree (yea); or it may combine with an incomplete phrase, as a determiner does, to yield a referring phrase. In addition, some languages conceivably have demonstrative verbs, prepositions, and conjunctions. But in all cases to be a demonstrative is to function linguistically and hence to enjoy syntactic powers. This is not how quotation marks work, however.

(i) THE EMPTY QUOTATION ARGUMENT AGAIN. The notion of a referring term is that it can combine with a predicate to form a complete grammatical sentence. But quotation marks do not do this.

(3) " " is a word.

As established in Section 1.1ii, *quoted matter is necessary* for making quotation referential. The very same evidence now yields another conclusion, that *quotation marks are not sufficient* for making quotation referential.[2]

---

[2]   This argument is anticipated by Gomez-Torrente (2001: 130). I wish to generalize it (Gomez-Torrente, p. 135, thinks that it does not apply against C&L's theory), to emphasize it, to point out the two distinct conclusions, to consider how paratacticians might respond to at least one of them (§1.1ii), and to deny Gomez-Torrente's assertion that it extends against my own approach (§3). For still more sound argumentation against the reference and paratactic theses, see Botterell & Stainton (2005: §2.1).

(ii) THE REDUNDANCY ARGUMENT. Recanati (2001: 654) and Wertheimer (2005: fn 13) argue that, though (8) is well-formed, its purported equivalent (8′) is not.

(8) The word "emu" is fun.
(8′) The word that is fun. emu

Bennett (1988: 417) anticipates the point and denies that it is a problem: after all, he suggests, (9) and (10) have the same semantic value, but that does not preclude them from combining.

(9) the composer of *Parsifal*
(10) Richard Wagner
(11) the composer Richard Wagner

Likewise, by implication, "the word" can logically combine with a quotation, as in (8), even if a quotation mark is a demonstrative referring term. (That "the word" cannot combine with "that" in (8′) would have to be explained by appeal to some rules of surface grammar.)

This defense is far from convincing, however. In the first place, in drawing a parallel between (8) and (11), Bennett ignores their prima facie difference. If they are fundamentally alike, why do they *seem* so different? In the second place, though (9) and (10) co-refer, neither is even a partial synonym, analysis, or logical form of the other. Their information values differ, and so (11) is not redundant. Truly redundant appositives would be deviant:

(12) the composer the composer of *Parsifal*
      the musician the composer of *Parsifal*

Since (8) is not deviant, quotation marks cannot contain the sense "the word." Moreover, it looks like this argument can be extended to other proposed analyses. Since (13) is acceptable but (13′) is not, quotation marks cannot mean what Davidson, in (2′), says they do.

(13) The expression type of which "emu" is a token is fun.
(13′) The expression type of which the expression type of which that is a token is fun. emu

(iii) NO JOKING MATTER. Another problem for the Demonstrative Theory is that in many cases it cannot interpret speech ascriptions.

(14) "You've got to be kidding," I laughed.
(14′) I laughed that. You've got to be kidding

Because "laugh" is intransitive, (14′) is meaningless. But (14) is meaningful. Therefore (14, 14′) cannot be equivalent.

Demonstratives needn't be singular terms. Were they to take the form of deictic adverbs then (14) would mean

(14″) I laughed thus. You've got to be kidding

The problem here is that "thus", if it referred, would refer to some manner; yet the displayed item is a sentence, not a manner. Demonstrative Theorists may correctly observe that sentences can be mentally associated with manners, but this move is puzzling. If Demonstrative Theorists are willing to invoke such pragmatic associations, why are they not willing to do so earlier in the game, before attributing unobservable logical forms to quotation marks in the first place?

(iv) THE EXCESS-TERM ARGUMENT. Recanati (2001: 654) observes that quotation marks can be used even in the absence of a matrix sentence, where referring terms should be out of place. Such free-standing quotation frequently appears in novels, I would add, for instance in Philip Roth's *Portnoy's Complaint*:

(15) "Alex, I want an answer from you …"
    "Nuhhh, nuhhh."

According to Demonstrative Theorists, (15) contains dangling referring terms, and is equivalent to:

(15′) This. Alex, I want an answer from you …
    This. Nuhhh, nuhhh.

Quotation marks are used in (15) to ascribe words to parties not explicitly identified and to indicate dialog boundaries. But referring terms do not serve this function, as illustrated by the deviance of (15′). Therefore the items serving this function, the quotation marks, are not referring terms. And if quotation marks are not referring terms in (15), there is no reason to think that they are elsewhere either.

(v) THE MISSING-TERM ARGUMENT. Whereas novelists routinely use unascribed dialog inside quotation marks, which appears to refute the Demonstrative Theory, playwrights routinely use unascribed dialog without quotation marks, and this too poses a problem for the Demonstrative Theory. Consider, for instance, Joseph Heller's *We Bombed in New Haven*:

(16) STARKEY Is it [the mission] dangerous?
   MAJOR Not for those who survive.

Demonstrative Theorists must make a choice. One option is to recognize normal font as marks of quotation when it is set in opposition to capitalized character names. In this case (16), equivalent to (16′) and hence (16″), would fall to the excess-term objection:

(16′) Starkey. "Is it dangerous?"
   Major. "Not for those who survive."
(16″) Starkey. This. Is it dangerous?
   Major. This. Not for those who survive.

In response to (16′), which cannot be taken literally, Demonstrative Theorists may posit a pragmatically understood "says" in each line. But if they are willing to do that, why not posit a pragmatically understood "says that" in (16)? And if "that" is but pragmatically understood in (16), font does not express it.

   Alternatively, Demonstrative Theorists might opt to regard contrastive font as linguistically inessential. In this case, (16) amounts to:

(16*) Starkey. Is it dangerous?
   Major. Not for those who survive.

This constitutes plain mentioning – quotation without quotation marks, if you will. Yet Demonstrative Theorists deny the existence of plain mentioning.

1.3   Plain Mentioning is Legitimate

   I believe that quotation marks disambiguate material that can intrinsically be either used or mentioned (not by selecting a sense, but by guiding to an understanding). It follows that even unmarked matter can be mentioned, i.e. plain mentioning as in (17) is possible.

(17) Cats has four letters.

In saying that (17) is possible, I mean that it is grammatical, though not necessarily grammatical in the same way as (17′).

(17′) Cats have four legs.

My claim rather is that the syntactic well-formedness of (17) is comparable to that of (17″), though of course they differ in literary acceptability.

(17″) "Cats" has four letters.

Later, in Section 2, I explain how (17′, 17″) rely on very different principles of construction. The same difference applies to (17′) and (17).

After arguing that plain mentioning is in fact well-formed, I defend the thesis from unsound criticisms and then appeal to reflective equilibrium. On this issue depends the plausibility of the Demonstrative Theory.

(i) THE USE ARGUMENT. To settle any debate over grammar, it would help to make our ideas of grammar explicit. I propose the following principle: if speakers regularly and unapologetically use construction C, then C is grammatical. Note first of all that this is intended as a criterion, not a definition or explication; and like criteria generally are, this one is defeasible. (Regularly and unapologetically using construction C because one is ordered to at gunpoint, or doing so in fits of religious mania – "speaking in tongues" – does not count as evidence for C's grammaticality.) Note too that the principle is not biconditional. A construction may be grammatical even if no one ever uses it, for it may be recognizably false, too long for human breath, rude or taboo, etc.

Now the evidence strikes me as perfectly straightforward. First, plain mentioning is widespread. Second, plain mentioning is resistant to change. After telling my linguistics students that they absolutely must use quotation marks when citing words, I invariably get some who fail to do so. (When questioned, they will sometimes say that quotation marks were inappropriate because what was meant was obvious.) Third, plain mentioning can be found in expertly written, professionally copy-edited texts. Lynn Truss, an authority on punctuation, writes of Woody Allen's character:

(18) He just wanted to know how to spell Connecticut. [2004: 130]

And Paul Dickson conforms to the practice found in books put out by many fine publishers when he writes:

(19) Chang is the most common name in the world. [1996: 196]

Indeed, when the word "name" appears in the subject rather than the predicate – when the listener can expect a name mentioned rather than used – quotation marks are not merely omissible; they are positively deviant:

(20) My name is "Paul."

Even those who pretend to the greatest rigor sometimes see no difference between using quotation marks, and not. In his experience with great logicians, such as Lewis and Sheffer, Quine (1986: 10) writes: "I had ever and again to recur to the theme of use versus mention. A little clarity of mind proves not always to suffice for the purpose." All of this is evidence that plain mentioning is no performance error. The product of competence, it is grammatical.

Finally, it is widely agreed that in speech one can mention a word without vocally marking it in any special way, i.e. one can plain mention it. It follows, to the extent that written language is a record of spoken language, that written language may also be plain mentioned yet grammatical.

(ii) A QUESTION-BEGGING CRITICISM. Cappelen & Lepore – henceforth C&L – argue against the possibility of plain mentioning. Recall that (17) is "Cats has four letters."

> Consider a language E*...E* has no mention-quotation distinction, and so [17] is ungrammatical in E*. Ask yourself: could a speaker assertively utter a token of [17], and her audience still understand what she means by her token? Should we expect that speakers of E* might occasionally omit...quote marks? The answer is trivially "yes". E* speakers could omit quote marks whenever what's meant is obvious...If E* speakers can omit quote marks and still get across what they mean, then the fact that we omit quote marks is no evidence that we are not ourselves E* speakers...[1999a: §1–2]

This argument is endorsed by Predelli (2003), who does not address my neighboring response to it in Saka (1999). Namely, on the face of it C&L contradict themselves. They posit (α) that language E* has no mention-quotation distinction (in my sense of mention and quotation), that is its speakers invariably quotation-mark their mentionings; and at the same time (β) that E*'s speakers occasionally omit quotation marks when mentioning.

Perhaps C&L mean (α') that E* has no *grammatical* mention-quotation distinction, that is its speakers invariably quotation-mark their mentionings when speaking grammatically; and (β') E*'s speakers may omit quotation marks when mentioning as long as "what's meant is obvious", although doing so is ungrammatical. But C&L err in thinking that obviousness licenses ungrammatical utterances. Whenever a grammatical subject in English denotes the established topic of a conversation, what's meant is obvious yet systematically not omitted outside of marked genres such as notes to oneself. Also, telegraphic language (not to be confused with elliptical language, which is perfectly grammatical) is usually clear in meaning, and certainly saves on breath, and yet telegraphic speech is generally not found except in telegrams, in headlines, in classifieds, and among some aphasics. In short, principle (β') does not describe English; if plain mentioning is ungrammatical in E* then E* is clearly distinguishable from English, where plain mentioning is widely, regularly, and unapologetically used.

More fundamentally, in stipulating a language that has no mention-quotation distinction, C&L invoke a premise that I am not willing to grant. Quotation marks are forms that a language may or may not possess. In contrast, mentioning is a function; it is what people do with language, not a feature of the language itself. In speaking or writing *any* language whatsoever, therefore, I can choose to mention one of its expressions regardless of whether I use a quotational form. There is no such thing as a possible language which lacks the mention-quotation distinction, and in assuming it C&L beg the question.

(iii) THE AMBIGUITY CRITICISM. If plain mentioning is possible then (21) is ambiguous – which is not to say that it encodes distinct meanings, but that it allows for distinct understandings: an objectual reading (the font known as Arial is elegant) and a metalinguistic reading (the name of the font is elegant).

(21) Arial is elegant.

Demonstrative Theorists criticize this ambiguity view, treating it as absurd (C&L 1999a: 744, Caplan 2002). I do not see why they feel this way unless they think all ambiguity is lexico-syntactic. But such a restricted view of ambiguity matches neither that expressed by the Identity Theory nor that of ordinary language. (Mona Lisa's smile is ambiguous without being lexically or syntactically so.)

Not incidentally, Demonstrative Theorists must themselves posit systematic ambiguity, given that they treat (22) and (22′) as equivalent.

(22) "You are either with us or against us" is an Orwellian lie.
(22′) (a) You are either with us or against us. (b) That is an Orwellian lie.

Apparently (22) is true while (22′) is self-contradictory – (a) contradicts (b). If (22′) is not to be self-contradictory, (a) must lack assertoric force. Yet in ordinary contexts (a) possesses assertoric force. Since some tokens of (a) are assertoric and some are not, (a) is ambiguous.

(iv) THE CRITERION OF SECOND-ORDER EXPLANATION. I judge plain mentioning to be grammatically well-formed while Demonstrative Theorists do not. To decide between us, you should look at the theoretical considerations for supporting one judgment over the other. But you should look further, too. You should look for the stories each side can give to explain the intuitions of the other (p. 15).

Here is mine. As a general rule, if you know an effective means for doing something that you value, you will frown upon those who willfully refuse to adopt it, you will regard their choices as erroneous. Using quotation marks is an effective means of being explicitly precise, which is of value to scholars; hence it is easy for scholars to condemn language that does not use it. The fact that plain mentioning might be eschewed by certain speakers is no evidence of its ungrammaticality.

Is it credible that smart people can be confused by the distinction between ungrammaticality on the one hand and stylistic infelicity, flouting of scholarly practice, and other sorts of ill-advisedness on the other? Our long sorry history proves that it is so. Many among the educated elite have railed against "ain't", saying that it isn't a word, when in fact its real problem is prudential. Speakers who use the word lose social status, they do not violate grammar.

To summarize, some regard (17–19) as well-formed and some do not. The best theory not only justifies one side but also explains the existence of divergent intuitions. On my account, those who accept (17–19) attend to the grammar while those who reject it are distracted by other felicity conditions. So far as I know, C&L cannot account for divergent intuitions. They cannot say, for instance, that those who reject (17–19) attend to grammar while others accept (17–19) because some ungrammatical constructions are assertable. For as a general rule, ungrammatical constructions are *not* regularly and unapologetically assertable.

(v) THE SIGNIFICANCE OF PLAIN MENTIONING. If thesis (c) is mistaken then that serves as additional argument against the paratactic and reference theses (a, b). For given that plain mentioning is possible, (17″) would keep its meaning even if stripped of its quotation marks, setting aside differences in ambiguity.

(17″) "Cats" has four letters.

But in that case, for purposes of grammaticality and interpretability, quotation marks need not add truth-conditional content to the sentences that they are in (modulo ambiguity). Hence so-called semantic accounts of quotation, including the Demonstrative Theory, are at best superfluous.

1.4 The Use-Mention Distinction is Relevant

The use-mention distinction bears on our understanding of quotation. First I argue that neglecting the distinction keeps us in the dark, then I argue that respecting the distinction is illuminating.

(i) AGAINST NEGLECTING THE DISTINCTION. Recall that the Demonstrative Theory treats (22) and (22′) as equivalent, yet (22′) appears to be self-contradictory.

(22) "You are either with us or against us" is an Orwellian lie.
(22′) (a) You are either with us or against us. (b) That is an Orwellian lie.

Davidson responds that (a) is not asserted, it is merely "said." What does it mean to say something? Davidson seems to suggest that saying is non-intentional, that it amounts to uttering, when he defines quotation as a relation to an expression *shape*. The problem is that the objects of utterance, mere syllables, are neither true nor false. If quotation is defined by reference to uttering then (22) claims that sounds as sounds can be false, when in fact it seems that only interpretations of sounds, or sounds relativized to interpretations, have truth-value. Davidson himself appears to acknowledge this elsewhere when he says that truth-values are borne by structural descriptions. On the other hand, if saying is more than flapping one's gums, to say is to make an assertion, pose a question, issue a directive, exclaim, attribute words to others, cite, or do something meaningful. But if one explains quotation in terms of saying and saying in terms of attributing or citing, one doesn't get very far. The resulting account of quotation is circular or at best incomplete.

C&L do spend one sentence on mentioning: "expression e is mentioned in an utterance u just in case the token of e occurring in u is produced in order to be demonstrated so as to talk about tokens that same-token it" (1997: fn 8). Not only does this formulation contain minor flaws – e.g. speakers talk, expressions do not, and even then speakers do not always talk about the expressions that they mention – more to the point, in consigning their discussion to a brief footnote C&L marginalize the essential relation between quoting and mentioning.

(ii) FOR RESPECTING THE DISTINCTION. I believe that by examining the use-mention distinction, specifically how it develops both historically and in the individual, we find evidence for the correct theory of quotation.

I treat the use-mention distinction as a matter of how language is used. This distinction, being independent of the lexico-grammatical peculiarities of languages, presumably applies to all languages; a speaker of any language can intend to draw attention to an expression. This is true even for a language without quotation marks. Such is easy to imagine, for ancient languages lack quotation marks, as do juvenile versions of modern languages. (It is because of lacking quotation marks that Chrysippus was able to equivocate, "If you say something, this comes out of your mouth; but you say wagon; therefore, a wagon comes out of your mouth"; Inwood & Gerson 1988: 78.)

Now imagine that you, a child, wish to write that you've learned a new word one day, "uranium". You start by writing, "I learned a new word today". How do you finish?

(23) It is this. uranium
(24) It is this: uranium.

(25) It is this, uranium.
(26) It is URANIUM.
(27) It is uranium.
(28) It is "uranium".

I grant that (23) and (24) are real possibilities. This shows that it is possible
to mention by means of paratactic demonstrating, though it does not show
that such is either necessary or typical, nor that this is how quotation
works. A more common and natural way for children to write is probably
(25), which, though demonstrative, is not paratactic. Also to be expected
would be (26) and (27). Those children who underline, box, capitalize, or
otherwise fancify the quoted matter, as in (26), are inventing their own
marks of quotation, perhaps though not necessarily as an effort to represent
in writing some feature of speech. It is the naturalness of the likes of (27)
that establishes that proto-language, be it juvenile English or Old English,
does not grammatically require either demonstrative reference to that which
is mentioned nor paratactic separation of that which mentions from that
which is mentioned.

The question now is this: in the development from ancient to modern
language, or from juvenile language to mature, which hypothesis is most
plausible for explaining current conventions of quotation?

(α) Elite speakers (editors and whatnot), realizing the ambiguity of (27),
first took (27) and secondly supplemented it with innovated disambiguating punctuation.

(β) Speakers first took (23), secondly replaced the ordinary demonstrative with quotation marks, thirdly moved the quoted matter into
the sentence at syntactic form but not logical form, and fourthly
banished (27) as a way of mentioning – and all in perfect synchrony.

The answer, of course, is that simplicity overwhelmingly favors (α).

(iii) SUMMARY. The Identity Theory, whereby quotation marks signal
disambiguating intent, makes several predictions. First, slapdash writers
oblivious to possible ambiguity will frequently omit quotation marks.
Second, quotation marks will be omitted even by careful editors in cases,
such as written plays, where ambiguity is systematically not a problem.
Third, if quotation marks were added by some amateur playwright, as in
(16**), they would be regarded as inelegant by those familiar with the norms
of playwrighting, but not as uninterpretable.

(16**) STARKEY: "Is it dangerous?"
MAJOR: "Not for those who survive."

Fourth, as first noticed by Wertheimer (1999), it will be unusual to find quotation marks around non-linguistic material, for lack of ambiguity.

(29) The color within the square, □, is white.

These facts and others favor the Identity Theory over the Demonstrative Theory.

Most crucially, the ill-formedness of example (3) establishes the integrity thesis, that quotations include their quoted matter, and it also refutes the reference thesis, that quotation marks are referring terms.

(3) " " is a word.

Sections 1.1 and 1.2 mount additional evidence for the same conclusions, and they furthermore support each other: if either section is correct, that would count as support for the other.

Section 1.3 observes that (19) is not the result of performance error, it is grammatical.

(19) Chang is the most common name in the world.

Furthermore, if (19) is grammatical then we seem to have a word being used in reference to itself, in accordance with pragmatic versions of the Identity Theory. We certainly do not have demonstratives doing the referring. All of this suggests that the simplest account of (30) is that it too has no demonstrative referring terms.

(30) "Chang" is the most common name in the world.

This conclusion is reinforced in Section 1.4, which speculates on the transition from a primitive language to one having quotation.

2.   The Attitudinal Theory

A speaker S may use any expression token (e.g. this particular inscription: cat) and in so doing ostend or make manifest it and various items associated with it (including the inscription-*type* "cat", the pronunciation /kæt/, the concept CAT, and the extension of cats). When S adds quotation marks, S conveys the presumed intention to pick out something other than the customary referent, either instead of it or in addition to it. These ideas are explained below (§2.1, §2.2) and their consequences are drawn out in application to a variety of quotations: scare-quoting (§2.3), metalinguistic citation (§2.4), reported speech (§2.5, §2.6), and echo-quoting, titles, and more (§2.7).

2.1 Ostension and Construction: Principle (P)

Every time you vocalize you vibrate the air, and in so doing you make manifest to your audience certain phonetic phenomena. The phonetic phenomena, in turn, activate phonological representations in the audience, which in turn trigger recognition of lexical entries including conceptual content and projections of syntactic structures (multiple sets thereof in the case of lexico-syntactic ambiguity), eventuating in referential models. What's more, the route from sound to referent is robust. Thus, I can plead "don't think of an elephant", and you will think of an elephant (Lakoff 2004). All I have done is present some ink, but the ink, or more directly speaking your perception of it, willy-nilly caused you to think of something other than the ink. In short, speech acts directly ostend sounds and thereby deferringly ostend, according to principles of association hardwired in the human mind, lexemes and mental models.

The foregoing is a false idealization, of course, assuming as it does that language comprehension works entirely bottom-up. Still, it is accurate enough for the sake of illustrating some facts of ostension and association, and for introducing my thoughts on conceptual content and referential models.

A "referential" model is one aspect of a mental model (see references in Chapter 1.3.10). Strictly speaking, mental models do not contain referents at all. Being in the mind, they are subjective and may be populated by phantasmagoria. Nonetheless, for present purposes mental models can be said to correspond to the world (or not) and to serve as objects of thought (belief, speculation, desire,...). They are partially language-independent, such that speakers of different languages have similar, though not identical, kinds of models (Gumperz & Levinson 1996). They are far from sentence-like, standing in a relation to contextualized sentences that is many-many, contra truth-conditional semantics.

Mental models are built and revised according to perception, according to inference, and according to *instructions as provided by linguistic concepts.* Because concepts relate to aspects of referential models, they might be said to have "extensions", internalistically construed.

Interpretation, or the construction of mental models, involves opportunistic problem-solving and invention. We use whatever tools and resources are at hand in order to figure out speaker's intent, and we do so according to constraints, for instance we follow the preference ordering of using what is most salient first (Sperber & Wilson 1986, Carston 2002).

I begin with a simple example. In saying (31) the speaker ostends (a–d).

(31) Anna sees Bob.
(31a) /Anna sees Bob/
(31b) [Anna] [sees] [Bob]
(31c) ANNA SEES BOB
(31d) |Anna sees Bob|

The phonological form in (a) activates the lexical items in (b), which trigger the concepts in (c), which serve as instructions for building/accessing the model specified in (d). What's more, the audience attends to the sequencing of what is ostended, knowing that such is relevant to semantic structure: [Anna] is ostended at time or position t_1, [sees] at t_2, and [Bob] at t_3. The verb [sees] contains the instruction to look left (earlier) for the subject and right for the object. Knowing this allows us to get to the model in (d), the "proposition" that Anna sees Bob, in a loose sense of the word.

In implementing the instructions provided by conceptual content, the audience does not select from a pre-established range of possible models, but actively constructs one (or more) using imagination and intelligence. Yet conceptual content is executed *automatically*. This, the primary principle of all language use, has a corollary that can be formulated as follows in terms of the speaker [cf. the Use Hypothesis of Predelli (2005: 153)].

(P) In uttering any expression x, S defeasibly intends for the audience to execute x's lexico-syntactically specified conceptual content.

Principle (P) will combine with principle (Q) to explain much about quotation.

2.2   Use and Mention: Principle (Q)

Use and *mention* have both vernacular and technical senses. In the vernacular, to mention is simply to refer to; and to use, make use of, or employ an expression is to speak some syllables or scrawl some scratch-marks with any number of intentions, or none at all. With certain intentions, however, we get use and mention in the following technical senses.

(U) Speaker S uses an expression x if and only if:
   (i) S produces a token of x, thereby ostending an open-ended number of items associated with x; and
   (ii) S intends to refer to the extension of x.

(M) Speaker S mentions an expression x if and only if:

    (i) S produces a token of x, thereby ostending an open-ended number of items associated with x; and

    (ii) S intends to refer to something associated with x other than its extension, e.g. x's form, associated lexemes, or conceptual structure.

This analysis calls for several clarifications.

(i) The use-mention distinction is neither exclusive nor exhaustive. An expression may be simply used (32), simply mentioned (33), or simultaneously used and mentioned (34).

(32) Motown is the home of some good music.
(33) "Motown" alludes to Detroit's motor industry.
(34) I grew up near "Motown".

In addition an expression may go neither used nor mentioned, e.g. when emitted by parrots.

(ii) What do I mean by reference? Recanati (2001: 648) suggests that reference requires predication. This is mistaken, however. If I scream "my baby!" while my neighbors keep me from running into my burning house, then I refer to my baby without predicating anything of it. It seems sufficient, for referring one's audience to x, to "pick out" x or to draw the audience's attention to x. In the case of *linguistic* reference, the speaker refers by means of a conventional *verbal* element. In short, the predication of an element is not necessary for its being referential, although it is sufficient.[3]

(iii) How is it possible, if using involves ostending an extension, to use particles such as "the," which have no extension? The answer is that though the extension of a particle in isolation cannot be picked out, it can nonetheless be characterized abstractly: the extension of "the" in a given sentence P is that which "the" contributes to the extension of P, which in turn is a (represented) kind of state of affairs.

(iv) My analyses invoke speaker intentions. If intention were dropped from (U) then the first word in (33) would mistakenly count as used; and if intention were dropped from (M) then, arguably, no word would ever count as mentioned.

---

[3] Technical distinctions could be drawn among reference, denotation, extension, and so on. In this section, however, such terms are used not only loosely (so as to accommodate the mentalism set forth in §2.1) but also broadly and interchangeably.

Because I invoke intentions, Cappelen & Lepore (1999a: 746) accuse me of Humpty-Dumptyism. This charge actually smears together two distinct doctrines: first that intentions contribute to meaning, and second that intentions can arbitrarily be whatever one wants them to be. Though the former is my position, the latter is not, for intentions in general are constrained by expectations. In particular, linguistic expectations depend both on internalized norms built up from summations of experience with others in one's language community and on general principles of cognition. (You cannot intend to fly no matter how hard you want or try or set your mind to. You can intend to do only that which you believe you are capable of doing, and in this way intending differs from desiring, hoping, and attempting; you cannot use the word "glory", as Humpty Dumpty does, in order to mean 'a knock-down argument'.) Derogatory imputations of Humpty-Dumptyism misapprehend the nature of intention.

To suppose that intentions play some role in linguistic phenomena is not necessarily to advocate Gricean intention-based semantics, which would indeed be controversial. My commitment to a modicum of intentionalism is rooted in the unexciting idea that when I say "pepperoni" I refer to either pepperoni or green pepper depending on something vaguely intentional, be it my intention (e.g. to speak English or German); the intention ascribed to me by my interpreter; some mutually recognized intention; the social/physical context of my utterance, as constituted by intentional norms (e.g. being in England or in Germany); etc. [cf. Predelli (2005: §3)]. When C&L (2005b: §2) deny altogether the relevance of intentions and context to semantic function, they seem to forget that words have meaning only in languages, and that a word cannot be in a language unless it is connected to some intentional agent, be it speaker or interpreter.[4]

Thus concludes my general framework and definition of use/mention. I turn now to quotation, which formally marks the mentioning function.

(Q) In uttering an expression in quotation marks, S defeasibly mentions it.

Primary principle (P) and quotational principle (Q) combine to help explain the interpretation of scare quotes, metalinguistic citation, discourse reports, and so forth.

---

[4] Certain other objections to intentionalism, though widespread, are non-starters [cf. Bach (1992), Garcia-Carpintero (2005: 92)]. By the way, it's worth noting that Lewis Carroll sided with Humpty Dumpty's first doctrine (Gardner 1960: 269) – the position is not manifestly absurd, nor can it be ruled out by fiat or by tendentious definitions of semantics.

2.3 Scare Quotes

Speakers draw attention to their word choices for any number of editorializing reasons. A textbook author may implicitly mean 'here is jargon, don't forget it'; a scholar may mean 'here is loose language, and I recognize it as much'; the haughty may mean 'here is slang I do not identify with'. To *alert* the audience to such pedagogical, cautionary, and distancing intents, the speaker uses *scare* quotes.

> (35) The earth is an "oblate spheroid" rather than a sphere. [Asimov 1988: 296]

In saying (35), S draws attention to (i) the proposition that the earth is an oblate spheroid rather than a sphere, and (ii) the term [oblate spheroid]. Just as it is up to the audience to infer why (i) is being made manifest – it could be for assertion, reminding, hypothesizing, or whatnot – so it is up to the audience to infer why (ii) is being made manifest.

We might say as a first approximation, then, that expressions containing quotations have two components of meaning. The first is just the kind of meaning that all plain expressions have, the kind that derives from (P) as presented at the end of Section 2.1. The second derives from the specifically quotational principle (Q) from the end of Section 2.2. Putting together (P) and (Q) yields:

> (PQ) In uttering an expression having quotation marks, S defeasibly intends for the audience to execute its conceptual content *and* to refer to something related to the quoted portion other than its extension.

Accordingly, in saying (35), Asimov intends for us to execute the instructions encoded in THE EARTH IS AN OBLATE SPHEROID RATHER THAN A SPHERE, that is to construct the thought that the earth is an oblate spheroid rather than a sphere, and also to attend especially to the term [oblate spheroid]. Perhaps we are supposed to realize that it is being implicitly defined, perhaps we are supposed to remember it, perhaps Asimov has some other reason in mind.

To repeat the lesson of Section 2.1, customary non-quotational use of language is automatic. Now, adding quotation marks allows for a new use that may but need not displace the old. In treating the quoted matter in (36) as a sort of noun phrase, I do not treat it as *only* a noun phrase; if logical forms existed, that of (36) would be not (36′) but more nearly (36″).

> (36) Quine says that quotation "is anomalous".

(36′) Quine says that quotation Annabel Lee.

(36″) Quine says that quotation is anomalous. Annabel Lee

Hence the criticism of C&L (1999a: 748), Simchen (1999: 331), and Abbott (2005: 19) is unsound.[5]

Yet principle (PQ) might be questioned on other grounds.

(37) Jack "fortuitously" bumped into Jill.

According to (PQ), S uses (37) to mean that Jack fortuitously bumped into Jill, and that we are to pause over the word choice "fortuitously". But it doesn't seem that (37) means that Jack fortuitously bumped into Jill. Thus there is an intuitive difference between two uses of scare quotes. In the *strict* case, (36), the quoted matter is both mentioned and literally used; in the *loose* case, (37), the quoted matter is mentioned and only figuratively used.

To solve the problem of loose-speech scare quotes, I shall sketch the following *resemblance* account. As mentioned, due to the laws of human linguistic competence, verbal stimuli are associated with words, concepts, and extensions; for example "fortuitously" is associated with /fortuitously/, [fortuitously], FORTUITOUSLY, and |fortuitously|. Because associations are also based on the more general cognitive principle of resemblance, there is a mentally apprehended relation between that which is strictly F and that which comes close to being F. Thus, if Jack meets Jill, and the encounter has the appearance of being both accidental and fortunate but is actually contrived or unfortunate, then the meeting resembles a fortuitous one without being so; it is quasi-fortuitous. Hence the results of reading (37) include the following sequences.

(37a) JACK /fortuitously/ BUMPED INTO JILL

(37b) JACK [fortuitously] BUMPED INTO JILL

(37c) JACK FORTUITOUSLY BUMPED INTO JILL

(37d) JACK QUASI-FORTUITOUSLY BUMPED INTO JILL

---

[5] Simchen (1999: 331) attributes to me the thesis that "quotation signals the exclusion of one aspect of the ordinary use of expressions – the extension". My actual words were: "quote marks *generally* [i.e. typically, not universally] ... rule out customary reference as the intended interpretation. Thus, the speaker who uses quote marks announces 'I am not (*merely*) using expression X but am mentioning it' " (1998: 127, italicization added; point elaborated on p. 115, implied on p. 126, and stressed on p. 133). My exposition could have been clearer, but my position then as now is that quotation marks signal mentioning, and that mentioning is compatible with using. For Abbott (2005) to indicate otherwise, contrary to unequivocal clarification in personal correspondence, is contumelious.

It's not possible to execute (a) or (b). Executing (c) and (d), however, does yield propositions.

(37e) |Jack fortuitously bumped into Jill|
(37f) |Jack bumped into Jill in a way that resembles the fortuitous|

The quotation marks in (37) signal that something other than (e) is intended, the reasonable candidate being (f). Meanwhile (P) tells us that (e) is defeasibly intended too, though in this case there is a defeater. Because (e) entails (f), there would be no reason for using quotation marks had the speaker intended both; indeed, there is a pragmatic implication from (f) to (g), which positively contradicts (e).

(37g) |Jack bumped into Jill in a way that resembles the fortuitous without being fortuitous|

The exact relation among (37, e–g) can be understood in various ways. (i) One option takes the fundamental, literal meaning of a sentence as given by principle (P). (P) tells us that (37) means (e), hence under the given scenario (37) is false. At the same time, because of (Q), (37) implies or otherwise conveys (g). Since speakers do sometimes deliberately make false statements for the sake of a larger conversational good, it is understandable how (37) might be false yet assertable. (ii) An alternative option is to say that (37) generates at least two propositions, one true and one false, in effect a false conjunction. Again it is understandable how (37) might be felicitous so long as (g) is true. (iii) Perhaps, analogous to cases of ambiguity, (37) generates two propositions, where only one counts as a truth-evaluable intended reading on any given occasion. This accommodates the intuition that (37) is true. (iv) Finally, my own inclination, we might say that deciding among (i–iii) is bogus because the notion of truth is not sufficiently determinate for (37) to be either true or not.

Any *one* of (i–iv), if correct, promises to save my project from the apparent counter-example of (37). In sum, loose-speech scare quotes are consistent with my overall project.

2.4 Metalinguistic Citation

Sometimes speakers draw attention to their words in order to say something about them.

(38) "Greets" is a verb.

In saying (38), according to (PQ), S defeasibly intends for us to execute (a) while attending to (b):

(38a) GREETS IS A VERB
(38b) [greets]

In executing IS A VERB (or any other predicate) at t_2, the audience looks left to t_1 for a thing-like referent to play subject. The audience finds GREETS being executed; but the execution of GREETS, far from identifying a subject, tells us to look further left for *its* subject. In short, GREETS does not "fit" IS A VERB; the execution of conceptual content (b) does not build a model.

At the same time the audience does find at t_1 thing-like referents, including the lexeme [greets] and the concept GREETS (which is distinct from the result of executing the concept). In this way (38) instructs us to construct the thought that [greets], the word, is a verb and GREETS, the idea, is a verb. It's not likely that anyone would take the latter seriously, of course, because it's obviously false; but that it could in principle be intended is illustrated by puns:

(39) *Marriage* is not a word, it's a sentence.

Readings include that the lexeme [marriage] is a kind of clause, that [marriage] is a penalty, that the state of being married is a kind of clause, and that the state of being married is a penalty. Because the first three are categorically false while the last one is true for some (not me), the last one will normally be taken as the intended reading. It is because the first one is simultaneously an available reading, however, that (39) gets its humor.

Even without quotation marks, ostensions make expressions available for serving as referent. In some contexts the audience will be unable to decide upon the intended readings. For instance, (40) and (41) are ambiguous.

(40) Arial is elegant.
(41) *Arial* is elegant.

The meanings of (40, 41) overlap but are distinct. Setting aside scare-quote readings, the meaning of (40) encompasses, or is neutral between, an object-level reading and a meta-level reading: you may utter it to indicate either that a certain font is elegant or that a certain name is. The meaning of (41) encompasses first- and second-order meta-level readings: you may utter it to indicate either that a certain name is elegant or that a certain way of marking quotation is elegant – for example if you are debating the esthetics of apostrophes versus italics you may write (41). In turn, (41) overlaps with but is distinct from:

(42) *"Arial"* is elegant.

This allows for a second-order meta-level reading, as when we are exemplifying italics, and a third-order meta-level reading, as when we are discussing the esthetics of quote-marks-within-quote-marks (should we use two apostrophe pairs, should we alternate between apostrophes and italics,...?). In sum, because any expression x can be read as either used or mentioned, the meaning of x overlaps in part but not whole with the meaning of x', where x' is just like x except for one extra layer of quotation marks or one fewer.

Actually (40) allows for readings of indefinitely high orders, though it does not work the other way around: (42) does not permit a purely object-level reading. My explanation for this is that association is not symmetric. In particular, in the right context a bare expression may be associated with its third-order quotation even though a third-order quotation is never associated with an object-level interpretation, all things considered. For if the object-level interpretation were intended, it would be inexplicable why the writer uses multiple layers of quotation marks.

Of course (41) allows for an object-level interpretation when we read it as scare-quoting, and likewise (42) allows for a first-order reading, etc. Unfortunately, to spell out fully the interactional effects of scare-quoting and metalinguistic citing, along with the interactions of all other sorts of quotation, would demand exponentially more exposition.

2.5   Mixed Discourse Reports

Following Fauconnier (1994), I take indirect discourse reports like (43) as instructions for one to construct a "space" of propositions, the subjective world consisting of what one believes Hillary to say to be the case, that is inferentially insulated from the rest of one's cognitive system.

(43) Hillary said she would consider running for president.

I extend the theory by considering direct discourse (44) and mixed discourse (45).

(44) Hillary said, "I would consider running for president."
(45) Hillary said she would "consider running for president".

In saying (45), speaker S does exactly what S does in saying (43), plus a little more: S ostends instructions for constructing a thought in which Hillary said that Hillary would consider running for president and S also pointedly ostends the words "consider running for president". S never asserts that these words are Hillary's. S's statement (45) would be true even if:

> (46) Hillary's only utterance was "I'll think about competing for the highest office".

My claim is distinguishable from others in the literature. On the one hand, many take it that (45) both refers to the phrase "consider running for president" and predicates something of it. C&L (1999b: 211) go so far as to allege that such is "obvious". It follows that mixed quotation and indirect quotation are inequivalent. On the other hand, Stainton (1999: 275) and Recanati (2001: 658) deny that (45) either refers to words or says anything about them and furthermore both hold that "mixed quotation is equivalent to indirect quotation – give or take some mimicry". In the middle, I propose that in saying (45) S refers to words, but does not actually say anything of those words.[6] I also disagree that the essential difference between mixed quotation and indirect quotation depends on the presence or absence of mimicry; indirect quotation may use exactly the same words and even same voice as the original source and be indirect for all that. The difference is that mixed quotation linguistically *signals* an act of mimicry whereas indirect quotation does not.

More specifically, I deny that (45) asserts that the quoted matter represents the original speaker verbatim. My rejection of this "Verbatim Assumption", being controversial, calls for additional positive arguments (i–ii) and rebuttals of unsound criticisms (iii–viii).[7]

(i) THE PARITY ARGUMENT. It is usually admitted that (45) can be true even if Hillary's only utterance is in Flemish. When Hillary is Flemish, the relation between her exact words and those in (45) is merely pragmatic; so by parity I argue that even when Hillary speaks English, the relation between her exact words and those in (45) is merely pragmatic. So long

---

[6]   The disagreement is rooted in one's understanding of reference; see §2.2ii.

[7]   C&L believe that they avoid commitment to the Verbatim Assumption because they appeal to unconstrained notions of "same-saying" and "same-tokening". But their position allows same-tokening to be coextensive with, or even broader than, same-saying: indirect discourse reports would mistakenly entail the corresponding direct discourse. Related criticisms have been registered by Tsohatzidis (1998), Elugardo (1999), Stainton (1999), Saka (2004), and Reimer (2005: fn 16).

as the speaker has some recognizable reason for drawing attention to the very words "consider running for president" – for instance, if S is mocking a prior speaker's choice of words in reporting Hillary's speech – then S may very well say (45) without asserting or even implying that the cited words came out of Hillary. In the absence of such recognizable reasons, the implication that "consider running for president" were Hillary's actual words would be the only implication available, but for all that it remains an implication.

(ii) THE RARITY ARGUMENT. Accurate verbatim quotations are extraordinarily rare (Lehrer 1989 and Clark & Gerrig 1990: §8). This means, given the Verbatim Assumption, that nearly all direct discourse reports are false. Yet accepting such systematic falsehood contradicts the principle of charity, which directs us to interpret statements as mostly true. Thus the empirical evidence devastates the Verbatim Assumption, at least for those who subscribe to the principle of charity as Davidsonians do.

(iii) THE INTUITION OBJECTION. For Reimer (2005: §1), a report like (45), under condition (46), "just sounds false". The inference from that, some would make, is that it *is* false, and that because of the Verbatim Assumption. While Reimer recognizes that intuitions of truth-conditions are unreliable, I would like to emphasize the point still more. Consider:

(47) In 1982 President Reagan returned from a trip to Latin America. "Well, I learned a lot," he told reporters. "You'd be surprised. They're all individual countries." [Slansky 1989: 55]

What is the relation between Reagan's utterances of (a) "Well, I learned a lot" and (b) "You'd be surprised"? For the typical subscriber of the Verbatim Assumption, (47) intuitively entails that (a) preceded (b) and did so without any intervening utterance on Reagan's part. But no extant theory allows that such is the case. Therefore intuitions favoring the Verbatim Assumption are hardly impressive.

(iv) THE NEGATION OBJECTION. If my claim is correct – that (45) is assertorically though not implicationally equivalent to (43) – then it would seem that (45′) should entail (43′).

(45′) Hillary didn't say that she would "consider running for president".
(43′) Hillary didn't say that she would consider running for president.

Yet (45′) seems to be the narrower statement, entailed by but not entailing (43′). It relates Hillary to specific word choices whereas (43′) does not.

I could argue that, contrary to intuition, (45′) actually does entail (43′). Pragmatic implications are widely known for befogging the semantic facts, and here we simply have another case of their doing so. Evidence for this line comes from the fact that (43″) seems to be possible.

(43″) Hillary didn't say that she would consider running for president, she said that she would think about competing for the highest office.

For those who hold that indirect discourse is truth-conditionally looser than quotation-marked discourse, however, (43″) is contradictory. This again suggests that intuition is not a reliable guide to entailment relations.

More fundamentally I would argue that negation is not always a truth-functional operator over propositions. Instead of asking the platonist's question, "what does negation do?" I ask the empirical naturalist's question, "how do speaker/hearers use negation?" I suggest, as a first approximation, that if S negates P then S denies P, and that one denies not only falsehoods but also statements deemed misleading or inadequately representative of the facts. Consequently if S says (45′), S denies (45); and to deny (45) it is sufficient for S to regard (45) as misleading rather than false.

(v) THE LAWYER'S OBJECTION. Surely if S testified to (45), in writing and in a legal setting, and if S did so knowing (46), and if the difference between (45) and (46) somehow spelled the difference for Hillary between conviction and exoneration, then S would be guilty of perjury. In reply, I say that judges and jurors typically care about ordinary honesty, as opposed to deception, rather than literal truth as opposed to falsehood [cf. Neisser (1981)]. Moreover, there are legal facts involving language that are nonetheless non-linguistic: if you sign a document, you legally bind yourself to its terms, but that does not mean that you wrote or said or even cognized what is in the document. Thus any objection to my claim based on legal practice is misconceived.

(vi) THE CONVENTION OBJECTION. "If a convention establishes itself for saying P in order to imply Q, then doesn't asserting P count as asserting Q? It is a regular, widespread, and publicly known practice to use quotation marks to imply exact word attribution. Therefore quotation marks assert exact word attribution."

I acknowledge that quotation marks conventionally imply *approximate* word attribution (the professional standard in journalism is for reporters to pare down, clean up, and "correct" quotations). Furthermore, a full under-standing of quotation requires understanding exactly what the conventions are and how they vary across language communities. Court recorders, for instance, commit, expect, and tolerate far more departures from the original source than scholars do, whereas practices among scholars range from the judicious to the mindlessly pedantic (e.g. preserving typographical errors while adding "[sic]", and fretting over insignificant variation in capitalization).

However, I deny that conventional implications amount to assertions. Flagging one's mailbox in the United States systematically implies that there is outgoing mail to be picked up; yet the flag does not *assert* "here is mail to be picked up." Adding a verbal dimension hardly changes matters: saying "hello" implies friendliness, but it does not assert "I am being friendly". For there to be assertion, there must be sufficiently rich verbal structure to signal reference and predication. Quotation marks do not have this.

(vii) THE PRESUPPOSITION OBJECTION. Reimer (2005: §3(a)) points out that non-assertoric content may contribute to the truth-conditions of a sentence. For instance, (48) does not assert that any caterpillars are furry-footed, but does entail it.

(48) Ferocious furry-footed caterpillars are friendly.

Can it be that (45), though it does not assert that Hillary used certain words, nonetheless entails it?

I think not. The problem is not merely lack of assertion, it is lack of subject-predicate structure. We can say that (48) expresses, in part, the proposition that certain caterpillars are furry-footed – because, after all, it contains the one-place predicate "furry-footed" in appropriate juxtaposition with its subject argument "caterpillars". In contrast we cannot say that (45) expresses the proposition that Hillary uttered certain words, for it does not contain the predicate "utter". [It contains "says", but "says" does not specifically relate to word choice, as shown by (43).] What's more, if (45) entailed that Hillary used particular words without asserting so, (45) would *presuppose* that Hillary used those words, just as (48) presupposes that some caterpillars are furry-footed. But if Hillary did indeed use those words then (43) would be true. In other words, the purported presuppositional content would entail the assertoric content! This, though logically tenable, is a peculiar position to hold.

(viii) THE CANCELLABILITY OBJECTION. C&L (2005b: 66) claim that the verbatim implication of quoted discourse cannot be cancelled; to (45) you cannot consistently add, "but Hillary never used *consider running for president*". However, this view relies upon several problematic presuppositions and overlooks relevant data. First, it assumes that some cancellations are linguistically self-contradictory, which cannot be if Quine is right about there being no analytic statements. (I myself do not endorse Quine on this point, but many or most do.)

Second, C&L assume that quotation is ambiguous, for cancellation does work if (45) is read in terms of scare quotes or echo quotes (cf. [52] below). Only by treating scare quotes and echo quotes as semantically distinct from discourse quotes can C&L begin to make their case. But positing unevinced ambiguity is methodologically unsound. (C&L themselves deny that their distinction counts as semantic ambiguity but only by adopting an eccentric view: that there is no semantic ambiguity between discourse quotes and scare quotes even though one has a semantic value that the other lacks.)[8]

Third, C&L miss Clark & Gerrig's example:

(49) She said, "he's a pain in the neck", only she didn't say "neck".

This is interesting because it's not clearly a case of either scare quoting or echo quoting.

Fourth, C&L assume that non-cancellability is evidence of linguistically semantic content, though it's not. When I assert P I cannot consistently cancel the implication that I believe P; yet "I believe P" is not part of the content of P. When I produce my name on a contract, I may subsequently contradict myself by saying that I won't pay, yet "I will pay" is no part of the content of my name. In general, C&L are wedded to a compositional truth-conditional theory of meaning. This approach is tendentious if not untenable.

2.6   Direct Discourse Reports

Direct discourse differs from mixed discourse. The biggest differences, superficially, involve quotational scope and viewpoint-shifting.

(44) Hillary said, "I would consider running for president".
(45) Hillary said she would "consider running for president".

In (44) the scope of quotation is the full subordinate clause and the pronoun is interpreted according to the context of Hillary's speech act. In (45) the scope of quotation is sub-clausal and the pronoun is interpreted according to the context of S's speech act. These differences are far from simple and invariable, however. First, original indexicals are sometimes preserved even without quotation-marking.

---

[8]   Gomez-Torrente (2005: §ii), admitting that there are apparent examples of cancellability, correctly notes that they "cannot convince someone who does not accept that all uses of the quotation marks have the same meaning." However, this does not put the two sides of the issue on an even par. For the assumption of ambiguity carries the burden of proof; univocality is the default assumption.

(50) Preachers say do as I say, not as I do. [John Selden]

Second, especially in older writing, direct discourse sometimes loses original tense.

(51) We said, "we were ready." [the source words being "we are ready"; Francis Bacon, *New Atlantis*]

Third, quotations can take full scope even in cases that I regard as non-direct.

(52) Lucian Freud seems to attest that "Here I stand, I can do no other".

The fact that Lucian Freud is a famous painter, the word choice "attest" instead of "say", and the use of "seems to" all work to suggest that Lucian Freud did not utter the quoted matter but rather conveyed, by painting, a sentiment that can be rendered by the quoted words. The report is quote-marked both because it shifts viewpoint and because it echoes or alludes to Martin Luther's famous line.

One reason for denying that (52) is a case of direct discourse is that it has a complementizer. In the case of indirect and mixed discourse (43, 45), "that" can equally appear or not, whereas adding "that" to (44) would change its deep syntax. This suggests to me that quoted matter in direct discourse, but not in mixed or indirect, functions as direct object, contra Munro (1982). In saying (44), S draws attention first to (a) and then to (b, c).

(44a) HILLARY SAID
(44b) I WOULD CONSIDER RUNNING FOR PRESIDENT
(44c) [[I] [would] [consider] [running] [for] [president]]
(44d) |Hillary said [[I] [would] [consider] [running] [for] [president]]|

In (a), SAID looks right for instructions on identifying a direct object and finds (b) and (c). Because (b) directs the building of a proposition rather than an object, the concepts in (a, b) do not fit together. However, (a) fits together with (c) to form (d). Given that (c) requires HILLARY SAID in order to make a well-formed model, perhaps it is not surprising that its viewpoint preferentially indexes that of Hillary.

In contrast, in saying (45) S ostends (a–d):

(45a) HILLARY SAID
(45b) THAT SHE WOULD CONSIDER RUNNING FOR PRESIDENT
(45c) [[consider] [running] [for] [president]]
(45d) HILLARY SAID THAT SHE WOULD

Regardless of whether "that" is overtly uttered, it appears at the level of interpretation (one of the few covert elements widely accepted across syntactic schools). It combines with the subordinate conceptual content in (b) to form a direct object, thus making (a) fit with (b). The interpreter executes (a–b) as part of (45)'s meaning and, recognizing that (c) does not feed into (d), imaginatively seeks some other point or significance in S's ostending (c). Knowing the conventions of utterance attribution, the interpreter may assume that (c) was ostended for the sake of implying utterance attribution, but the interpreter will also know that, given the right context, S may have had a different motivation for quotation-marking, such as alluding to someone's famous words.

In summary, differences between mixed and direct quotation naturally fall out of the fact that a verb of saying does not take a sentence as direct object but rather a noun phrase or *that*-clause. Mixed and direct discourse reports do not include fundamentally separate kinds of quotation.

2.7   Other Conventions

My focus on pragmatic associations does not preclude conventional aspects of quotation. First, the combination of quotation marks with other punctuation marks traditionally follows peculiar rules. In prescribing (53) over (53′), conservative grammarians inexplicably separate, by comma, verb from direct object; they undermine the display aspect of quotation by mindlessly including punctuation inside of quotation; and thankfully they are opposed by progressives like Pullum (1991).[9]

(53) It takes three keystrokes to type, "yes."
(53′) It takes three keystrokes to type "yes".

Second, iterated quotation usually switches back and forth between double apostrophes and single. Third, quotation marks do not always come in pairs. If a character's speech is reported in two paragraphs, there will be an open-quotation mark for each and only one close-quotation mark, for a total of three. (For years I read novels thinking that the authors were making performance errors!) Fourth, different forms of quotation mark have prototypically characteristic uses – double apostrophes being used more for

---

[9]   If commas once served to signal mentioning –

(53″) It takes three keystrokes to type, yes.

– then the comma in (53) is a holdover of a practice that made sense prior to the advent of modern paired quotation marks. This hypothesis is open to testing by a historian.

direct discourse and for titles of short works, italics being used more for code-switching and titles of books.

Other conventions used in quotation involve editorial modifications. Sherwin Nuland, in *The Mysteries Within*, writes: "The fact is that [Jan] van Helmont's contention that the soul and mind are located in the stomach was the result of an insight gained while he was under the influence of a poison called wolfsbane ..." This allows for multiple readings. I may intend for the brackets to be recognized as a form of disquotation – as markers that "Jan" did not appear in Nuland's text – or I may intend to report that Nuland himself used brackets; and I may intend for the ellipses either to convey that I left something out of Nuland's text or to represent Nuland's own trailing off. Finally, in other texts, I may use "@$$#%&" either to report directly that someone used six shift-numeral keys or to report indirectly that they used some vulgarity to be left to the imagination.

These observations are worth making partly because Simchen (1999: 331) argues that editorial modifications pose a problem for my theory. In particular he challenges me to account for:

(54) Quine says that quotation has "[a]nomalous features."

Conforming to the associationism I have emphasized, I would say that any ostension of (54) deferringly ostends first (55) and then (56): for surely when you see "[a]nomalous" you think ANOMALOUS.

(55) QUINE SAYS THAT QUOTATION HAS
(56) ANOMALOUS FEATURES

The quotation marks instruct us to think of something associated with the quoted matter other than its extension. We might think of (a) the form /[a]nomalous features/; given the convention of brackets, we might think of (b) the form /Anomalous features/; if ignorant of the convention, we might ignore the brackets and think of (c) /anomalous features/; and in any case we are sure to think of (d) the nearest lexemes [anomalous] [features]. Of the items just listed, (d) fits with (55) to create the most creditable reading. Therefore the reasonable interpreter concludes that, in saying (54), S intends for us to execute (55) and to attend to (d). In addition, if we know the convention of brackets, we surmise that (d) reflects Quine's word choice modulo the bracketed portion.

2.8   Conclusion

To summarize, I offer a unified account of scare quotes (including loose, pedagogical, and distancing uses), echo quotes or allusions, quotation-marked metalinguistic citation, quoted discourse reports (both direct and mixed), and marked code-switching/borrowings and titles. Quotational principle (Q) tells us that quotation marks signal mentioning – that there is reference to something other than what is customary. In most cases, reference is to the quoted matter (or to some linguistic type with which it is associated); in the case of loose-speech scare quotes, reference is to something resembling the extension of the quoted matter. At the same time, primary principle (P) tells us that when utterances impinge on audiences, audiences automatically attempt to execute the conventionally associated lexico-syntactic conceptual structure; quoted matter is defeasibly used as well as mentioned. The use interpretation is defeated, however, when it is ungrammatical, as in the case of most citations and titles; and when it is pragmatically contradicted by the mention interpretation, as in the case of loose-speech scare quotes. In short, standard quotation marks always direct the audience to the same panoply of material: to the concepts that are automatically associated with the quoted matter and to "something else". It is up to the interpreter to conjure a model using higher-level reasoning not specifically provided by the particular words at hand. As a result, linguistic meaning underdetermines truth-conditions.

This view extends to my treatment of mixed and direct discourse. Quotation-marked direct discourse, as in (44), does not, in virtue of its linguistic meaning, entail that the reported subject used the actual words on display. (That the subject used *some* words follows not from the quotation marks but from the verb "say".)

(44) Hillary said, "I would consider running for president."

In other words, the following does not necessarily hold:

(57) S thinks "Hillary said, 'I would consider running for president' " ≡
     S thinks that Hillary uttered the words "I would consider running
     for president."

If (44) is nonetheless associated with truth-conditions requiring that Hillary uttered the words quoted, then such truth-conditions are contextually constructed by creative interpretation influenced by extra-linguistic customs of the sort seen elsewhere. (In signing a contract, S may promise to pay a mortgage even though S never says or writes that S will pay the mortgage. Likewise, in using direct discourse, S might report that Hillary used specified words without saying or writing that Hillary used them.)

I have taken indirect discourse as a given, using it as a basis upon which to suggest an analysis of quoted discourse. I thus invert the explanatory order of the popular inscription theory, which understands indirect discourse as a kind of transformed quotation [e.g. Scheffler (1954)]. Two considerations favor my analysis of discourse over the inscriptional account. First, it enjoys architectonic support from being part of a larger theory of quotation. Second, indirect discourse seems to me to be far more frequent than direct discourse, which suggests that indirect discourse is cognitively more basic.

My treatment of discourse assumes that English has a single lexeme [say]. In contrast, for C&L (1999b) the surface verb "say" encompasses two predicates, SAME-SAY and SAME-TOKEN, and for Gomez-Torrente (2005) English "say" is lexically ambiguous. C&L (2005b: §2) also posit ambiguity when they distinguish between discourse quotes and scare quotes. In short, the core of my theory of quotation (Q), supplemented by an independently motivated principle of language (P), appears to offer non-equivocational explanations for a broad variety of uses of quotation marks.

Still, my work leaves many problems unresolved. For starters, I am not happy with metaphorical appeals to concepts "fitting" together. In preliminary defense I could point out that better thinkers than I have relied on notions equally ill-defined. I might also mention that it is better to have an unfledged theory, which may or may not mature into a success, than rigorous precision that is rigorously wrong. Even so, my project does call for more elaboration.

Furthermore, if quotation marks mark mentionings, and if mentionings include irony (Jorgensen et al. 1984), then why is written irony rarely if ever marked by quotation, especially given that spoken irony frequently carries special tonal markings? And why do poetry, allusions, and wordplay often go without quotation marks? Speakers surely wish to draw attention to word choice in their deliberate rhymes and puns. If quotation marks serve to draw attention to word choice, why then do they not use quotation marks? In the rhymes of spontaneous speech, perhaps speakers do not use quotation marks because quotation marks are rarely used in speech at all; in writing, perhaps poets do not use quotation marks because it goes without saying that literary appreciation requires attending to form, content, and the relation between them. (Indeed, even many essayists and novelists choose their words with such care that they want the word choice to be noticed.) Perhaps written literature is a *game* that readers do not want given away.

Chapter 8

LIARS AND TRUTH-TELLERS

The liar paradox demonstratively refutes our ordinary conception of truth, reference, or both. How this is so and why it matters are explained in Section 1. Afterwards I consider various attempts at constructing a new theory of truth. First I survey the leading projects of the truth-conditionalists, and explain why I find them unconvincing or otherwise unhelpful (Sects. 2–7), and then I present my own attitudinal account and illustrate how it solves not only the Liar but related puzzles as well.

1.   The Pi Paradox

A paradox poses a sort of theoretical dilemma, presenting us with inconsistent theses each of which is hard to give up. In the case of the Liar, common sense insists on the following.

(1) CLASSICAL LOGIC: Every statement is either true or not true; no statement is both true and not true; and every provable theorem is true.

(2) THE EFFABILITY THESIS: Every grammatical declarative sentence can be used to make a statement or express a proposition, and every such sentence can be described and named.

(T) THE NAIVE T-SCHEMA: For every term Φ designating sentence P, Φ is true ≡ P.

Given the effability thesis, we can give the name "λ" (lambda) to the liar sentence "λ is false".

λ   λ is false.

Substitution of λ into the T-schema yields a seeming contradiction:

(X) λ is true $\equiv \lambda$ is false.

Classical logic confirms (X) as a genuine and unacceptable contradiction.

Glanzberg (2001: 217) contends that not only does a viable solution to the liar exist, but viable solutions exist in great number and are easy to come by; Eklund (2005: §vi) doubts that solving the Liar "has any more philosophical significance than solving a chess problem"; and most books devoted to truth in general mention the Liar only nominally, if at all, and without acknowledging any of the relevant literature [e.g. Vision (2004), Armour-Garb & Beall (2005), Blackburn (2005)]. Yet the significance of contradiction (X) cannot be underestimated. It means that the enunciated theses – which are not only widely held but central to our understanding of language, logic, and truth – are jointly untenable; hence *at least one of them must give way*. The liar paradox is thus no mere parlor trick, but a remarkable instrument for philosophical inquiry. Its eventual resolution, whatever that may be, will have profound consequences.

As a point of clarification, I should say a word about what the liar paradox, and contradiction (X), do *not* mean. Despite what is frequently said, they do not mean that "true" is an inconsistent predicate. For otherwise calling a statement true would be equivalent to calling it false and not false, in which case any attribution of truth, including that of the liar sentence, would simply be self-contradictory, i.e. unproblematically false. The paradox also does not mean that our *language* is inconsistent, whatever that might mean. It is neither the truth *predicate* nor the totality of English grammar and vocabulary that is inconsistent, but rather the truth *theory* as encapsulated by the joint theses (1, 2, T).

There is, therefore, a crisis in the theory of truth. Moreover, it spills over to theories that invoke truth, as TC semantics does. TC semanticists, recognizing what's at stake, sometimes try to insulate themselves by saying that they are not really talking about truth at all, but about a related concept, one which we might call *schmuth*. Practitioners of this strategy include Lycan (1984: 191) and, here, Davidson:

> Even if we hold there is some important sense in which moral or evaluative sentences do not have a truth value . . ., we ought not to boggle at:
> [β] "Bardot is good" is true iff Bardot is good. [1967: 31]

This position not only impugns the honesty of truth-based semantics, it nullifies its content. For instance, if we accept that "Bardot is good" lacks truth-value, then in order for (β) to be a meaningful statement, we must interpret not only "true" in a strange way, but "iff" as well; for ordinarily, "iff" is evaluable only when its two arguments each has a truth-value. In reply one might suggest that we replace the ordinary notion IFF with some new concept SCHMIFF. However, the requisite properties of the new concept are even more mysterious than those of "meaning". The big attraction of Davidsonian semantics was supposed to be that it replaces "Φ means that P" by "Φ is true iff P", materially (truth-functionally) understood. But now it looks like it doesn't really do this!

More significantly, it is not just the *truth*-schema that pies semantic theory, but *any* equivalence of the following form, where π is an arbitrary predicate:

(Π) Φ is π ≡ P.

Thus, contrary to a great deal of the literature [e.g. Horwich (1993), Engel (2002: 48)], the pragmatist, coherentist, verificationist, correspondence, and coy (fraudulent?) schmuth claims are all contradicted by liar sentences of their own.

(3) P ≡ Φ promotes the satisfaction of goals.
λ_3 λ_3 does not promote the satisfaction of goals.
(4) P ≡ Φ is an element of a maximally coherent system.
λ_4 λ_4 is not an element of a maximally coherent system.
(5) P ≡ Φ is verifiable.
λ_5 λ_5 is not verifiable.
(6) P ≡ Φ corresponds to reality.
λ_6 λ_6 does not correspond to reality.
(7) P ≡ Φ is schmue.
λ_7 λ_7 is not schmue.

In general, "Φ is π ≡ P" can always be defeated by a liar sentence which says of itself that it's not π. The relevance of the Liar, then, extends far beyond the disquotational and realist theories of truth, and henceforth when I speak of truth and the naive T-schema (T) I mean any Π-schema generally and any property π that satisfies Π.

If it is to escape incoherence, TC semantics must find a way to successfully honor its commitment to truth (or to π). Specifically, it must satisfy the following ADEQUACY CONDITIONS. (i) It must first and foremost convincingly resolve the liar paradox. It must reject either classical logic, the effability thesis, or the naive T-schema; and, as a corollary of the criterion of second-order preference (p. 15), it should introduce a new and admissible set of principles to help explain the appeal of whatever is displaced. Furthermore, it must accomplish task (i) while operating within the strictures of TC semantics. That is to say, (ii) any proposal for replacing classical logic, the effability thesis, or the naive T-schema must be conducive to identifying natural-language meaning with truth-conditions. In particular, (iii) the replacement theory must be explicable by truth-conditions (or π-conditions). As I shall argue over the next few sections, however, the available proposals for dealing with the Liar all offend against conditions (i–iii) in one way or another.

While there are too many proposed solutions to the liar paradox for me to canvass them all, practically all of them fall into a few families, and for each family I can say a little bit about the most prominent representatives. I shall have to skimp on detail, but I can say enough, I hope, for you to understand my general reasons for thinking that none of the leading theories do what they need to do for the purposes of TC semantics.

Most proposed solutions are formulated in terms of truth-conditions, or at least might be, and thus will be accepted as satisfying adequacy condition (iii). They include Significance theories, which reject the effability thesis; Gap theories, which variously reject bivalence and the law of excluded middle; Dialethic theories, which effectively reject the law of non-contradiction; and the Hierarchy, Deictic, and Revision theories, which all reject the naive T-schema. These theories are not all incompatible, it should be noted; the Significance, Gap, and Hierarchy theories in particular often intertwine.

2.   The Significance Theory

Many commentators claim that the liar sentence cannot be used to express a genuine proposition [Donnellan, Ushenko, Whitely, Bennett, all cited in Burge (1979: fn 17); also Wittgenstein (1921: §4.442), Bar-Hillel (1966), Sommers (1969), and Rescher (2001: Chap. 10). One elaboration of this idea adverts to the myth of category errors (Saka 1998a: Chap. 3.2). Another elaboration holds that since paradox appears to rely on self-reference, self-reference is somehow linguistically illegitimate. Reflexive sentences fail to make statements and hence are without truth-value, perhaps even without meaning; thus "λ is true $\equiv \lambda$ is false" is as harmless as "jklp is true $\equiv$ asdfr".

The claim cannot be about grammar, of course. Liar sentences are well-formed syntactically, morphologically, and phono/typographically; and even if "λ" be questionable, it is easy to find liar sentences that are lexically impeccable ("the very sentence I am now producing does not express a true statement"). As a claim about semantics or pragmatics, however, the

Significance Theory requires more discussion. For in order to understand "λ is false", one arguably does need to identify the referent of "λ"; and in order to grasp the referent of "λ" one arguably does need to understand the statement "λ is false". Thus, in some cases self-reference might present a circle that is impossible to break into; such reference is "ungrounded" (Kripke 1975).

Castigation of self-reference strikes me as misguided, however. To begin with, it is not clear that self-reference is necessary for paradox. For instance, the Loop Liar consists of mutually referring statements.[1]

> (8) Nixon states the following and nothing but the following: "What Jones says is true."
> (9) Jones states the following and nothing but the following: "What Nixon says is false."

If Nixon's statement is true then Jones's statement is true, which makes Nixon's statement false. If Nixon's statement is false then Jones's statement is false, which makes Nixon's statement true. Either way, contradiction. Hence the Loop Liar indicates (i) that paradox can arise on the basis of contingent matters of fact rather than on anything intrinsic to the given linguistic forms, and (ii) that it arguably happens without self-reference. Other arguments against the "mystique of self-reference", to use Sorensen's phrase, can be found in Chihara (1979: 603), Gupta & Belnap (1993: 273), Simmons (1993: 5), Yablo (1993), and Sorensen (1998). Simmons and Yablo, for instance, give us the Infinite Liar:

Imagine an infinite sequence of sentences $S_1, S_2, S_3 \ldots$, each to the effect that every subsequent sentence is false:

> (S_1) For all $i > 1$, (S_i) is false,
> (S_2) For all $i > 2$, (S_i) is false,
> (S_3) For all $i > 3$, (S_i) is false, ...

Suppose (S_1) is true. Then *everything* subsequent on the list is false, including (S_2). But the falsity of (S_2) amounts to the claim that some S_i is true for $i > 2$, which is a contradiction. So suppose (S_1) is false. Then something else on the list is true, call it (S_n). But (S_n), by the same reasoning as above, likewise leads to contradiction.

Priest (1997) argues that finitely stated Infinite Liars are actually self-referential, and Beall (2001) argues that there is no reason to believe that

---

[1] My example comes from Kripke (1975: 54), but it should be acknowledged that the idea goes back to Buridan at least.

any infinite set of unstated propositions, absent self-reference, generates semantic paradox. Even so, self-reference is insufficient for paradox. It is not just possible but normally easy to refer to expressions without interpreting or understanding them ("*Kuviasungnerk* is Inuit for something"; "The teacher's explanation went right over my head"; "I can't decipher your handwriting; what does this sentence say?"). More particularly, Kripke (1975) argues that, due to the work of Goedel, there is nothing logically or mathematically suspicious about self-reference per se. I would add that there is nothing empirically suspicious, either: the universal statements of science refer to everything, including themselves, and hence commit self-reference. For example, "All birds have feathers" translates as $(\forall x)(x$ is a bird $\rightarrow$ x has feathers) – "It is true for everything, including this very statement, that if it is a bird then it has feathers." Now one might object to the canonical rendition, preferring instead quantification over restricted domains. But outside of science too self-reference is common fare and normally unproblematic. I once asked someone why she believed in Christianity and she said, "Because the Bible says it's the word of God." In other words, taking the Bible as one conjunction of statements, the biblical statement BS says that BS is true. Although this fails as justification, it succeeds as a claim: it refers and it appears to be truth-valued, whether true or false. In short, any attempt to deny the propositionality of a liar sentence must explain how it is that paradoxical self-reference differs from legitimate cases of logical, scientific, and ordinary self-reference.

The Significance Theory is furthermore vulnerable to a criticism due to Gupta & Belnap (1993): If "all Cretans are liars" doesn't express a proposition, then belief ascriptions do not report propositions, e.g. "St Paul believed that all Cretans were liars". But to sever the link between belief contents and propositions is to make a radical move calling for considerable justification or at least elaboration, which Significance theorists have not attempted to produce.

According to Significance theorists, the Liar hinges on equivocation. If "λ" refers to a sentence then it is unproblematically neither true nor false because sentences are not truth-bearers (propositions are). If "λ" purports to refer to a proposition then it fails because in fact no proposition is picked out. But this, though it give a coherent response to liar sentence λ, falls to a "strengthened" version of the Liar:

λ_8 Sentence λ_8 does not express a true proposition.

Instantiation into (T) yields:

(X) The proposition expressed by sentence λ_8 is true $\equiv$ sentence λ_8 does not express a true proposition.

This is contradictory. (a) By familiar reasoning, we can't take λ_8 as either true or false. Therefore, the Significance theorist concludes, (b) λ_8 does not express a proposition. Therefore (c) λ_8 does not express a true proposition. (d) But conclusion (c) says precisely what λ_8 says, and so the Significance Theory is self-defeating. The Significance theorist can maintain a consistent position only by neither asserting nor believing λ_8; but if no one asserts or believes λ_8, then the Significance Theory is left without advocates.

Sentence λ_8, and for that matter effability thesis (2), might be questioned by opponents of abstract propositions. However, λ_8 can be read in non-platonistic ways, for instance pleonastically (Schiffer 2003); alternatively, it can be reworded. Some rewording or other, in terms of truth-bearers, must be possible for those who believe in truth-bearers.

So far I have argued that the Liar does not in fact involve reference failure, and indeed cannot do so given the Strengthened Liar. It thus fails to satisfy adequacy condition (i). But let's suppose I'm mistaken about this, and that the Significance Theory can save the traditional concept of truth by abandoning the naive conception of reference. Then TC semantics, at least in the usual form of model-theoretic and truth-theoretic semantics, would still be in a jam. For these theories are referentialist, invoking the reference relation; and reference is not what we think it is, according to the theory under view. It thus fails to meet adequacy condition (ii).

3.   The Gap Theory

According to the supervalued system of van Fraassen (1966, 1968) and the three-valued system of Kripke (1975), it's possible for a statement to be neither true nor false. By taking λ to be neither true nor false, the apparent contradiction "λ is true $\equiv$ λ is false" turns out undefined on the left-hand side, undefined on the right-hand side, and therefore perfectly coherent.

That not everything is either true or false is certainly correct. After all, the universe contains many items which are neither true nor false: banana splits, for instance, are neither true nor false. Certain objects are just not the sort of thing to which "is true" or "is false" can rightfully apply. So perhaps some statements are neither true nor false, and surely pseudo-statements – declarative sentences that fail to express complete propositions – are neither true nor false. But at the same time I want to insist that everything in the universe is either true or not true. A banana split, by being neither true nor false, is ipso facto not true. Likewise the liar sentence, if it were neither true nor false, would consequently be not true. In other words, bivalence does not necessarily hold because an object could either possess some value besides "true" and "false" or lack truth-value altogether (in which case it is, let us say, *other*); yet the law of excluded middle remains in force because a (pseudo-)statement that is *other* is either true or not true. As a result we get another Strengthened Liar.

λ_9 λ_9 is not true.

Substituting into the naive T-schema gives:

(X) λ_9 is true $\equiv \lambda_9$ is not true.

By familiar reasoning, if λ_9 is true then λ_9 is not true, a contradiction; and if λ_9 is false then λ_9 is true, another contradiction. So let's suppose λ_9 is neither true nor false. In that case, the right-hand side of (X) is true. Yet the left-hand side is false. Therefore the equivalence fails, and the Gap Theory leaves the Liar on the loose.

Gap theorists will disagree. They may insist that if λ_9 is neither true nor false then the left-hand and right-hand sides are both neither true nor false. To do this they may distinguish variously between negation and denial, predicate and sentence negation, internal and external negation (Bochvar 1939), "exclusion" and "choice" negation (van Fraassen 1969), or ordinary and metalinguistic negation (Horn 1989). In the one case "Φ is not true" entails "¬P;" in the other it does not.

But this move, in itself, does no good, for in stating the liar sentence we could perfectly well specify that we are using classical negation – the paradox-generating kind by which "P is neither true nor false" does entail "P is not true". In reply, Gap theorists must locate the source of paradox within classical negation, denying that it's coherent.

Is there evidence that negation is incoherent? According to Rescher (2001: 203), the Self-Negation Liar, without mention of truth, yields paradox:

λ_{10} not-λ_{10}

(X) λ_{10} is true iff not-λ_{10}

Rescher is mistaken, however. First, even though *sentence* λ_{10} avoids mentioning truth, the *paradox* does not. For the paradox is generated not by λ_{10} alone but by its conjunction with something like (T), which does mention truth. Second, even then the Self-Negation Liar does not yield contradiction because it is not well-defined. If λ_{10} is a sentence, it cannot serve as grammatical subject on the left-hand side of (X). If λ_{10} is a term that names a sentence then it cannot be negated and the right-hand side is ill-formed. I conclude that there is no special reason to impugn classical negation.

Most importantly, Gap theorists must distinguish between object- and meta-language [see Sainsbury (1988: 125)]. They claim, in effect, that the solution to the Liar is ineffable, which runs afoul of adequacy condition (iii); and their distinction thwarts the aims of natural-language semantics, if adequacy condition (ii) is to be satisfied (see §5).

4.   The Dialethic Theory

C.S. Peirce [as reported in Michael (1975)], Priest (1979–1993), Dowden (1984), various contributors in Priest et al. (1989), Woods (2003), and possibly Chihara (1979) regard the Liar as "dialethic", meaning both true and false at once.[2] Such a position is unacceptable in classical logic, for in classical logic a single contradiction devastatingly entails that *every* proposition and its negation is true. Therefore dialethists call for paraconsistent logic, which, by quarantining little inconsistencies, preserves the health of the theory as a whole.

Some paraconsistent logicians acknowledge not solving the Liar, e.g. Rescher & Brandom (1980). Among work that does aim at the Liar, the most renown is by Graham Priest, who motivates his approach as follows.

> Each sentence has a set of situations where it is applicable . . .Now the uses of various sentences are, of course, interconnected. But natural language being what it is, we should not necessarily expect the pieces of language to fit together neatly, like some multi-dimensional jigsaw puzzle. There may well be mismatches. In particular, the conditions of application of a sentence may well overlap those of the application of its negation, especially if the world arranges itself in an unkind fashion. At such spots in the weft and warp of language we have dialetheias. [1987: 85]

This would be more persuasive if learning a predicate did not seem to automatically accompany a grasp of its negation.

Be that as it may, for Priest the semantic value of a proposition is taken as a set: when P is strictly true, $|P| = \{T\}$; when P is strictly false, $|P| = \{F\}$; and when P is both true and false, $|P| = \{T, F\}$. Since truth and falsity vary independently of each other, the value of each truth-functional connective

---

[2] I prefer the term "dialethism" to Priest's "dialetheism" on the grounds that it comports better with the already established "alethic" (not "aletheic"), it is more euphonious, and it is no form of *theism*.

requires two different specifications – one for truth, the other for falsity. The specifications are as follows.[3]

Negation:

$T \in |{\neg}P|$ iff $F \in |P|$

$F \in |{\neg}P|$ iff $T \in |P|$

Conjunction:

$T \in |P\&Q|$ iff $T \in |P|$ and $T \in |Q|$

$F \in |P\&Q|$ iff $F \in |P|$ or $F \in |Q|$

Disjunction:

$T \in |PvQ|$ iff $T \in |P|$ or $T \in |Q|$

$F \in |PvQ|$ iff $F \in |P|$ and $F \in |Q|$

Implication:

$T \in |P \rightarrow Q|$ iff $F \in |P|$ or $T \in |Q|$

$F \in |P \rightarrow Q|$ iff $T \in |P|$ and $F \in |Q|$

Personally, I find Priest's project pleasingly audacious, a healthy antidote to prejudice, and probably useful for certain applications. As a solution to the Liar, however, it categorically does not work. Consider the following display [cp. Smiley (1993)]:

λ_{11} λ_{11} is not true only.

According to dialethism, every statement is either true only, false only, or dialethic, i.e. both true and false. Which category does λ_{11} fall into? It's clear that every option leads to self-contradiction.

> (10) Assume that λ_{11} *is true only*. Then the displayed claim is true. But the displayed claim is that λ_{11} *is not true only*. Hence λ_{11} is true only and not true only. Contradiction!

---

[3]   In addition to the truth-functional conditional defined here, Priest uses a relevance conditional. I will not go into its details, however, since the exact nature of the conditional plays no part in my critique of dialethism.

(11) Assume that λ_{11} *is false only*. Then the negation of the display is true. But that negation is that λ_{11} *is true only*. Hence λ_{11} is false only and true only. Contradiction!

(12) The position of the dialethists: Suppose λ_{11} *is both true and false*. Therefore λ_{11} is false. Therefore the negation of λ_{11} is true. The negation of λ_{11} states that λ_{11} *is true only*. But λ_{11} can't be both true-and-false on the one hand and true-only on the other. Contradiction!

The bare fact of self-contradiction, of course, does not upset the dialethist. "If I were attempting to produce a consistent theory of the inconsistent, this [the likes of λ_{11}] would be fatal," writes Priest (1987: 111). "However, the aim of the enterprise is not to eliminate contradictions but to accommodate them."

The problem with this move is that it has implications that even paraconsistent logicians must reject. The italicized results of (12), for instance, translate into the formal theory as (13) and (14):

(13) $|\lambda_{11}| = \{T, F\}$
(14) $|\lambda_{11}| = \{T\}$

By the transitivity of identity, (13) and (14) jointly entail (15). This entailment follows regardless of whether (13, 14) are taken to be true-and-false or true-only.

(15) $\{T\} = \{T, F\}$

But (15) serves as a reductio against dialethism, and therefore the Dialethic Theory cannot satisfy adequacy condition (i).

The dialethist simply cannot bite the bullet and accept (15) as true (as well as false). To begin with, it does too much violence to our intuitions. One might accept Priest's argument that the liar sentence can be both true and false (at the same time and in the same way) because after all the liar sentence strikes us as a paradoxical claim that demands some revision in the way we ordinarily think. However, there is nothing prima facie paradoxical about (15), and to insist that it's anything other than a simple falsehood seems wild. More importantly, if (15) were really true then we wouldn't be able even to comprehend the Dialethic Theory, which goes to so much trouble to distinguish truth-only from truth-and-falsity.

As if this weren't enough, consider the following variant on the Liar.

λ_{12} λ_{12} is false only.

Again, λ_{12} must be either true only, false only, or true-and-false.

(16) If λ_{12} is true only, it is true, and we must accept what it says, namely that it's false only. Hence it is both true only and false only.

(17) If λ_{12} is false only, it is false, and we must negate what it says, arriving at "λ_{12} is not false only". But if it's not false only then it's true. Hence it's both false only and true.

(18) If λ_{12} is true-and-false then it's true, and we must accept what it says, namely that it's false only.

Again, dialethists claim (18), which translates as:

(19) $|\lambda_{12}| = \{T, F\}$
(20) $|\lambda_{12}| = \{F\}$

By the transitivity of identity, (19) and (20) yield (21):

(21) $\{T, F\} = \{F\}$

What's more, (15) and (21) yield (22):

(22) $\{T\} = \{F\}$

Thus the semantic value of all truths is the same as the semantic value of all falsehoods. Any proposition accorded a truth-value at all will get evaluated as both true and false.

So far I have followed the dialethist in assuming (12) and (18). Rejecting these assumptions for (10) or (11) on the one hand, and (16) or (17) on the other, leads to precisely the same conclusion. (The proofs extend the pattern established here.) The only remaining possible dialethic move is to call (22) both true and false. But this isn't at all helpful, for the status of (22) as both-true-and-false wouldn't change the fact that (22) allows for the assignment of $\{T\}$ to *all* propositions, true and false. This proves that dialethism is not just paraconsistent but degeneratively inconsistent, unacceptable on the dialethist's own terms, and violative of adequacy condition (i).

In reply to the Strengthened Liar, Priest (1993: 50) suggests two ways out. One way frankly admits the inadequacy of his semantics and proposes instead an infinite number of truth values – the elements in the power set, iterated without end, of $\{T, F\}$. Although Priest plausibly asserts that this approach "accommodates extended liars of any ordinal level", to be confident of that we would need to know more than the number of so-called dialethic (actually poly-alethic) truth-values; we would need to know the poly-alethic logic of negation. Aside from that, I do not see how polylethic semantics can accommodate liars extended to the limitless transfinite levels.

Priest alternately suggests revising his set-theoretic semantics in terms of a valuation relation ("in the obvious way"), and he adds that the two formulations "do *exactly* the same job". Of course, if this be right then my reductio against set-theoretic dialethism sinks relation-theoretic dialethism too. The failure of the latter, in its own terms, is moreover established by Bromand (2002), and the whole approach is criticized by Littmann & Simmons (2004).

5.   The Hierarchy Theory

The classical approach to dealing with the Liar is to postulate a hierarchy of types or languages, as Russell (1908), Tarski (1933), Quine (1961), and countless textbooks do. Under the Russell scheme, each proposition within a given language gets assigned to a type; under the more popular Tarski scheme, each proposition among a set of languages gets assigned to a language. In general, any statement that refers to another is at a higher "level" than it. These restrictions mean that *Tarskians do not really accept (T)*; they accept, instead:

(T_i) Φ is true$_i$ $\equiv P_j$, for $i > j$.

Applying T-schema (T_i) to λ, we get (OK).

(OK) λ is true$_2$ $\equiv \lambda$ is false$_1$.

In other words, λ is true at one level, false at another. Since truth and falsity contradict each other only if they have the same subscript, paradox disappears.

One difficulty for the hierarchy approach is that language does not naturally come in "levels", and contingent Liars demonstrate that there is no natural way to assign them. Although paradox is avoided if Nixon's statement (8) is at a higher level than Jones's (9), or vice versa, how are we to know which statement is higher than the other? Indeed, how are we to know that the two statements, which are contingently related to each other, are *necessarily* at different levels? There is nothing in either the structure of language or the context of utterance to decide the issue. Granted, arbitrary stipulations would work for artificially constructed languages; but for natural languages they would, at best, be a distortion of the linguistic facts. What's more, even if natural language could be stratified in the appropriate way, such stratification would entail that there's no single concept of truth. There would be separate predicates "true$_1$", "true$_2$", "true$_3$", etc., one for each language in the never-ending hierarchy, each with a distinct meaning and hence incapable of intertranslation with each other and with what we think of as foreign synonyms such as "vrai" and "wahr". Therefore it looks like the Hierarchy Theory fails to meet adequacy condition (i).

Finally, the Hierarchy Theory relies on a vicious distinction between object- and meta-language. If your object-language contains the truth predicate "true$_1$", then to define it you need to invoke "true$_2$" within the meta-language; but to define "true$_2$", you need to invoke "true$_3$" within some meta-meta-language; etc. Thus, if you want a theory for every language that you use, you must ascend an infinite number of levels, each with its own truth predicate. Since it's impossible for anyone to know an infinite number of primitive predicates, it's impossible for anyone to know the absolute meta-language. This view, which effectively treats linguistic meaning as an object outside of nature and unfit for rational investigation, offends against both naturalism and adequacy condition (iii).

Ulm (1978), Priest (1987: 88), and McGee (1992: 159) rightfully reject Hierarchy theories for distinguishing as they do between object- and meta-language. But then McGee enunciates the Requirement of the Integrity of Language, which goes too far: "It must be possible to give the semantics of our language within the language itself". This methodological constraint mistakenly assumes objectivism, the claim that perspective either does not matter or can be transcended, when in fact the idea of a view from nowhere contradicts naturalism. Suppose that languages L_1 and L_2 cannot give their own respective semantics, but that each can express the other's (compare: you and your friend cannot see your own respective eyeballs, but you can see each other's). This would not make semantic theory any less scientific, any less subject to test, or any less doable than if it were objective. I conclude that object-/meta-language distinctions are acceptable, but only when they are not viciously regressive.

6.   The Contextualist Theory

Whereas Hierarchy Theories postulate lexical ambiguity, others postulate pragmatic ambiguity. For contextualist or deictic theories of truth, pragmatic ambiguity is located in the truth predicate, for contextualist theories of reference it is located in the subject term, and for contextualist theories of assertion it is located in the speech act.

6.1   Tokens & Truth

Just as "Kilroy was here" and "Kilroy was not here" are consistent so long as the two uses of "here" refer to different locations, or the two uses of "was" refer to different times, so too "λ is true $\equiv \lambda$ is not true" is consistent so long as "true" on the left-hand side points to a different context or "situation" than the "true" on the right-hand side. Burge explains that "true" and "false" are

> indexical in the sense that their extensions are not fixed, but vary systematically depending on their context of use. Thus the predicates are not strictly constants, though they may be and often are treated as such for a fixed context. They are not variables either, since we do not quantify over them... "true" is a schematic predicate. In a given context "true" takes on a specific extension, and in that context we can represent "true" with a predicate... subscripted numerically. [1979: 100]

Barwise & Etchemendy (1987) similarly compare uses of "true" to uses of definite descriptions and universal quantifications, which are implicitly limited to contextually determined domains.

The problem for the Contextualist Theory is to assign indices in a consistent way so that you never get "Φ is true$_i$ $\equiv$ Φ is false$_j$," where $i = j$. It can't be that every separate statement gets its own index, for then disagreement would never be possible.

A: The cat in the hat is back.$_1$
B: The cat in the hat's not back.$_2$
A: I hear you – the cat in the hat is back!$_3$
B: The cat in the hat is *not* back!$_4$
A: You're absolutely right.$_5$ Oh, by the way, the cat in the hat is back.$_6$
B: *The cat in the hat is not back!*$_7$
A: You know something? I've been mistaken all along.$_8$ In fact, the cat in the hat's not back.$_9$ And something else: the cat in the hat is back.$_{10}$ And one last thing, which I've never said before: the cat in the hat is back.$_{11}$

Because of their separate indices, these statements are all consistent. (One might assign a truth index to each claim to truth or assertion, as Parsons (1974) does, or only to each explicit mention of truth, as Burge does. In case of the latter, you can simply put each sentence in quote marks, append "is true", and you will get a dialog with exactly the same surface disagreement, deep-structure consistency as you find here.)

So the Contextualist Theory demands that attributions of truth sometimes get different indices (to avoid the liar paradox) and sometimes the same (in order to make genuine disagreement possible). How are indices to be meted out? One possibility is to say that "true" as used in T-sentences always refers to a distinguished context c which no other use of "true" can refer to.

(T_c) Φ is $true_c \equiv P$.

Instantiation of the appropriate liar sentence successfully yields a non-contradiction:

(OK) λ is $true_c \equiv \lambda$ is not $true_1$.

However, this strategy fails for two reasons. First, it does not resolve the Loop Liar. Second, it doesn't seem to make sense to say that reference to context c can be made only by T-sentences. It seems that I can say λ_{12}, "λ_{12} is not true in any context or at any level", which entails the contradiction that λ_{12} is $true_c$ iff λ_{12} is not true in any context or at any level.

Burge demurs:

> But $[\lambda_{12}]$ is not an English reading of any sentence in our formalization. Our theory is a theory of "true", not "true at a level". From our viewpoint, the latter phrase represents a misguided attempt to quantify out the indexical character of "true"; it has some of the incongruity of "here at some place". No relativization will deindexicalize "true". Even in such English phrases as "true at a level", the indexes occur implicitly on "true". [108]

I'm not convinced by this account, however. In the first place, "here at some place" strikes me as perfectly good in the context of "Hello, 911? I've crash-landed here some place in the Amazon, and I need help." It is also clearly good when the modifier is read as unrestrictive ("here, at some place"). In the second place, the reference of ordinary indexicals appears to be under a great deal of speaker control. By using "then", for instance, I can refer to any time I choose, past or future, simply by having the right intention so long as it is reasonably clear to my audience. Even such a context-bound indexical as "me", in my mouth, can refer to anyone or anything at all, if it's in the context of direct quotation. (My venus fly trap is probably saying right now, "Feed me!") By analogy, we should be able to construct liar statements that refer paradoxically.

But there is a deeper concern. We understand why the reference of ordinary indexicals varies from context to context: it is because of their character, to put a label on it (Kaplan 1977). The character of "I" is that it indexes the speaker, the character of "now" is that it indexes a period of time encompassing the moment of speech, the character of "here" is that it indexes a place proximal to the speaker. But what is the character of truth? What is its constant nature that makes the extension change from context to context?

Relatedly, if "true" is context-relative like "here" and "there", and "now" and "then", and "I" and "you", what gives the illusion that it's otherwise? That is to say, why has it not been obvious that "true" is indexical, as it has always been obvious that pronouns and demonstratives and tense inflections are? This is not to suggest that appearances make for reliable guides, for appearances do in fact often deceive. Rather, any complete and correct theory must explain not only what is true, but also, either directly or by reference to some other theory, why illusions appear the way they do. For example, if optics did not explain why a half-submerged oar appears to bend just at the surface of the water, we would not be so justified in our conviction that oars are rigid bodies; and if not for our understanding of wishful thinking, gullibility, propensities for hyperbole, the indoctrination of children before they can think critically, and outright fraud, then reports of divine miracles would carry more weight than they actually do. By the same token, if we are to believe that the seeming context-independence of truth is an illusion, we need to have some story as to how this illusion comes about. A mere gesture at a story would put me at ease, but not even this is to be had. As it stands, the Contextualist Theory fails to meet adequacy condition (i), and in comparison to its rivals it fails the criterion of second-order preference (p. 15).

6.2   Tokens & Reference

Because the liar sentence is paradoxical, it is neither true nor false, and because it is neither true nor false, it is not true. This conclusion is important, and should be displayed:

(23) λ is not true.

Now (23) has just been asserted as part of serious discourse; neither joke nor mere supposition, it is true, or at least we regard it as such. But (23) says no more and no less than λ itself does. In asserting (23), we assert that λ *is true* – another important conclusion that calls for display:

(24) λ is true.

Yet (23) and (24) contradict each other, and there is no reason to privilege one over the other. Therefore Significance theorists reject both, Dialethists embrace both, and contextualists posit pragmatic ambiguity. According to Parsons, Burge, Barwise & Etchemendy, (23) and (24) are compatible because distinct extensions are carried by the two tokens of "true". According to Gaifman (1992), Clark (1999) and Goldstein (2001), (23) and (24) are compatible because distinct extensions are carried by the two tokens of "λ".

Familiar objections resurface: How can tokens be assured the right references? What indeed *is* the right reference? Why have we no intuitive access to the "character" of the λ types, and why have we no intuition that they exist? If the reported judgments are correct that (23) and (24) are strictly true, why do only "token relativists" share them? And above all, how can token relativism overcome its own super-strengthened liar? Gaifman acknowledges that his work admits "black holes", a fancy term for super liars, while Weir (2000, 2002) soundly presses the super-liar objection against the whole contextualist approach.

6.3   Tokens & Assertions

Gauker (2003: Chap. 9) rejects truth-conditions in favor of assertability-conditions, which allows him to say that λ is neither assertable nor deniable. As we will see, this comes close to my own position, that we should neither believe nor doubt λ, but with a difference. Because belief and doubt are subjective states of mind, while for Gauker assertability and deniability are objective, I will be able to escape strengthened versions of the liar whereas Gauker succumbs to the following:

α   α is not assertable.

Realizing that α is a threat, Gauker counters by denying that we can ever talk about the context we are in. The logical form of α, if you will, is "α is not assertable in c", and we can neither assert it nor deny it without occupying some context other than c.

The proposed solution baffles me, since for Gauker a context is a *set of sentences* (namely the set that accords with the right actions regarding the conversation's goals; Chapter 1.3.8). What does it mean for a speaker to be in a set of sentences? And regardless of the set that one is "in", *why* can't we talk about whatever context we choose to? Gauker's solution, in short, is susceptible to some of the same objections as truth-conditional forms of the Contextualist Theory.

7.   The Revision Theory

When confronted with the Liar, we often take a hypothetical attitude toward it: If it's true, then what? If it's false, then what? And as we follow the consequences of our initial hypothesis, we find ourselves switching truth-assignments back and forth. This practice, which I'm sure is familiar to anyone who has played with the Liar, is taken by Revision theorists as constitutive of the concept of truth.

Valuable works in Revision Theory include Herzberger (1982), Gupta (1982), Belnap (1982), Gupta & Belnap (1993), and Yaqub (1993). These represent the concept of truth as an iterating rule of revision r. If the outputs of successive applications of r(P) always stabilize at truth or always stabilize at falsity, then P is true or false. If r(P) sometimes stabilizes at truth and sometimes at falsity, as it does for the Truth-teller, then P is capricious. If r(P) does not stabilize then P is paradoxical.

A potential problem for the Revision Theory is raised by Azzouni (1995). Azzouni asks us to imagine two distinct Liars:

λ_{13} λ_{13} is not true.
λ_{14} λ_{14} is not true.

Now what is their relation? Are they equivalent?

(?) λ_{13} is not true $\equiv \lambda_{14}$ is not true.

On the one hand, since each side by itself is paradoxical, it might seem that the value of the left-hand side equals the value of the right, and (?) should be true. On the other hand, it might seem that the whole should be paradoxical. It can also be argued that (?) is capricious. My own position holds that it's undecidable because there is no fact of the matter. The Revision Theory, however, does not enjoy this luxury. The various formal systems of stability semantics are all forced to one verdict or another, and it so happens that they mostly disagree with each other. Now if you agree that there is no fact of the matter, then you must reject the Revision Theory, at least all available versions thereof.

What's most significant about the Revision Theory is that it regards the naive T-schema as inapplicable to the Liar. But the naive T-schema applies to whatever possesses truth-conditions, according to available TC theories of meaning. From this and the assumption that truth-conditions constitute meaning, it follows that the liar sentence is meaningless. Yet this cannot be, for a meaningless string of marks could not have stirred philosophers of language over the millennia as the liar sentence has. I conclude that the Revision Theory is incompatible with available TC semantics taken as a theory of natural language. If you accept the Revision Theory then you reject the truth-conditional analysis of the meaning of the Liar and hence offend against adequacy condition (ii); and if you reject the Revision Theory along with the other approaches surveyed here then you leave TC semantics without a coherent conception of truth, thus offending against adequacy condition (i).

8.   The Attitudinal Theory

To review, the canvassed solutions to the liar paradox are all unsatisfactory. The elimination of λ from natural language, aside from its arguable
inadequacy as a response to the Loop and Infinite Liars, is untenable
because λ is in fact a meaningful statement. The Gap Theory, which inter-
prets statements under a three-valued or supervalued logic, either falls to
the Strengthened Liar or is ineffable and hence utterly unknowable. The
Hierarchy Theory posits countless homonymous or subscripted truth predicates, which fails to describe natural language, and it also posits a countless
number of meta-languages, which also fails to describe natural language. The
Contextualist Theory, implausibly assuming indexicality without character,
has trouble with the Loop Liar and the Strengthened Liar.

By no means does my brief critique of the leading Liar literature demonstrate that the available approaches to solving the liar paradox are doomed to
necessary failure. But by pointing out that enormous labor has gone into the
task of finding a solution that is generally acceptable to truth-conditionalists,
repeating some common criticisms, and adding to them, I have tried to show
that the situation is ripe for an alternative kind of approach.

The general attitudinal framework, recall, analyzes meaning by recognizing that content and container are inseparable: in principle, *that*-clauses
are always embedded under some propositional attitude or another, and the
analysis of a *that*-clause must always explicitly acknowledge as much.

8.1   The Liar Paradox

As I see it, truth-conditional T-schemas fail because they assume a sort of
objectivism; they assume that the analysis of truth need not make essential
and explicit reference to some subject who thinks about truth. They need to
be rejected in favor of the following attitudinal T-schema:

(T_ψ) S thinks "Φ is true" $\equiv$ S thinks that P.

Instantiation by the original Liar yields:

(OK)   S thinks "λ is true" $\equiv$ S thinks λ is false.

If S thinks λ is true then S thinks λ is false; and if S thinks λ is false
then S thinks λ is true. Either way, S is highly irrational. But this is not at
all paradoxical because there is a difference between an inconsistent state
of affairs and an inconsistent system of beliefs. The former, by its very
nature, cannot obtain, yet the latter is not only possible but common, even
ubiquitous. That every human being surely holds contradictory beliefs is a
mark against protoplasmic brains, not against the attitudinal theory of truth.

While S is irrational in holding either "λ is true" or "λ is false", S can easily escape irrationality by not having any direct beliefs about λ's truth-value at all, not even that λ is without truth-value. S *can*, however, consistently think both that λ is paradoxical or troublesome, and that S cannot consistently believe either that λ is true or that λ is false. To think that λ is paradoxical is not to think that λ is neither true nor false, it is to think that merely supposing λ would commit one to inconsistency.

If λ cannot be rationally held, and if being subordinated to a propositional attitude is necessary to meaningfulness as I have urged, then you might ask whether λ is meaningful. The answer is an overdetermined yes. First, λ is meaningful because it consists of meaningful parts in a meaningful composition. Even if the composition is problematic for the theory of truth, it is still significant. Second, λ is meaningful because it can rationally fall under a variety of non-doxastic attitudes, for instance "wonder, suspect, suppose" (in contrast to attitudes like "accept, believe, maintain"). Third, λ is meaningful because it can be rational for one to report that someone else believes it. When I report to you that Priest believes λ then – despite Priest's inconsistency – *my* belief is impeccable. Thus the components of my belief, including λ, are meaningful. The Liar is meaningful because it *can* be believed, whether rationally or not. Irrationality does not make a belief into a non-belief or a meaningless belief (Chap. 3.3).

The attitudinal account also applies to the Loop Liar. The situation, recall, is this.

(8) Nixon states the following and nothing but the following: "Every thing Jones says is true."
(9) Jones states the following and nothing but the following: "Everything Nixon says is false."

What is a subject to think? Since the answer depends entirely on who the subject is, we will need to make a number of assumptions. (a) Circumstantial positioning: let's say that subject S happens to be present when Nixon and Jones make their respective statements; S thus *hears* what is said. (b) Idealization of language: let's say that S speaks English and does not commit any performance errors; S thus *understands* what is said. (c) Idealization of credulity: let's say that S is no skeptic, S does not wonder whether S's perceptions are the toys of a mad demon; S thus *believes* that what is being said is being said. (d) Idealization of time: let's assume that S's beliefs all take place at once; in other words, degradation of memory

will be ignored along with other forms of corruption of beliefs. With S thus
identified we can say the following:

(25) S believes that Nixon states "Everything Jones says is true."
(26) S believes that Jones states "Everything Nixon says is false."

From the attitudinal T-schema we can also infer:

(27) S believes that 'Nixon states "Everything Jones says is true"' is true.
(28) S believes that 'Jones states "Everything Nixon says is false"'
      is true.

At this point a second principle of credulity kicks in: when S understands
someone to be saying something, S normally believes it. [Research on
propaganda shows that even when you regard a statement as invalid at
the time of hearing it, the fact of hearing it will increase your chance of
believing it later; Pratkanis & Aronson (1992).] Supposing that that happens
in the present case, from (27) we can infer:

(29) S believes everything Jones says is true.

This can be taken two ways. Under the opaque reading, it claims that S
has the thought "Everything Jones says is true", which does not entail that
S has any thought about Jones's particular statements. Nonetheless, since
S does believe that what Jones says is "Everything Nixon says is false", S
may easily infer "Everything Nixon says is false." Hence:

(30) S believes that everything Nixon says is false.

Under the transparent reading, "everything Jones says", in (29), can be
directly substituted by "everything Nixon says is false". Under either
reading, then, (30) holds. Given that (30) and (25) hold, it follows that

(31) S believes "everything Jones says is true" is false.

Now (29) and (31) ascribe contradictory beliefs to S. But again, this is a
sign of irrationality, not of paradox. If S wishes to be rational, S need simply
refuse to hold the beliefs "Everything Nixon says is true", "Everything Jones
says is true", and their negations.

Turning to the Strengthened Liar, note that the TC account of truth is
defeated by statements that say of themselves "I am not (strictly) true"
while Gauker's assertability-conditional account is defeated by statements
that say of themselves "I am not assertable". So how does my account fare

with statements that say of themselves "I cannot be thought" or "I am not believed by S"?

λ_{15} S does not believe λ_{15}.
λ_{16} No one believes λ_{16}.

Substitution yields:

(OK_{15}) S believes λ_{15} is true $\equiv$ S believes S does not believe λ_{15}.
(OK_{16}) S believes λ_{16} is true $\equiv$ S believes no one believes λ_{16}.

Both cases are similar. (i) If the left-hand side were true then the right-hand side would have to be true. But this is legitimate, since there is nothing contradictory about actually believing that P while mistakenly believing that you do not believe P. It would represent an epistemic failing for S, more specifically a lack of self-understanding, if the components in (OK_{15}) were true; for in that case S would have a false belief about S's own mental state. But a false belief in the mind of S is no inconsistency in the notion of truth. (ii) If the left-hand side were false then the right-hand side would have to be false. This too is legitimate, since S may have no beliefs one way or the other regarding λ_{15}. This in fact is the position of the rational subject.

Once you recognize that the rational subject has no beliefs regarding λ_{15}, you will be tempted to believe that you yourself have no beliefs regarding λ_{15}. But if you succumb, you will make the right-hand side true, hence the left-hand side will be true, hence you *will* have beliefs regarding λ_{15} – and they will be inconsistent. By trying to believe everything that is true, then, you defeat rationality. (And by trying to experience everything that is good, you defeat happiness.) In other words, we get a LIMITATIVE THEOREM: *no one can know or believe all and only truths*. If you believe λ_{15}, it will be false, and if you fail to believe it then λ_{15} will be true. This sort of claim, though staggering, is neither self-contradictory nor unheard of. It finds parallels in strands of mystical thought, and furthermore is reminiscent of the Goedelian gulf between truth and provable belief.

In addition to universally unknowable truths there are local blindspots. While *I* cannot rationally hold the following belief, *you* can:

(32) Paul Saka does not believe (32).

Nor can I rationally hold the following, for it is just a telescoped-out formulation of the same proposition:

(33) Paul Saka does not believe that Paul Saka does not believe (32).

The truth of (32) and (33), though not consistently demonstrable within my system, is accessible to yours. Generally speaking, for *any* subject S there are truths inherently beyond S's ken that others can recognize; and there is at least one sort of belief, namely $\lambda_{15/16}$, that no one can correctly hold.

In denying that the naive T-schema holds, I deny what intuitively appears to be the case. This by itself is perfectly acceptable; indeed, the fact that the naive T-schema, classical logic, and the effability thesis are incompatible proves beyond all question that intuition must give way at some point or another. But to be convincing, any theory claiming that some appearance is mere illusion needs to explain how such illusion is possible or comes about. In the case at hand, the explanation, I think, is straightforward. (a) I posit the attitudinal T-schema (T_ψ). This is not only encouraged by attitudinal semantics, it's something that TC semanticists can accept as well. (b) Now according to (T_ψ), the mental state characterized by "Φ is true" holds precisely when the mental state characterized by "P" holds. (c) Therefore the beliefs "Φ is true" and "P" are co-extensive. In other words, (T) holds because (T) follows from (T_ψ). (d) But the inference from (b) to (c) is illegitimate. This inference may seem compelling, as discussed in Chapter 4.13, but it is unlicensed by formal logic, it seems to rely on the tendentious container-content metaphor of the mind, and it can be criticized by counter-examples. In conclusion, (T_ψ) is verified by common sense; (T) is refuted by the Liar; and the fact that (T_ψ) explains the appeal of (T) lends support to the thesis of attitudinal semantics that the concept of truth not only includes attitudinal equivalences, but is exhausted by attitudinal equivalences.

I would now like to mention how the attitudinal account captures some of the insights of the other proposed solutions to the Liar. To begin with, my account shares with the Contextualist Theory the idea that language is inherently situated, that it is essentially indexical (Perry 1979) and embodied (Johnson 1987). For Burge, it is inherent in the sense that you can't "quantify out" the indexicals, that "no relativization will deindexicalize" your language. For me, the situatedness of language is inherent in the sense that for any expression Φ_1, its accurate description Φ_2 must describe Φ_1's context of use, while Φ_2 itself will take place in some context of use. Another similarity is that the Contextualist Theory and mine agree that two tokens of λ can have distinct values. They differ, however, in that the Contextualist Theory ascribes distinct objective values (true, false) while mine ascribes distinct subjective values (held true, held false). Another difference is that Deictic theorists regard only some words, notably "true", as indexical, while I regard all uses of language as situated.

The Attitudinal Theory also resembles the Gap Theory in two regards. First, both agree that some propositions lack truth-conditions. But whereas the Gap Theory denies objective truth-values only to "pathological" statements, I claim that all statements are in the same boat: as expressions of non-platonic thoughts, they are subjective and without independent standing. Second, the Gap Theory treats statements as valued true, valued false, and not (truth-)valued; the Attitudinal Theory analogously treats statements as believed true, believed false, and not believed, thus capturing the intuition that there is a "gap". There is a difference, however. While the Gap Theory posits a single category of "without truth-value", the Attitudinal Theory posits two kinds of non-belief: you can fail to believe P and independently you can fail to believe ¬P. You may fail at both or at just one.

The Attitudinal Theory can further explain the intuition behind the Dialethic Theory, that the Liar is both true and false. If for whatever reason you think that λ is true, then according to the attitudinal T-schema you will also think that λ is false (and vice versa). Reflection will then allow you to combine your two thoughts, that λ is true and that λ is false, into the single thought that λ is true and false.

Attitudinal semantics, recall, is not limited to talking about beliefs; it generalizes over many propositional attitudes.

(34) S ψ "Φ is true" $\equiv$ S ψ P.

In particular, ψ may be supposition: "S supposes that λ is true $\equiv$ S supposes that λ is false." In thinking about the liar statement one typically works by hypothesis. You say to yourself, "Let's suppose that λ is true..." But this entails, initially unbeknownst to you though true nonetheless, that you suppose that λ is false. In working through the Liar you do simultaneously hold "λ is true" and "λ is false" – but you hold them as suppositions and generally not as beliefs. Once you recognize the inconsistency you reject the suppositions, only to pick them up again later whenever you rethink the paradox. These attitudinal facts may erroneously seem to suggest the Dialethic, Deictic, or Revision Theories.

The attitudinal T-schema (T_ψ), *S thinks "Φ is true" $\equiv$ S thinks that P*, can also be rendered as follows:

(T'_ψ) ψ_S("Φ is true") $\equiv$ ψ_S(P)

This notation brings out its structural similarity to the work of Gauker (2003) and McGee (1989, 1992). For Christopher Gauker, the

T-schema refers to assertability, and assertability is always relative to some context c:

$$(T \vdash_c) \quad \vdash_c (\Phi \text{ is true}) \equiv \vdash_c P$$

For Vann McGee, the T-schema takes a proof-conditional form, where "$\vdash_v$" indicates provability relative to Vann's vagueness logic (Saka 1998a: Chap. 5.3):

$$(T \vdash_v) \quad \vdash_v (\Phi \text{ is true}) \equiv \vdash_v P$$

On all three accounts, talk about truth is replaced by other talk: talk about believed truth, talk about assertable truth, and talk about provable truth. As a result Gauker's and McGee's systems, like mine, effectively allow for truth gaps while remaining strictly bivalent. But these similarities are overshadowed by the fact that the notions of objective assertability and factive provability open themselves up to the Strengthened Liar, whereas the notion of belief does not.

Finally, it should be noted that my subject-oriented solution of the liar paradox enjoys a qualified precedent. Zeno Vendler writes:

> If you ask, "But what about *the* statement that all Cretans are liars?" I reply that there is no such thing *in abstracto*. Statements always belong to a person; they are somebody's statements. [1972: 209]

Likewise my approach views statements as intrinsically subordinated to subjects, as *embodied* and hence concrete. However, Vendler goes on unnecessarily to add that the liar sentence cannot be used to make a meaningful assertion or to express a belief.

The remaining sections mention other problem areas that I believe can be resolved in the same way as the Liar. These involve the comparatively neglected truth-teller, omniscience, and performative paradoxes, plus well known logico-semantic paradoxes.

8.2   The Truth-Teller

According to conventional wisdom, statement τ (tau) is interesting because you can consistently regard it as either true or false, with nothing in logic, linguistic convention, or the nature of the cosmos to decide between the two.

τ This sentence is true.

Whereas the Liar is incoherent, being contradictory if true and contradictory if false, the Truth-teller is *super-coherent*, being always consistent with everything other than its own negation.

The Truth-teller, however, is more than merely interesting. In the first place, it serves as a test case for solutions to the Liar. If the Significance Theory blames self-reference for leading to incoherence in the case of λ, can it also appeal to self-reference in explaining super-coherence in the case of τ? If the Dialethic Theory calls the Liar both true and false, and banana splits neither, can it find an appropriate characterization for the Truth-teller? In general, any satisfying account of the Liar should have something plausible to say about the Truth-teller. For the most part, however, they sit silent on the matter.

Second, according to TC semantics, the meaning of a statement P is equal to or at least dependent on the truth-conditions of P; and the truth-conditions of P constitute a function that maps from the state of the world to a truth-value. Hence the Truth-teller, which is meaningful, ought to express a function that maps from reality to the true or the false. Because it does not do so, however, meaning cannot be identified with TCs. Thus, though it be less dramatic, *the Truth-teller undermines TC semantics as much as does the Liar.*

In reply the TC theorist might claim that meaning is at least a *relation* between possible worlds and truth-values, with τ mapping onto both truth and falsity. But this amounts to dialethism, and if we refuse the Dialethic Theory as a solution to the Liar, we shouldn't want it here either.

My own account of the Truth-teller, at a *first* approximation, is that S can rationally believe τ, rationally disbelieve τ, or rationally refrain from believing one way or the other. The reason for this is that there is no direct empirical or logical or other pressure to ascribe a particular truth-value to τ. In particular, the value of τ is not determined by (T_ψ):

(35) S thinks "τ is true" $\equiv$ S thinks that τ is true.

Consequently it is not irrational to believe τ or its negation. Since the choice is indifferent, it is moreover not irrational to believe neither.

More precisely, a complete epistemology must choose among the various "not irrational" options. If you live by the rule "Maximize the number of your coherent beliefs", then it will be rational for you to believe either τ or its negation or possibly both. If you live by "Minimize the number of your worthless beliefs", it will be rational for you to believe neither. The latter is prescribed when you widen your evidential base so as to include not only direct observations and the constraints of logic but also the theorizing of attitudinal semantics, which regards truth-values as not matters of objective fact. Thus, the possible epistemic stances toward the Truth-teller are not ultimately equi-rational.

There is nothing new to my observation that nothing could conceivably count either for or against the truth of the Truth-teller. But having made this observation, the traditional truth-theorist would continue: "So what is it *really*?" In contrast I insist that truth is a subjective predicate, that ascriptions of truth are implicitly subsumed under attitudes. There is nothing else that can or need be said about the truth of the Truth-teller aside from what people do think about its truth, what criteria they do use in deciding what to believe about its truth, and what criteria they should use, from any given point of view.

8.3   The Omniscience Paradox

Suppose that you make the following statement about God:[4]

(G)   God does not know that what I am now speaking is the truth.

From this we can prove that God does not know everything. (a) You cannot be lying, by reductio. For when you lyingly assert (G) then (G) is false. But if (G) is false, then God *does* know that you are speaking the truth. But if God *knows* that you are speaking the truth, then you *are* speaking the truth. But if you are speaking the truth, then you are not lying. (b) Therefore, in saying (G), you speak the truth. But then (G) is true, in which case God does not know that you speak the truth. Since God is by definition omniscient, this too is self-contradictory.

My paradox can be taken in two ways. On the one hand, it works as a reductio against the possibility of an omniscient being. It is, if you buy the naive theory of truth and knowledge, a deductively valid disproof of the existence of *God*, meaning any absolute god. On the other hand, you may insist that omniscience, whether real or imaginary, is a coherent concept, in which case my argument works as a new reductio, in addition to the liar paradox, of the naive theory of truth and knowledge.

It is not clear to me how your average account of the Liar is supposed to resolve the omniscience paradox. I count as one of its virtues the fact that the attitudinal approach applies straightforwardly. S either believes (G); believes ¬(G); or has no direct beliefs one way or the other about the truth of (G). Let's consider these in turn.

(36) S believes God does not know that what you were then speaking was the truth.

---

[4]   A non-self-referential version of (G), involving human knowledge, is anticipated in Sorensen's 1988 tour de force.

For S to believe that God does not know something is, under the intended conception of "God", akin to S's believing that squares do not have sides, or that unicorns do not have horns. It is to hold a conceptual anomaly, and in that regard it is irrational.

(37) S believes ¬(God does not know that what you were then speaking was the truth), i.e. S believes God knows that what you were then speaking was the truth.

Truth-conditional epistemology holds that "X knows that P" entails P. Attitudinal epistemology claims rather that "S thinks X knows that P" entails "S thinks P" (p. 107). From this principle and (37), it follows:

(38) S believes that what you were then speaking was the truth.

But what you were speaking then is (G). Therefore:

(39) S believes (G), i.e. S believes God does not know that what you were then speaking was the truth.

Since beliefs (37, 39) are contradictory, S is irrational. In conclusion, for S to be rational S must hold neither (G) nor ¬(G); S must hold no direct beliefs about (G) at all.

8.4   Other Paradoxes

Russell (1903) asks us to imagine the class of all classes that are not members of themselves, call it c. From this the malignant contradiction follows that $c \in c$ iff $c \notin c$. For this reason, class c has been treated as the Liar has: as fixed in a hierarchy of types, as meaningless. My earlier objections to the truth-conditional liar solutions apply here as well. Instead I suggest that set-theoretic axioms, like all propositions, may best be understood as embodied – as embedded under propositional attitudes – yielding the benign "contradiction" that S thinks that $c \in c$ iff S thinks that $c \notin c$. We therefore have justification in restricting uses of the concept of c without pretending that it does not exist.

There is a large consensus that Russell's paradox has been resolved, the diagnosis being that there is no such thing as the set of all sets not members of themselves. In contrast, there is no consensus regarding the Liar. Intuitively, however, those who think about the set of all sets not members of themselves and those who think about the liar sentence are thinking analogous thoughts. This analogy is captured by attitudinal semantics.

Finally, my framework promises to yield analogous resolutions of Grelling's paradox, on heterological or non-self-applying terms; of Berry's paradox, "the least integer not nameable in fewer than nineteen syllables"; and of Richard's paradox, which uses diagonalization to give a finite specification of a number that is not finitely specifiable. The fact that attitudinal semantics offers a unified kind of solution to disparate paradoxes stands as a point in its favor [cf. Priest (2000)].

CONCLUSION

(i) CREDIT WHERE CREDIT IS DUE. Needless to say, my assault on truth-conditionalism does not imply that it is utterly worthless. As a going theory it possesses virtues, for instance insights that can be accommodated by cognitive semantics. (This helps explain why scientific methodo- logy demands that rivals pay attention to one another; p. 17) Indeed, many truth-conditional analyses convert almost mechanically into attitudinal analyses. Davidson's powerful treatment of events (1), for instance, corresponds to the attitudinal claim (2):

(1) "Sue passionately kissed Kim" is true $\equiv \exists x$ (kissed [sue, kim, x] & passionate[x]).
(2) S thinks "Sue passionately kissed Kim" $\equiv$ S thinks that $\exists x$ (kissed [sue, kim, x] & passionate[x]).

Conversion does not always work, as demonstrated by connotation, ambiguity, the liar paradox, and so forth, but it works often enough to justify mining it.

My program makes contact with many sources too. First there is Descartes, whose internalism is congenial to mentalist semantics (although Descartes himself held that beliefs about God and perfection entail the existence of God and perfection, a view which can be seen as a forerunner to Putnam's anti-skeptical argument, rejected in Chapter 4.6). Then there's Locke, whose idea idea stands in sharp opposition to the referential theory. I oppose such referentialism partly because of my conviction that language can be used even in ignorance of the external world (consider for instance the output of AI programs such as ELIZA): semantics and metaphysics are independent (Devitt 1992).

The idea idea continues with Berkeley, where it is part of a broader idealism, and with Hume. Although Hume is not known for contributing to semantic theory, his "non-cognitivist" positions on causality and on morality – a term devised by partisans who assume that cognition involves objective truth-conditions – clearly invoke non-referentialist semantics. Hume's theory of causality, for instance, might be glossed as:

(3) S thinks "event A causes event B" ≡ S's thought, that A happens, regularly precedes S's thought that B happens.

This is not the way that Hume puts the matter, and it is not necessarily what he would endorse, but I think that it succeeds in capturing a good deal of what he was after while at the same time escaping the standard objection to equating necessary causation with constant conjunction.

Non-cognitivist ethics remains alive and well, as witnessed by Ayer (1936), Stevenson (1937, 1945), Hare (1952), Gibbard (1990), and Johnson (1992). I would suggest that attitudinal semantics provides for a way of understanding what it means for a moral statement to be expressive rather than descriptive, and yet at the same time open to debate, contra relativism. It also, incidentally, provides one way of understanding instrumentalism in the philosophy of science, irrealism in the theory of truth, and subjectivism more generally. My only objection to non-cognitivist ethics resides in the way non-cognitivist ethicists segregate moral and non-moral statements. If attitudinal semantics is correct, then *all* statements are non-cognitivist, in the operative sense. Exemplifying my point, Kant expounds a constructivism that might be assimilated to attitudinal semantics [cf. Johnson (1987)].

Kant's challenges to naive realism and to the roles of truth and truth-conditions recall another Continental thinker, Nietzsche, who writes:

> Let us thus define our task – the value of truth must for once be experimentally *called into question*. [*On the Genealogy of Morals* III: §25; see also *Beyond Good and Evil*, §1, and Stich (1990: Chap. 5)]

More seriously, by rejecting the relevance of truth as objectivistically understood, my project makes contact with pragmatism and its disparagement of truth as transcendentally understood. Peirce writes:

> You only puzzle yourself by talking about this metaphysical "truth" and metaphysical "falsity", that you know nothing about. All you have any dealings with are your doubts and beliefs, with the course of life that forces new beliefs upon you and gives you power to doubt old beliefs. If your terms "truth" and "falsity" are taken in such senses as to be definable in terms of doubt and belief and the course of experience . . . well and good . . . But if by truth and falsity you mean something not definable in terms of doubt and belief in any way, then you are talking about entities of whose existence you can know nothing, and which Ockham's razor would clean shave off. [1905: 257]

Not coincidentally, Peirce's treatment of truth is accompanied by a stand on meaning:

> The entire intellectual purport (significance, meaning) of any symbol consists in the total of all general modes of rational conduct which, conditionally upon all the possible different circumstances and desires, would ensue upon the acceptance of the symbol. [1905: 290]

Like the writings of Hume, Peirce's could be interpreted as implying if not advocating some sort of attitudinal semantics.

Peirce influenced James, of course, who had a major impact on Quine, it turns out [see Quine (1986: 6)]. Now Quine, one of my heroes, is connected to a number of doctrines, on top of pragmatism and relativism, that can be compared and contrasted with my own: semantic nihilism, semantic behaviorism, truth-conditionalism, deflationism, and verificationism. To begin with, Quine emphasizes that sentences do not have meanings (1980: 12, 22). That sounds like semantic nihilism, but Quine accepts the property of meaningfulness, denying only meanings as individual entities. I like the sentiment, but not Quine's way of putting it, for only a referentialist would imagine that saying "sentences have meanings" commits one to the existence of meanings as individual (non-syncategorematic thing-like) entities.

Quine's anti-entity stance appears to vanish when he identifies the meaning of an observation sentence with its stimulus meaning, which is an ordered set and hence an entity. Specifically, for speaker S and observation pronouncement P, the stimulus meaning of P is the ordered pair consisting of P's affirmative and negative stimulus meanings – the sets of stimuli that would provoke S to assent to, or dissent from, P (1960: §8). The appeal to stimuli that *would* provoke assent sounds intensional, but Quine explains that "dispositions to speech are for me actual enduring states of nerves". Given that Quine also regards cognitive states as identical to neural states (1986: 429), presumably there is a mapping in at least one direction between the claims of (dispositional-)behavioral semantics and the claims of attitudinal semantics.

However, Quine's reductionism is just an article of faith. Given our current state of knowledge, it seems more productive to me to ground behavioral counterfactuals in psychological states than in neuro-states. First, you know the meaning of the observation sentence "An elephant is in the room", and you know which stimuli would tend to prompt assent, but do you know how to describe those stimuli? Using the vocabulary of neurology, I could hardly begin ("S assents when S's retinal rods ... "); but using the vocabulary of psychology, I can begin ("S assents when S thinks ... ") and continue ("there is a very large, gray, long-nosed, ... "). Second, behaviorist semantics draws clumsy distinctions among observation sentences, eternal sentences, and so forth. Though epistemologically relevant, semantically they deserve a uniform framework, as attitudinal semantics provides.

Quine's behaviorist semantics is a version of causal role semantics or CRS, though it appears to be duplex rather than pure (p. 32). Quine writes:

> Ideally . . . two sentences mean the same proposition when they are true in all the same possible worlds . . . But still this idea affords us no general way of equating sentences in real life. [1970: 4]

This can be understood in a variety of ways. Perhaps the first statement admits ontic truth-conditionalism while the second denies epistemic truth-conditionalism; perhaps the first statement admits truth-conditional semantics as a theory of a logically perfect language while the second one denies it of natural language; perhaps the first statement is a careless concession while the second one stakes Quine's actual position; perhaps, in line with Quine's otherwise stated deflationism, the first statement merely acknowledges consequences of the disquotational T-schema while the second statement denies that they contribute to a theory of meaning.

Quine's occasional allusions to truth-conditions make sense, vis-a-vis a substantive theory of meaning, given that Quine sometimes expresses a holistic kind of verificationism:

> The Vienna Circle espoused a verification theory of meaning but did not take it seriously enough. If we recognized with Peirce that the meaning of a sentence turns purely on what would count as evidence for its truth, and if we recognize with Duhem that theoretical sentences have their evidence not as single sentences but only as larger blocks of theory, then the indeterminacy of translation . . . is the natural conclusion. [1969: 80]

However, I do not see how verificatonism squares with deflationism.

To recap, I find many strands of thought in Quine. I like his anti-entity stance; indeed I believe it is justified in view of the argument from ignorance (Chap. 2). I like the naturalism of his CRS, although I think that his rejection of a conceptual or mentalist version of CRS is not justified. I believe he did not always keep CRS distinct from verificationism specifically or truth-conditionalism generally, and I believe the latter made him regard the indeterminacy of reference as almost paradoxical. But the indeterminacy thesis – that reference is relative to a translation manual, a conceptual scheme, or a subject's way of thinking – comports well with the subjectivism of attitudinal semantics.

Deep parallels allegedly run between Quine and Wittgenstein. For instance, although I've never seen this mentioned in the literature, pragmatism appears to have influenced the later Wittgenstein as much as it did Quine. In the opening lines of his *Blue Book*, Wittgenstein suggests that we can answer the question "What is length?" by asking "How do we measure length?" and that we can likewise get at the answer to "What is meaning?" by asking some different, empirical question. The different question that I suggest is "How do we ascribe meaning?"; and to answer it, I suggest, we need to further ask "How do we ascribe beliefs, desires, disdain, and other attitudes?" Of course Wittgenstein is also known for emphasizing that the meaning of an expression is to be found in its use. This slogan, if taken as a claim about what constitutes meaning, happens to be incompatible with mentalist semantics, which holds that an expression may possess meaning even if it's idly contemplated by a solitary castaway. Taken as a methodological injunction, however, Wittgenstein's slogan simply states the empiricist principles that underlie my work.

The early Wittgenstein is famous for recognizing limits to what can be said, and in this way the conclusion of the *Tractatus* anticipates my own limitative theorem (p. 239). The later Wittgenstein is famous for comparing language to a toolbox, which I think is right, and to denying that the meaning of "game" is truth-conditional, and in this too he anticipates my work (Chap. 2).[1]

I say only that Wittgenstein "anticipates" my work because he has not been a direct influence and because my own work differs from his in both substance and method. First, I do not think that language is much like a game. Speakers are "players" who make "moves" according to rules, it is true; but, paradigmatically, speakers do not enter into language communities voluntarily, speaking is not an end in itself, speakers do not engage in make-believe or compete against other speakers for linguistic points, and so forth. The Wittgensteinian metaphor is arresting, but I question its systematic usefulness, as I imagine Wittgenstein himself would.[2]

Second, I do not question the value of systematic philosophizing. Where Wittgenstein evidently believed that philosophy serves as nothing but ad hoc therapy, I believe that philosophical inquiry is continuous with scientific inquiry, that it has given us grand theories of which some appear to be true, and that it holds the promise of yielding additional useful theories, some of them dealing with language.

Third, I reject Wittgenstein's private-language argument. According to one interpretation, Wittgenstein argues that if any language were internal

---

[1] As an antidote to Wittgenstein's game claim, I heartily recommend Suits 1978.

[2] Wittgenstein's actual position (1953: §7) is that language-games are primarily "those games by means of which children learn their native language" (though I doubt that children learn to speak from playing games), and that by extension language-games are "primitive languages" themselves, such as Wittgenstein's contrived "slab" language (though I doubt that it is importantly like English). Wittgenstein left it to his followers to conceive of genuine natural languages as themselves games.

and idiosyncratic then there would be no objective norms regarding its proper and improper uses, which is allegedly absurd. From the perspective of an empirical naturalist, however, the argument begs the question. The natural order consists of facts, not values, except where values are kinds of subjective fact. We can criticize a given use of language because *we* don't like it, but as an object in itself it can only be described.

Fourth, I do not think that language is a "form of life". Indeed, I don't even know what a form of life is. I believe in *ways* of life, I believe that they interact with the language one speaks, and I believe that philosophy of language has much to learn from sociology and social psychology. I do not believe, however, that one's language can render religious belief "not [assertably] unreasonable" (Wittgenstein 1967: 58), nor do I see that distinct "forms of life" prevent the theist and atheist from contradicting each other.

Perhaps Wittgenstein embodied a form of life. Certainly he personified a particular ethos, which may or may not be admirable. However, I believe that philosophers, whether they succeed as paragons or not, should at least articulate their philosophy according to rational standards. I myself shall eschew oracular pronouncements in favor of reasoned arguments, documented references, and the most direct prose that I can muster, and I promise never to write a book just for those who have already shared my thoughts.

(ii) RETROSPECT AND PROSPECT. Classical logic, the naive T-schema (T), and the effability thesis of Chapter 8 are incompatible, and therefore at least one is mistaken. I claim that it is (T) which is in error, I observe that the untenability of truth-conditional truth makes truth-conditionalism untenable, and I explain (T)'s deceptive attractiveness as parasitic on the genuine soundness of the attitudinal T-schema (T_ψ). The resulting attitudinal conception of truth differs in important ways from the old conception. These two different conceptions of truth may be called the *objectivist* and the *subjectivist*. The objectivist conception claims that every proposition is either true or false (or neither) regardless of what anyone thinks about it, and that we possess the power to speak of such truth-values even if we can't always ascertain them. The subjectivist in contrast claims that truth and falsity, as predicates of sentences, statements, and beliefs, are just like sentences, statements, and beliefs themselves: they are products of agent subjects and hence are ultimately grounded in some subject's beliefs. To put it another way, the difference between "P" in (4) and "P" in (5) is not the difference between belief and fact, and it is not the difference between "P" as embodied in some historical subject and "P" as platonic object. Rather, it's the difference between "P" as explicitly embodied in X and "P" as implicitly embodied in the writer and the readers of this page.

(4) X thinks that P.
(5) P.

The objectivist conception of truth, in short, is contravened by the liar paradox.

The rejection of objectivist truth entails the rejection of TC semantics. TC semantics is also challenged by the findings reported in Chapter 7, on quotation, in Chapter 6, on ambiguity, and in Chapter 5, on pejoratives. The orthodox theory of meaning cannot be sustained, and something else is required. What I propose, attitudinal semantics, is described and defended in Chapters 3 and 4. Even if I be mistaken about attitudinal semantics, truth-conditional semantics remains untenable, according to the Argument from Ignorance in Chapter 2.

Chapter 1 suggests that semantic theory is responsible for addressing the research areas repeated here.

translation	indexicality
intentionality	vagueness
information, truth	ambiguity
inference	anomaly
intensionality	prototypicality
compositionality	perspective
illocutionary force	register
lexical relations	figurative speech
presupposition	connotation
implicature, impliciture	diachrony
thematic roles	

So far I have argued that attitudinal semantics can provide better accounts of connotation, ambiguity, and aspects of truth than TC semantics, and I have made programmatic claims regarding illocutionary force (Chap. 3.2.1), anomaly (Saka 1998a: Chap. 3.2), intensionality (Chap. 5.9xiv), and the nature of compositionality (Chap. 7.3.1). In addition, intentionality, indexicality, perspective and prototypicality positively seem to invite mentalist analyses. Carrying them out remains as future work.

(iii) CODA. What can explain the popularity of TC semantics, and the resistance to attitudinal semantics? One answer, I think, can be found in the joke about the drunkard who searches under a lamp post for his house key; that's not where he dropped it, but it's easier to see there than on the porch. Likewise, TC semantics generates a lot of light. This is a virtue, and it is to the credit of TC semantics that it is clear enough and precise enough for us to see that within its scope meaning is not to be found. Instead of basking in the light, however, it would serve us better to look elsewhere, even if that means fumbling in the dark.

REFERENCES

Note: All university presses are located at their respective universities.

Abbott, Barbara. 2005. "Some notes on quotation." *Belgian Journal of Linguistics* 17: 13–26.

Akiba, Ken. 2005. "A unified theory of quotation." *Pacific Philosophical Quarterly* 86: 161–71.

Allan, Keith & Kate Burridge. 1991. *Euphemism and dysphemism.* Oxford UP.

Almog, J., J. Perry, & H. Wettstein, eds. 1989. *Themes from Kaplan.* Oxford UP.

Alston, William. 1983. "Christian experience and Christian belief." In Plantinga & Wolterstorff.

——. 1991. *Perceiving God.* Cornell UP.

——. 2000. *Illocutionary acts and sentence meaning.* Cornell UP.

Altman, Andrew. 1994. "Speech acts and hate speech." *An Ethical Education* (ed. Sellers). Berg.

Anderson, Michael, Yoshi Okamoto, Darsana Josyula, & Don Perlis. 2002. "The use-mention distinction and its importance to human-computerinteraction." *Proceedings of EDILOG: the Sixth Workshop on the Semantics and Pragmatics of Dialog.*

Antony, Louise. 2003. "Rabbit-pots and supernovas." In Barber.

Aqvist, Lennart. 1965. *A new approach to the logical theory of interrogatives.* Uppsala UP.

Armour-Garb, Bradley & J.C. Beall, eds. 2005. *Deflationary truth.* La Salle, IL: Open Court.

Asimov, Isaac. 1988. *The relativity of wrong.* New York: Doubleday.

Atlas, Jay. 1978. "On presupposing." *Mind* 87: 396–411.

——. 1989. *Philosophy without ambiguity.* Oxford UP.

——. 2005. *Logic, meaning, and conversation.* Oxford UP.

Austin, J.L. 1940. "The meaning of a word." In his *Philosophical papers.* Oxford UP, 1961.

——. 1962. *How to do things with words.* Harvard UP.

Avramides, Anita. 1989. *Meaning and mind.* MIT Press.

Ayer, A.J. 1936. *Language, truth, and logic.* New York: Dover edition, no date.

Azzouni, Jody. 1995. Review of Yaqub. *Mind* 104.

Bach, Emmon & Robert Harms, eds. 1968. *Universals in linguistic theory.* New York: Holt, Rinehart& Winston.

Bach, Kent. 1987. *Thought and reference.* Oxford UP.

——. 1992. "Paving the road to reference." *Philosophical Studies* 67: 295–300.

——. 1994. "Conversational impliciture." *Mind and Language* 9: 124–62.

——. 1997. "Do belief reports report beliefs?" *Pacific Philosophical Quarterly* 78: 215–41.

——. 1999. "The myth of conventional implicature." *Linguistics and Philosophy* 22: 327–66.

—— & Robert Harnish. 1979. *Linguistic communication and speech acts.* MIT Press.

Baghramian, Maria, ed. 1998. *Modern philosophy of language.* Washington DC: Counter-point.

——. 2004. *Relativism.* London: Routledge.

Baker, C.L. 1978. *Introduction to generative-transformational syntax.* New York: Prentice-Hall.

Baker, G.P. & P.M.S. Hacker. 1984. *Language, sense & nonsense*. Oxford: Blackwell.

Baker, Lynne. 1987. *Saving belief*. Princeton UP.

Ballmer, Thomas & Manfred Pinkal, eds. 1983. *Approaching vagueness*. Amsterdam: North-Holland.

Barber, Alex, ed. 2003. *Epistemology of language*. Oxford UP.

Bar-Hillel, Yehoshua. 1966. "Do natural languages contain paradoxes?" In his *Aspects of language*. Jerusalem: Magnes.

Barker, Stephen. 2004. *Renewing meaning*. Oxford UP.

Bar-on, Dorit, Claire Horisk, & William Lycan. 1999. "Deflationism, meaning, and truth-conditions." *Philosophical Studies* 101: 1–28.

Barwise, Jon & John Etchemendy. 1987. *The liar*. Oxford UP.

Barwise, Jon & John Perry. 1983. *Situations and attitudes*. MIT Press.

Bates, Elizabeth & Brian MacWhinney. 1979. "A functionalist approach to the acquisition of grammar." In *Developmental pragmatics* (eds. E. Ochs & B. Schieffelin). New York: Academic Press.

Beall, J.C. 2001. "Is Yablo's paradox non-circular?" *Analysis* 61: 176–87.

——, ed. 2003. *Liars and heaps: new essays on paradox*. Oxford UP.

Beaver, David. 2001. *Presupposition and assertion in dynamic semantics*. Stanford, CA: CSLI Publications.

Belnap, Nuel. 1982. "Gupta's rule of revision theory of truth." *Journal of Philosophical Logic* 11: 103–16.

Belnap, Nuel & Thomas Steel Jr. 1976. *The logic of questions and answers*. Yale UP.

Benbaji, Yitzhak. 2004. "A demonstrative analysis of 'open quotation'." *Mind and Language* 19: 534–47.

——. 2005. "Who needs semantics of quotation marks?" *Belgian Journal of Linguistics* 17:27–49.

Bennett, Jonathan. 1976. *Linguistic behavior*. Cambridge UP.

——. 1988. "Quotation." *Nous* 22: 399–418.

Bezuidenhout, Anne. 1997. "Pragmatics, semantic underdetermination, and the referential/attributive distinction." *Mind* 106: 375–409.

——. 2002. "Truth-conditional pragmatics." *Philosophical Perspectives* 16: 105–35.

Bianchi, Claudia. 2004. *The semantics/pragmatics distinction*. Stanford, CA: CSLI Publications.

Blackburn, Simon. 1984. *Spreading the word*. Oxford UP.

——. 2005. *Truth: a guide*. Oxford UP.

Block, Ned. 1986. "Advertisement for a semantics for psychology." In *Midwest Studies in Philosophy* X (eds. P. French, T. Uehling, & H. Wettstein). U. of Minnesota Press.

Bloomfield, Leonard. 1933. *Language*. New York: Holt, Rinehart & Winston.

Bochvar, D. 1939. "On a three-valued logic..." Translated in *History and Philosophy of Logic*, 1981.

Boer, Steven. 1979. "Meaning and contrastive stress." *Philosophical Review* 88: 263–98.

Bogdan, Radu, ed. 1986. *Belief*. Oxford UP.

——, ed. 1991. *Mind and common sense*. Cambridge UP.

Bohnert, Herbert. 1945. "The semiotic status of commands." *Philosophy of Science* 12: 302–15.

Borg, Emma. 2004. *Minimal semantics*. Oxford UP.

Botterell, Andrew & Robert Stainton. 2005. "Quotation: compositionality and innocence without demonstration." *Critica* 37: 3–33.

Brandom, Robert. 2000. *Articulating reasons*. Harvard UP.

Bromand, Joachim. 2002. "Why paraconsistent logic can only tell half the truth." *Mind* 111: 741–49.

Brown, Penelope & Stephen Levinson. 1987. *Politeness*, 2nd edn. Cambridge UP.

Burge, Tyler. 1979. "Semantic paradox." In Martin.

Cann, Ronnie. 1993. *Formal semantics*. Cambridge UP.

Caplan, Ben. 2002. "Quotation and demonstration." *Philosophical Studies* 111: 69–80.

Cappelen, Herman & Ernie Lepore. 1997. "Varieties of quotation." *Mind* 106: 429–50.

——. 1998. "Reply to Tsohatzidis." *Mind* 107: 665f.

——. 1999a. "Reply to Saka." *Mind* 108: 741–50.

——. 1999b. "Semantics for quotation." In Murasugi & Stainton. Revised edition of 1997.

——. 2005a. *Insensitive semantics*. Oxford: Blackwell.

——. 2005b. "Varieties of quotation revisited," MS edition. *Belgian Journal of Linguistics* 17: 51–76.

Carnap, Rudolf. 1947. *Meaning and necessity*. U. of Chicago Press.

Carston, Robyn. 2002. *Thoughts and utterances*. Oxford: Blackwell.

Chambers, J. et al., eds. 2001. *Handbook of language variation and change*. Oxford: Blackwell.

Channell, Joanna. 1993. *Vague language*. Oxford UP.

Cherniak, Christopher. 1986. *Minimal rationality*. MIT Press.

Chierchia, Gennaro & Sally McConnell-Ginet. 2000. *Meaning and grammar*, 2nd edn. MIT Press.

Chihara, Charles. 1979. "The semantic paradoxes: a diagnostic investigation." *Philosophical Review* 88: 590–618.

Chomsky, Noam. 1965. *Aspects of the theory of syntax*. MIT Press.

——. 1986. *Knowledge of language*. New York: Praeger.

——. 2000. *New horizons in the study of language and mind*. Cambridge UP.

Christensen, Niels. 1967. "The alleged distinction between use and mention." *Philosophical Review* 76: 358–67.

Churchland, Paul. 1988. *Matter and consciousness*, 2nd edn. MIT Press.

Clapin, Hugh, ed. 2002. *Philosophy of mental representation*. Oxford UP.

Clark, Eve. 1974. "Normal states and evaluative viewpoints." *Language* 50: 316–32.

Clark, Herbert. 1992. *Arenas of language use*. U. of Chicago Press.

Clark, Herbert & Richard Gerrig. 1990. "Quotations as demonstrations." *Language* 66: 764–805.

Clark, Michael. 1999. "Recalcitrant variants of the liar paradox." *Analysis* 59: 117–26.

Cohen, L. Jonathan. 1985. "A problem about ambiguity in truth-theoretical semantics." *Analysis* 45: 129–34.

——. 1981. "Can human irrationality be experimentally demonstrated?" *Behavioral and Brain Sciences* 4: 317–70.

Copp, David. 2001. "Realist-expressivism." *Social Philosophy and Policy* 18: 1–43.

Corazza, Eros. 2004. *Reflecting the mind*. Oxford UP.

Cresswell, Max. 1978. "Semantic competence." *Meaning and translation* (eds. F. Guenthner & M. Guenthner-Reutter). London: Duckworth.

——. 1983. "A highly impossible scene: the semantics of visual contradictions." *Meaning, use, and the interpretation of language* (eds. R. Bauerle et al.). Berlin: Walter de Gruyter.

——. 1985. *Structured meanings*. MIT Press.

——. 1994. *Language in the world*. Cambridge UP.

——. 1996. *Semantic indexicality*. Dordrecht: Kluwer.

——. 2003. "Semantics." *International encyclopedia of linguistics*, 2nd edn. Oxford UP.

Cruse, D.A. 1986. *Lexical semantics*. Cambridge UP.

——. 2002. *Lexikologie/lexicology*. Berlin: Mouton de Gruyter.

Cummins, Robert. 1991. "Methodological reflections on belief." In Bogdan.

——. 1996. "Systematicity." *Journal of Philosophy* 93: 591–614.

Davidson, Donald. 1967. "Truth and meaning." In his 1984.

——. 1970. "Semantics for natural languages." In his 1984.

——. 1973a. "In defence of convention T." In his 1984.

——. 1973b. "Radical interpretation." In his 1984.

——. 1974. "On the very idea of a conceptual scheme." In his 1984.

——. 1975. "Thought and talk." In his 1984.

——. 1976. "Reply to Foster." In his 1984.

——. 1977a. "The method of truth in metaphysics." In his 1984.

——. 1977b. "Reality without reference." In his 1984.

——. 1978. "What metaphors mean." In his 1984.

——. 1979a. "Moods and performances." In his 1984.

——. 1979b. "Quotation." In his 1984.

——. 1984. *Inquiries into truth and meaning*. Oxford UP.

——. 1990. "The structure and content of truth." *Journal of Philosophy* 87: 279–328.

——. 1993. "Method and metaphysics." In his *Truth, language, and history*. Oxford UP, 2005.

——. 1995. "The problem of objectivity." In his *Problems of rationality*. Oxford UP, 2004.

——. 2001. "What thought requires." In his *Problems of rationality*. Oxford UP, 2004.

—— & Gil Harman, eds. 1972. *Semantics of natural language*. Dordrecht: Reidel.

Davis, Steven & Brendan Gillon, eds. 2004. *Semantics*. Oxford UP.

Davis, Wayne. 1998. *Implicature*. Cambridge UP.

Deane, Paul. 1992. *Grammar in mind and brain*. The Hague: Mouton.

Dennett, Daniel. 1978. *Brainstorms*. MIT Press edition, 1981.

——. 1982. "Beyond belief." In his 1987 and in Woodfield 1982.

——. 1987. *The intentional stance*. MIT Press.

De Sousa, Ronald. 1971. "How to give a piece of your mind: or the logic of belief and assent." *Review of Metaphysics* 25: 52–79.

Devitt, Michael. 1981. *Designation*. Columbia UP.

——. 1991. *Realism and truth*, 2nd edn. Oxford: Blackwell.

——. 1996. *Coming to our senses*. Cambridge UP.

——. 2003. "Linguistics is not psychology." In Barber.

—— & Kim Sterelny. 1999. *Language and reality*, 2nd edn. MIT Press.

Dickson, Paul. 1996. *What's in a name?* Springfield, MA: Merriam-Webster.

Diessel, Holger. 1999. *Demonstratives*. Amsterdam: John Benjamins.

Donnellan, Keith. 1966. "Reference and definite descriptions." *Philosophical Review* 75: 281–304.

Dowden, Bradley. 1984. "Accepting inconsistencies from the paradoxes." *Journal of Philosophical Logic* 13: 125–30.

Dowty, David, Robert Wall & Stanley Peters. 1981. *Introduction to Montague semantics*. Dordrecht: Reidel.

Dummett, Michael. 1963. "Realism." In his *Truth and other enigmas*. Harvard UP, 1978.

——. 1973. *Frege*. London: Duckworth.

——. 1975. "What is a theory of meaning? I." In his 1993b.

——. 1976. "What is a theory of meaning? II." In his1993b.

——. 1978. *Truth and other enigmas*. Harvard UP.

——. 1993a. "Mood, force, and convention." In his 1993b.

——. 1993b. *The seas of language*. Oxford UP.

Eco, Umberto et al., eds. 1988. *Meaning and mental representation*. Indiana UP.

Eklund, Matti. 2005. "Metasolutions to the liar." Manuscript.

Ekman, Paul & Richard Davidson, eds. 1994. *The nature of emotions*. Oxford UP.

Elugardo, Reinaldo. 1999. "Mixed quotation." In Murasugi & Stainton.

Engel, Paul. 2002. *Truth*. McGill-Queen's UP.

Erteschik-Shir, Nomi. 1997. *The dynamics of focus structure*. Cambridge UP.

Erwin, Edward. 1970. *The concept of meaninglessness*. Johns Hopkins UP.

Evans, Gareth & John McDowell, eds. 1976. *Truth and meaning*. Oxford UP.

Fauconnier, Gilles. 1994. *Mental spaces*, 2nd edn. Cambridge UP.

——. 1997. *Mappings in thought and language*. Cambridge UP.

—— & Mark Turner. 2002. *The way we think*. New York: Basic Books.

Fawcett, Peter. 2003. *Translation and language*. Manchester: St Jerome.

Fellbaum, Christiane, ed. 1998. *Wordnet*. MIT Press.

Field, Hartry. 1972. "Tarski's theory of truth." In his 2001.

——. 1977. "Logic, meaning, and conceptual role." *Journal of Philosophy* 74: 379–409.

——. 1978. "Mental representation." In his 2001.

——. 1994. "Deflationist views of meaning and content." In his 2001.

——. 2001. *Truth and the absence of fact*. Oxford UP.

Fillmore, Charles. 1968. "The case for case." In Bach & Harms.

——. 1997. *Lectures on deixis*. Stanford UP.

Fine, Arthur. 1986. *The shaky game*. U. of Chicago Press.

Flynn, Charles. 1977. *Insult and society*. Port Washington, NY: Kennikat Press.

Fodor, Jerry. 1978. "Tom Swift and his procedural grandmother." Re-presented in Fodor 1981.

——. 1980. "Methodological solipsism considered as a research strategy." Re-presented in Fodor 1981.

——. 1981. *Representations*. MIT Press.

——. 1987. *Psychosemantics*. MIT Press.

Frege, Gottlob. 1892. "On sense and reference." *Translations from the philosophical writings of Gottlob Frege* (eds. P. Geach and M. Black), 3rd edn. Oxford: Blackwell, 1980.

——. 1918. "The thought." Translated in *Mind* 65: 289–311, 1956.

Gaifman, Haim. 1992. "Pointers to truth." *Journal of Philosophy* 89: 223–61.

Gamut, L.T.F. 1991. *Logic, language, and meaning*. U. of Chicago Press.

Garcia-Carpintero, Manuel. 1994. "Ostensive signs." *Journal of Philosophy* 91: 253–64.

——. 2004. "The deferred ostension theory of quotation." *Nous* 38: 674–92.

——. 2005. "Double-duty quotation." *Belgian Journal of Linguistics* 17: 89–108.

Gardner, Martin. 1960. *The Annotated Alice*. New York: Bramhall House.

Garfield, Jay & Murray Kiteley, eds. 1991. *The essential readings in modern semantics*. St Paul, MN: Paragon House.

Garver, Newton. 1965. "Varieties of use and mention." *Philosophy and Phenomenological Research* 26: 230–8.

Gauker, Christopher. 1986. "The principle of charity." *Synthese* 69: 1–25.

——. 2003. *Words without meaning*. MIT Press.

Geeraerts, Dirk. 1997. *Diachronic prototype semantics*. Oxford UP.
—— & Hubert Cuyckens, eds. 2005. *The Oxford handbook of cognitive linguistics*. Oxford UP.
Geurts, Bart & Emar Maier. 2005. "Quotation in context." *Belgian Journal of Linguistics* 17: 109–28.
Gibbs, Raymond. 1994. *The poetics of mind*. Cambridge UP.
Gillon, Brendan. 1990a. "Truth theoretical semantics and ambiguity." *Analysis* 50: 178–82.
——. 1990b. "Ambiguity, generality, and indeterminacy." *Synthese* 85: 391–416.
——. 2004. "Ambiguity, indeterminacy, deixis, and vagueness." *Semantics* (eds. S. Davis & B. Gillon). Oxford UP.
Glanzberg, Michael. 2001. "The liar in context." *Philosophical Studies* 103: 217–51.
Glock, Jans-Johann. 2003. *Quine and Davidson on language, thought, and reality*. Cambridge UP.
Goddard, L. & R. London: Routley. 1966. "Use, mention, and quotation." *Australasian Journal of Philosophy* 44: 1–49.
Goldman, Alvin. 1989. "Interpretation psychologized." *Mind and Language* 4: 161–85.
Goldstein, Laurence. 1984. "Quotation of types and types of quotation." *Analysis* 44: 1–6.
——. 2001. " 'Truth-bearers and the liar': a reply to Weir." *Analysis* 61: 115–26.
Gomez-Torrente, Mario. 2001. "Quotation revisited." *Philosophical Studies* 102: 123–53.
——. 2005. "Remarks on impure quotation." *Belgian Journal of Linguistics* 17: 129–52.
Goodman, Nelson. 1951. *The structure of appearance*. Harvard UP.
Gordon, R. 1986. "Folk psychology as simulation." *Mind and Language* 1: 158–71.
Gorfein, David, ed. 1989. *Resolving semantic ambiguity*. Springer.
——, ed. 2002. *On the consequences of meaning selection*. American Psychological Association.
Grandy, Richard. 1973. "Reference, meaning, belief." *Journal of Philosophy* 70: 439–52.
——. 1986. "Some misconceptions about belief." *Philosophical grounds of rationality* (eds. R. Grandy & R. Warner). Oxford UP.
Greenawalt, Kent. 1996. *Fighting words*. Princeton UP.
Greenberg, R. & S. Pyszczynski. 1985. "The effect of an overheard ethnic slur on evaluation of the target: how to spread a social disease." *Journal of Experimental Social Psychology* 21: 61.
Greenough, Patrick. 2001. "Free assumptions and the liar paradox." *American Philosophical Quarterly* 38.2: 115–35.
Grice, Paul. 1957. "Meaning." In his 1989.
——. 1967. "Logic and conversation." In his 1989.
——. 1968. "Utterer's meaning, sentence meaning, and word meaning." In his 1989.
——. 1969. "Utterer's meaning and intentions." In his 1989.
——. 1989. *Studies in the way of words*. Harvard UP.
Grim, Patrick. 1981. "A note on the ethics of theories of truth." In Vetterling-Braggin.
——. 1991. *The incomplete universe*. MIT Press.
Gross, Steven. 2001. *Essays on linguistic context sensitivity and its philosophical significance*. London: Routledge.
Gumperz, John & Stephen Levinson, eds. 1996. *Rethinking linguistic relativity*. Cambridge UP.
Gupta, Anil. 1982. "Truth and paradox." In Martin.
—— & Nuel Belnap. 1993. *The revision theory of truth*. MIT Press.
Haack, Susan. 1974. "Mentioning expressions." *Logique et Analyse* 17: 277–94.

Hahn, Lewis, ed. 1999. *The philosophy of Donald Davidson.* Chicago, IL: Open Court.

Haiman, John. 1978. "Conditionals are topics." *Language* 54: 564–89.

Hare, R.M. 1952. *The language of morals.* Oxford UP.

Harman, Gilbert. 1974. "Meaning and semantics." In his 1999.

———. 1975. "Language, thought, and communication." In his 1999.

———. 1982. "Conceptual role semantics." *Notre Dame Journal of Formal Logic* 28: 242–56.

———. 1987. "(Non-solipsistic) conceptual role semantics." In his 1999.

———. 1990. "Immanent and transcendent approaches to meaning and mind." In his 1999.

———. 1999. *Reasoning, meaning, and mind.* Oxford UP.

Harnish, R.M., ed. 1994. *Basic topics in the philosophy of language.* Prentice-Hall.

Harris, Zellig. 1991. *A theory of language and information.* Oxford UP.

Hartman, Rhonda. 1992. "Revitalizing group defamation as a remedy for hate speech on campus." *Oregon Law Review* 71: 855–900.

Hatim, Basil & Jeremy Munday. 2005. *Translation.* London: Routledge.

Hawkins, John. 1994. *A performance theory of order and constituency.* Cambridge UP.

Heim, Irene & Angelika Kratzer. 1998. *Semantics in generative grammar.* Oxford: Blackwell.

Henderson, David. 1996. "Epistemic rationality, epistemic motivation, and interpretive charity." *Protosoziologie* 89: 4–29.

Herzberger, Hans. 1982. "Notes on naive semantics." In Martin.

Higginbotham, James. 1999. "A perspective on truth and meaning." In Hahn.

———. 2006. "Truth and reference as the basis of meaning." *Blackwell guide to the philosophy of language* (eds. M. Devitt & R. Hanley). Blackwell.

Hirst, Graeme. 1992. *Semantic interpretation and the resolution of ambiguity.* Cambridge UP.

Holmes, Janet & Miriam Meyerhoff, eds. 2003. *Handbook of language variation and change.* Oxford: Blackwell.

Horn, Laurence. 1989. *A natural history of negation.* U. of Chicago Press.

Horwich, Paul. 1990. *Truth.* Oxford: Blackwell.

———. 1993. "Theories of truth." *A philosophical companion to first-order logic* (ed. R. Hughes). Indianapolis, IN: Hackett.

———. 1998. *Meaning.* Oxford UP.

———. 2005. *Reflections on meaning.* Oxford UP.

Hymes, Dell. 1972. "Models of the interaction of language and social life." *Directions in sociolinguistics* (eds. J. Gumperz & D. Hymes). New York: Holt, Rinehart & Winston.

International Linguistics Department. 1999. *Doing linguistics.* www.sil.org/linguistics/DoingLinguistics/contents.htm

Inwood, Brad & L.P. Gerson. 1988. *Hellenistic philosophy.* Indianapolis, IN: Hackett.

Jackendoff, Ray. 1983. *Semantics and cognition.* MIT Press.

———. 1985. "Information is in the mind of the beholder." *Linguistics & Philosophy* 8: 23–33.

———. 1987. "The status of thematic relations in linguistic theory." *Linguistic Inquiry* 18: 369–411.

———. 1992. *Languages of the mind,* chapter 6. MIT Press.

———. 2002. *Foundations of language.* Oxford UP.

Jackman, Henry. 2003. "Charity, self-interpretation, and belief." *Journal of Philosophical Research* 28: 143–68.

Jacquette, Dale, ed. 2003. *Philosophy, psychology, and psychologism.* Dordrecht: Springer.

Jennings, R.E. 2004. "The meanings of connectives." In Davis & Gillon.

———. 2007. "Logic, language, and the brain." *International Journal for Cognitive Informatics Natural Intelligence* 1: 66–78.

Johnson, Mark, ed. 1981. *Philosophical perspectives on metaphor*. U. of Minnesota Press.
——. 1987. *The body in the mind*. U. of Chicago Press.
——. 1993. *Moral imagination: implications of cognitive science for ethics*. U. of Chicago Press.
Johnson-Laird, Philip. 1983. *Mental models*. Harvard UP.
Jorgensen, Julia. 1990. "The psychological reality of word senses." *Journal of Psycholinguistic Research* 19: 167–90.
——. 1996. "The function of sarcastic irony in speech." *Journal of Pragmatics* 26: 613–34.
——, Dan Sperber, & George Miller. 1984. "A test of the mention theory of irony." *Journal of Experimental Psychology: General* 113: 112–20.
Kaplan, David. 1977. "Demonstratives." In Davis & Gillon.
Katz, Jerrold. 1981. *Languages and other abstract objects*. Totowa, NJ: Rowman & Littlefield.
——. 1990. *The metaphysics of meaning*. MIT Press.
——. 1996. "Semantics and philosophy." *The Handbook of contemporary semantic theory* (ed. S. Lappin). Oxford: Blackwell.
—— & Jerry Fodor. 1963. "The structure of a semantic theory." *Language* 39: 170–210.
Keefe, Rosanna. 2000. *Theories of vagueness*. Cambridge UP.
—— & Peter Smith, eds. 1997. *Vagueness: a reader*. MIT Press.
Kempson, Ruth. 1977. *Semantic theory*. Cambridge UP.
——. 1988. "Grammar and conversational principles." *Linguistics: the Cambridge survey* (ed. F. Newmeyer), v. II. Cambridge UP.
Kirby, D.M. & R.C. Gardner. 1973. "Ethnic stereotypes." *Canadian Journal of Psychology* 27: 127–43.
Kirkland, Shari, Jeff Greenberg, & Tom Pyszczynski. 1987. "Further evidence of the deleterious effects of overheard derogatory ethnic labels." *Personality and Social Psychology Bulletin* 13: 216–27.
Kittay, Eva. 1987. *Metaphor: its cognitive force and linguistic structure*. Oxford UP.
—— & Adrienne Lehrer. 1981. "Semantic fields and the structure of metaphor." *Studies in Language* 5: 31–63.
Kripke, Saul. 1975. "Outline of a theory of truth." In Martin.
——. 1980. *Naming and necessity*, 2nd edn. Harvard UP.
Kunne, Wolfgang. 2003. *Conceptions of truth*. MIT Press.
Kusch, Martin. 1995. *Psychologism: a study in the sociology of philosophical knowledge*. London: Routledge.
——. 2004. *Knowledge by agreement*, 2nd edn. Oxford UP.
Labov, William. 1972. *Sociolinguistic patterns*. U. of Pennsylvania Press.
Ladd, Robert. 1996. *Intonational phonology*. Cambridge UP.
Lakoff, George. 1970. "A note on vagueness and ambiguity." *Linguistic Inquiry* 3: 57–9.
——. 1972a. "Linguistics and natural logic." In Davidson & Harman.
——. 1972b. "Performative antinomies." *Foundations of Language* 8: 569–72.
——. 1987. *Women, fire, dangerous things*. U. of Chicago Press.
——. 1996. *Moral politics*. U. of Chicago Press
——. 2004. *Don't think of an elephant*. White River Jct, VT: Chelsea Green.
—— & Mark Johnson. 1980. *Metaphors we live by*. U. of Chicago Press.
——. 1998. *Philosophy in the flesh*. Basic Books.
Lambrecht, Knud. 1994. *Information structure and sentence form*. Cambridge UP.
Langacker, Ronald. 1986. *Foundations of cognitive grammar*. Stanford UP.

Larson, Richard & Gabriel Segal. 1995. *Knowledge of meaning*. MIT Press.

Latour, Bruno. 1987. *Science in action*. Harvard UP.

Laudan, Larry. 1984. "A confutation of convergent realism." *Scientific realism* (ed. J. Leplin). U. of California Press.

Laurence, Stephen. 1996. "A Chomskian alternative to convention-based semantics." *Mind* 105: 269–301.

——. 2003. "Is linguistics a branch of psychology?" In Barber.

Lea, Timothy. 1979. *Confessions from a haunted house*. London: Futura.

Lehrer, Adrienne. 1974a. Homonymy and polysemy: measuring similarity of meaning. *Language Sciences* 32: 33–9.

——. 1974b. *Semantic fields and lexical structure*. Amsterdam: North-Holland.

——. 1989. "Remembering and representing prose." *Discourse Processes* 12: 105–25.

—— & Eva Kittay, eds. 1992. *Frames, fields, contrasts*. Hillsdale, NJ: Lawrence Erlbaum.

LePore, Ernest 1994. "Conceptual role semantics." *A companion to the philosophy of mind* (ed. S. Guttenplan). Oxford: Blackwell.

—— & Barry Loewer. 1987. "Dual aspect semantics." *New directions in semantics* (ed. Lepore). San Diego, CA: Academic Press.

Levinson, Stephen. 1983. *Pragmatics*. Cambridge UP.

——. 2000. *Presumptive meanings*. MIT Press.

Lewis, David. 1970. "General semantics." In Davidson & Harman 1972.

——. 1974. "Radical interpretation." In his *Philosophical papers*. Oxford UP, 1983.

——. 1981. "What puzzling Pierre does not believe." *Australasian Journal of Philosophy*: 59: 283–9.

Liles, Bruce. 1971. An introductory transformational grammar. New York: Prentice-Hall.

Littmann, Greg & Keith Simmons. 2004. "A critique of dialetheism." *The law of non-contradiction* (eds. G. Priest et al.), Oxford UP.

Ludlow, Peter, ed. 1997. *Readings in the philosophy of language*. MIT Press.

Ludwig, Kirk. 2004. "Rationality, language, and the principle of charity." *The Oxford handbook of rationality* (ed. A. Mele), Oxford UP.

Luntley, Michael. 1999. *Contemporary philosophy of thought*. Oxford: Blackwell.

Lycan, William. 1984. *Logical form in natural language*. MIT Press.

——. 1998. *Judgement and justification*. Cambridge UP.

——. 1999. *Philosophy of language*. London: Routledge.

——. 2004. "On a defense of the truth-condition theory of meaning." www.unc.edu/~ujanel.

Lyons, John. 1977. *Semantics*, 2 vols. Cambridge UP.

MacCormac, Earl. 1985. *A cognitive theory of metaphor*. MIT Press.

Machery, Edouard, Ron Mallon, Shaun Nichols, & Stephen Stich. 2004. "Semantics, cross-cultural style." *Cognition* 92: B1–B12.

Mamet, David. 1995. Interview. *Playboy*, April.

Mar, Gary & Patrick Grim. 1991. "Pattern and chaos." *Nous* 25: 659–93.

Marcus, Ruth. 1981. "A proposed solution to a puzzle about belief." *Midwest Studies in Philosophy* 6: 501–10.

——. 1990. "Some revisionary proposals about belief and believing." *Philosophy and Phenomenological Research* 50: 133–53.

Margalit, Avishai. 1983. A review of Scheffler 1979. *Journal of Philosophy* 80: 129–37.

Martin, Robert L., ed. 1984. *Recent essays on the liar paradox*. Oxford UP.

Martinich, A.P., ed. 2001. *The philosophy of language*, 4th edn. Oxford UP.

Matsuda, Mari. 1989. "Public response to racist speech." *Michigan Law Review* 87: 2320–81.

Maudlin, Tim. 2004. *Truth and paradox*. Oxford UP.

Mauranen, Anna, ed. 2004. *Translation universals*. Amsterdam: John Benjamins.

McCawley, James. 1968. "The role of semantics in a grammar." In Bach & Harms.

McDowell, John. 1998. *Meaning, knowledge, reality*. Harvard UP.

McGee, Vann. 1989. "Applying Kripke's theory of truth." *Journal of Philosophy* 86: 530–9.

——. 1992. *Truth, vagueness, and paradox*. Indianapolis, IN: Hackett.

McGinn, Colin. 1982. "The structure of content." *Thought & object* (ed. Andrew Woodfield). Oxford UP.

——. 1991. *Mental content*. Cambridge: Blackwell.

Michael, Emily. 1975. "Peirce's paradoxical solution to the liar's paradox." *Notre Dame Journal of Formal Logic* 16: 369–74.

Miller, Alexander. 1998. *Philosophy of language*. Montreal: McGill-Queen's UP.

Miller, George & Philip Johnson-Laird. 1976. *Language and perception*. Harvard UP.

Montague, Richard. 1974. *Formal philosophy* (ed. R. Thomason). Yale UP.

Morris, Charles. 1938. *Foundations of the theory of signs*. U. of Chicago Press.

Munro, P. 1982. "On the transitivity of 'say' verbs." *Syntax & Semantics* 15: 301–18.

Murasugi, Kumiko & Robert Stainton, eds. 1999. *Philosophy and linguistics*. Boulder, CO: Westview Press.

Neale, Stephen. 1999. "Coloring and composition." In Murasugi & Stainton.

Neisser, Ulric. 1981. "John Dean's memory." *Cognition* 9: 1–22.

Nida, Eugene. 1975a. *Componential analysis of meaning*. The Hague: Mouton.

——. 1975b. *Language structure and translation*. Stanford UP.

Nisbett, Richard. 2003. *The geography of thought*. Free Press.

Noh, Eun-ju. 1998. "Echo questions." *Linguistics & Philosophy* 21: 603–28.

Nozick, Robert. 2001. *Invariances: the structure of the objective world*. Harvard UP.

Nunberg, Geoffrey. 1978. *The pragmatics of reference*. Linguistics dissertation, City U. of New York.

——. 1979. "The non-uniqueness of semantic solutions: polysemy." *Linguistics & Philosophy* 3: 143–84.

——. 1993. "Indexicality and deixis." *Linguistics & Philosophy* 16: 1–43.

——. 2006. *Talking right*. New York: PublicAffairs.

Nuyts, Jan. 2001. *Epistemic modality, language, and conceptualization: a cognitive-pragmatic perspective*. Amsterdam: John Benjamins.

Nye, Andrea, ed. 1998. *Philosophy of language*. Blackwell.

Ortony, Andrew, ed. 1993. *Metaphor and thought*, 2nd edn. Cambridge UP.

Parsons, Charles. 1974. "The liar paradox." In Martin.

Parsons, Kathryn. 1973. "Ambiguity and the truth definition." *Nous* 7: 379–94.

Parsons, Terence. 1982. "What do quotation marks name?" *Philosophical Studies* 42: 315–28.

Partee, Barbara. 1973. "The syntax and semantics of quotation." *Festschrift for Morris Halle* (eds. S. Anderson & P. Kiparsky). New York: Holt, Rinehart & Winston.

——. ed. 1976. *Montague grammar*. San Diego, CA: Academic Press.

Peacocke, Christopher. 1981. "Are vague predicates incoherent?" *Synthese* 46.

——. 1986. *Thoughts*. Oxford: Blackwell.

Pelletier, Francis. 1994. "The principle of semantic compositionality." In Davis & Gillon.

Perry, John. 1979. "The problem of the essential indexical." In *The problem of the essential indexical*, 2nd edn. Oxford UP, 2000.

Phillips, David. 1998. "The middle ground in moral semantics." *American Philosophical Quarterly* 35: 141–55.

Pietroski, Paul. 1999. "Compositional quotation." In Murasugi & Stainton.

——. 2003. "The character of natural language semantics." In Barber.

——. 2005. "Meaning before truth." In Preyer & Peter.

Plantinga, Alvin. 1983. "Reason and belief in God." In Plantinga & Wolterstorff.

——. 1993. *Warrant and proper function*. Oxford UP.

—— & N. Wolterstorff, eds. 1983. *Faith and rationality*. U. of Notre Dame Press.

Platts, Mark. 1997. *Ways of meaning*, 2nd edn. MIT Press.

Portner, Paul. 2005. *What is meaning?* Oxford: Blackwell.

Pratkanis, Anthony & Elliot Aronson. 1992. *Age of propaganda*. New York: W.H. Freeman.

Predelli, Stefano. 2003. "Scare quotes and their relation to other semantic issues." *Linguistics & Philosophy* 26: 1–28.

——. 2005. "'Subliminable' messages, scare quotes, and the Use Hypothesis." *Belgian Journal of Linguistics* 17: 153–66.

Preyer, Gerhard & Georg Peter, eds. 2005. *Contextualism in philosophy*. Oxford UP.

Priest, Graham. 1979. "The logic of paradox." *Journal of Philosophical Logic* 8: 219–41.

——. 1984. "The logic of paradox revisited." *Journal of Philosophical Logic* 13: 153–80.

——. 1987. *In contradiction*. Amsterdam: Nijhoff.

——. 1993. "Can contradictions be true? II." *Proceedings of the Aristotelian Society*, suppl. 67: 35–54.

——. 1997. "Yablo's paradox." *Analysis* 57:236–42.

——. 2000. "On the principle of uniform solution." *Mind* 109: 123–6.

——, Richard Routley & Jean Norman, eds. 1989. *Paraconsistent logic*. Munich: Philosophia Verlag.

Prior, Arthur. 1971. *Objects of thought*, p. 60. Oxford UP.

Pullum, Geoffrey. 1991. *The great Eskimo vocabulary hoax*. U. of Chicago Press.

Putnam, Hilary. 1975. "The meaning of 'meaning'." In his *Philosophical papers*, v. II. Cambridge UP.

——. 1978. *Meaning and the moral sciences*. London: Routledge.

——. 1988. *Representation and reality*. MIT Press.

Quine, W.V. 1940. *Mathematical logic*. Harvard UP.

——. 1943. "Notes on existence and necessity." *Journal of Philosophy*. Revised as "Reference and modality" in his 1980.

——. 1951. "Two dogmas of empiricism." In his 1980.

——. 1960. *Word & object*. MIT Press.

——. 1961. "A basis for number theory in finite classes." *Bulletin of the American Mathematical Society* 67: 391f.

——. 1969. *Ontological relativity*. Columbia UP.

——. 1970. *Philosophy of logic*. Englewood Cliffs, NJ: Prentice-Hall.

——. 1975. "Mind and verbal dispositions." *Mind and language* (ed. S. Guttenplan). Oxford UP.

——. 1980. *From a logical point of view*, 3rd edn. Harvard UP.

——. 1986. *The philosophy of W.V. Quine* (eds. L. Hahn & P. Schilpp). La Salle, IL: Open Court.

——. 1987. *Quiddities*. Harvard UP.

Read, Stephen. 1997. "Quotation and Reach's puzzle." *Acta Analytica* 19: 9–20.

Recanati, Francois. 2001. "Open quotation." *Mind* 110: 637–87.

——. 2002. "Unarticulated constituents." *Linguistics & Philosophy* 25: 299–345.

——. 2004. *Literal meaning*. Cambridge UP.

Reimer, Marga. 1996. "Quotation marks: demonstratives or demonstration?" *Analysis* 56: 131–41.

——. 2005. "Too counter-intuitive to believe? Pragmatic accounts of mixed quotation." *Belgian Journal of Linguistics* 17: 167–86.

Rescher, Nicholas. 2001. *Paradoxes*. Chicago, IL: Open Court.

——. & Robert Brandom. 1980. *The logic of inconsistency*. Totowa, NJ: Rowman & Littlefield.

Richard, Mark. 1986. "Quotation, grammar, and opacity." *Linguistics & Philosophy* 9: 383–403.

Rorty, Richard. 1991. *Objectivity, relativism, and truth: philosophical papers* v. 1. Cambridge UP.

Rosenberg, Alexander. 1991. "How is eliminative materialism possible?" In Bogdan.

Ross, Alan Ross. 1958. "A reduction of deontic logic to alethic modal logic." *Mind* 67: 100–103.

Ruhl, Charles. 1989. *On monosemy*. State U. of New York Press.

Russell, Bertrand. 1903. *The principles of mathematics*. Cambridge UP.

——. 1905. "On denoting." *Mind* 14: 479–93.

——. 1908. "Mathematical logic as based on the theory of type." *Logic and knowledge* (ed. R. Marsh). London: Allen & Unwin, 1956.

——. 1918. *The philosophy of logical atomism*. La Salle, IL: Open Court, 1985.

——. 1935. *Sceptical essays*. London: Unwin.

——. 1940. *An inquiry into meaning and truth*. London: Penguin.

Ryle, Gilbert. 1938. "Categories." *Logic and language* (ed. A. Flew). New York: Doubleday, 1965.

——. 1949. *The concept of mind*. U. of Chicago Press.

Sadock, Jerrold. 1978. "On testing for conversational implicature." *Syntax and Semantics* 9: 281–97.

—— & Arnold Zwicky. 1985. "Speech-act distinctions in syntax." *Language typology and syntactic description*, v. I (ed. T. Shopen). Cambridge UP.

Sainsbury, R.M. 1988. *Paradoxes*. Cambridge UP.

Saka, Paul. 1991. *Lexical decomposition in cognitive semantics*. Linguistics dissertation, University of Arizona.

——. 1998a. *Meaning and the ascription of attitudes*. Philosophy dissertation, University of Illinois, Urbana-Champaign.

——. 1998b. "Quotation and the use-mention distinction." *Mind* 107: 113–35.

——. 1999. "Quotation: a reply to Cappelen & Lepore." *Mind* 108: 751–4.

——. 2000. "*Ought* does not imply *can*." *American Philosophical Quarterly* 37: 93–105.

——. 2002. "Proof-conditional semantics and the liar paradox." Manuscript.

——. 2003. "The category mistake mistake." Manuscript.

——. 2004. "Speaking of quotations." Manuscript.

——. 2005. "Quotational constructions." *Belgian Journal of Linguistics* 17: 187–213. Reprinted in *Hybrid Quotations* (ed. P. de Brabanter), Amsterdam: John Benjamins, 2005.

——. 2006a. "The demonstrative and identity theories of quotation." *Journal of Philosophy* 103.9: 452–471.

——. 2006b. "Spurning charity." *Axiomathes* 17.

——. 2007a. "The argument from ignorance." *American Philosophical Quarterly* 44.2.

——. 2007b. Review of Barker 2004. *Mind* 116.1.

Salmon, Nathan. 1986. *Frege's puzzle*. MIT Press.

Sapir, Edward. 1944. "On grading." *Philosophy of Science* 2: 93–116.

Saussure, Ferdinand de. 1916. *Course in general linguistics* (trans. by Baskin), 1959. New York: Philosophical Library.

Scheffler, Israel. 1954. "An inscriptional approach to indirect quotation." *Analysis* 14: 83–90.

——. 1979. *Beyond the letter: a philosophical inquiry into ambiguity, vagueness, and metaphor in language*. London: Routledge & Kegan Paul.

Schick, Frederic. 2003. *Ambiguity and logic*. Cambridge UP.

Schiffer, Stephen. 1987. *Remnants of meaning*. MIT Press.

——. 2003. *The things we mean*. Oxford UP.

Schlesinger, George. 1994. "A central theistic argument." *Gambling on God* (ed. J. Jordan). Lanham, MD: Rowman & Littlefield.

Schutze, Hinrich. 1997. *Ambiguity resolution in language learning*. Stanford, CA: CSLI Publications.

Searle, John. 1965. "What is a speech act?" In *Philosophy of language* (ed. Searle). Oxford UP.

——. 1969. *Speech acts*. Cambridge UP.

——. 1978. "Literal meaning." In his 1979a.

——. 1979a. *Expression and meaning*. Cambridge UP.

——. 1979b. "Referential and attributive." In his 1979a.

——. 1983. *Intentionality*. Cambridge UP.

Segal, Gabriel. 2000. *A slim book about narrow content*. MIT Press.

Sellars, Wilfrid. 1963. "Some reflections on language games." In his *Science, perception, and reality*. London: Routledge.

Seuren, Pieter. 1998. *Western linguistics*. Oxford: Blackwell.

Seymour, Michel. 1994. "Indirect discourse and quotation." *Philosophical Studies* 74: 1–39.

Simchen, Ori. 1999. "Quotational mixing of use and mention." *Philosophical Quarterly* 49: 325–36.

Simmons, Keith. 1993. *Universality and the liar*. Cambridge UP.

Simon, Horst & Heike Wiese, eds. 2002. *Pronouns*. Amsterdam: John Benjamins.

Simon, Linda & Jeff Greenberg. 1996. "Further progress in understanding the effects of derogatory ethnic labels." *Personality and Social Psychology Bulletin* 22: 1195–204.

Slansky, Paul. 1989. *The clothes have no emperor*. New York: Simon & Schuster.

Smiley, Timothy. 1993. "Can contradictions be true? I." *Proceedings of the Aristotelian Society*, suppl. 67: 17–33.

Soames, Scott. 2002. *Beyond rigidity*. Oxford UP.

——. 2005a. "Naming and asserting." In Szabo.

——. 2005b. *Reference and description*. Princeton UP.

Sommers, Fred. 1969. "On concepts of truth in natural languages." *Review of Metaphysics* 23: 259–86.

Sorensen, Roy. 1988. *Blindspots*. Oxford UP.

——. 1998. "Yablo's paradox and kindred infinite liars." *Mind* 107: 137–55.

——. 2002. *Vagueness and contradiction*. Oxford UP.

——. 2004. "Charity implies meta-charity." *Philosophy & Phenomenological Research* 68: 290–315.

Sperber, Dan & Deirdre Wilson. 1986. *Relevance*. Harvard UP.

Stainton, Robert. 1996. *Philosophical perspectives on language*. Peterborough, ON: Broadview Press.

——. 1999. "Remarks on the syntax and semantics of mixed quotation." In Murasugi & Stainton.

Stalnaker, Robert. 1970. "Pragmatics." In Davidson & Harman 1972.

——. 1997. "Reference and necessity." In his *Ways a world might be*. Oxford UP, 2003.

Stanley, Jason. 2002. "Making it articulated." *Mind & Language* 17: 149–68.

——. 2005. "Semantics in context." In Preyer & Peter.

Stein, Dieter & Susan Wright, eds. 1995. *Subjectivity and subjectivisation*. Cambridge UP.

Stenius, Erik. 1967. "Mood and language-game." *Synthese* 17: 254–74.

Stenner, A.J. 1981. "A note on logical truth and non-sexist semantics." In Vetterling-Braggin.

Stevenson, C.L. 1944. *Ethics and language*. Yale UP.

Stevenson, Mark. 2002. *Word sense disambiguation*. Stanford, CA: CSLI Publications.

Stich, Stephen. 1986. "Are belief predicates systematically ambiguous?" In Bogdan.

——. 1990. *The fragmentation of reason*. MIT Press.

—— & Ted Warfield. 1994. *Mental representation*. Oxford: Blackwell.

Stockwell, Robert, Paul Schachter, & Barbara Partee. 1973. *The major syntactic structures of English*. New York: Holt, Rinehart & Winston.

Stove, David. 1991. *The Plato cult and other philosophical follies*. Oxford: Blackwell.

Strawson, P.F. 1950. "On referring." *Mind* 59: 320–44.

——. 1970. *Meaning and truth*. Oxford UP. In his 1971.

——. 1971. *Logico-linguistic papers*. London: Methuen.

Stroll, Avrum. 1998. *Sketches of landscapes*, chapter 2. MIT Press.

Suits, Bernard. 1978. *The grasshopper: games, life, utopia*. U. of Toronto Press.

Swart, Henriette de. 1998. *Introduction to natural language semantics*. Stanford, CA: CSLI Publications.

Sweetser, Eve. 1990. *From etymology to pragmatics*. Cambridge UP.

Szabo, Zoltan. 1999. "Introduction" to Murasugi & Stainton.

——, ed. 2004. *Semantics vs. pragmatics*. Oxford UP.

Talmy, Leonard. 2000. *Toward a cognitive semantics*, v. 1. MIT Press.

Tarski, Alfred. 1933. "The concept of truth in formalized languages." Translated in his *Logic, semantics & metamathematics*, 2nd edn. Indianapolis, IN: Hackett, 1983.

——. 1944. "The semantic conception of truth and the foundations of semantics." *Philosophical & Phenomenological Research* 4: 341–76.

Taylor, Charles. 1995. *Linguistic categorization*, 2nd edn. Oxford UP.

Taylor, John & Robert MacLaury, eds. 1995. *Language and the cognitive construal of the world*. Berlin: Mouton de Gruyter.

Taylor, Kriste. 1981. "Reference and truth: the case of sexist and racist utterances." In Vetterling-Braggin.

Tennant, Neil. 1987. *Anti-realism and logic*. Oxford UP.

——. 1997. *The taming of the true*. Oxford UP.

Tomasello, Michael, ed. 2003. *The new psychology of language*, 2 vols. Mahwah, NJ: Lawrence Erlbaum.

Translator, The. Serial. www.stjerome.co.uk.

Traugott, Elizabeth & Richard Dasher. 2002. *Regularity in semantic change*. Cambridge UP.

Travis, Charles. 1996. "Meaning's role in truth." *Mind* 100: 451–66.

——. 1997. "Pragmatics." *A companion to the philosophy of language* (eds. B. Hale & C. Wright). Oxford: Blackwell.

——. 2000. *Unshadowed thought*. Harvard UP.

Truss, Lynn. 2004. *Eats, shoots and leaves*. New York: Gotham Press.

Tsohatzidis, Savas, ed. 1990. *Meanings and prototypes*. London: Routledge.

——, ed. 1994. *Foundations of speech act theory*. London: Routledge.

——. 1998. "The hybrid theory of mixed quotation." *Mind* 107: 661–68.

Turner, Ken, ed. 1999. *The semantics-pragmatics interface from different points of view*. Oxford: Elsevier.

Tyler, Stephen. 1969. *Cognitive anthropology*. New York: Holt, Rinehart & Winston.

Ulm, Melvin. 1978. "Harman's account of semantic paradoxes." *Studies in Language* 2: 379–83.

Unger, Peter. 1975. *Ignorance*. Oxford UP.

——. 1983. "The causal theory of reference." *Philosophical Studies* 43: 1–45.

van Deemter, Kees & Stanley Peters. 1996. *Semantic ambiguity and underspecification*. Stanford, CA: CSLI Publications.

van Fraassen, Bas. 1966. "Singular terms, truth-value gaps, and free logic." *Journal of Philosophy* 63: 481–94.

——. 1968. "Presupposition, implication, and self-reference." *Journal of Philosophy* 65: 136–52.

——. 1969. "Presuppositions, super-valuations, and free logic." *The logical way of doing things* (ed. K. Lambert). Yale UP.

——. 1986. *The scientific image*. Oxford UP.

Vanderveken, Daniel. 1990. *Meaning and speech acts*. Cambridge UP.

——. 2004. "Success, satisfaction, and truth in the logic of speech acts and formal semantics." In Davis & Gillon.

Vendler, Zeno. 1972. *Res cogitans*. Cornell UP.

Vetterling-Braggin, Mary, ed. 1981. *Sexist language: a modern philosophical analysis*. Totowa, NJ: Littlefield & Adams.

Vision, Gerald. 2004. *Veritas*. MIT Press.

Wagner, Steven. 1993. "Why realism can't be naturalized." In *Naturalism* (eds. S. Wagner & R. Warner). U. of Notre Dame Press.

——. 1996. "Teleosemantics and the troubles of naturalism." *Philosophical Studies* 82: 81–110.

Warren, R.M. & R.P. Warren. 1970. "Auditory illusions and confusions." *Scientific American* 223: 30–6.

Washington, Corey. 1992. "Quotation." *Journal of Philosophy* 89: 582–605.

Weinreich, Uriel. 1964. "*Webster's Third*: a critique of its semantics." In his *On Semantics*. U. of Pennsylvania Press, 1980.

Wertheimer, Roger. 2005. "Signs of speech." Manuscript.

Weir, Alan. 2000. "Token relativism and the liar." *Analysis* 60: 156–70.

——. 2002. "Rejoinder to Laurence Goldstein on the liar." *Analysis* 62: 26–34.

Wierzbicka, Anna. 1972. *Semantic primitives*. Frankfurt: Athenaeum.

——. 1985. *Lexicography and conceptual analysis*. Ann Arbor, MI: Karoma.

——. 1987. *English speech act verbs*. San Diego, CA: Academic Press.

——. 1992. *Semantics, culture, and cognition*. Oxford UP.

——. 1996. *Semantics: primes and universals*. Oxford UP.

——. 1999. *Cross-cultural pragmatics*. Berlin: Mouton de Gruyter.

Wilkins, Wendy, ed. 1988. *Thematic relations* (*Syntax and Semantics* v. 21). San Diego, CA: Academic Press.

Williamson, Timothy. 1994. *Vagueness*. London: Routledge.

——. 2006. "Past the linguistic turn?" *The future for philosophy* (ed. B. Leiter). Oxford UP.

Wilson, Deirdre. 1975. *Presupposition and non-truth-conditional semantics*. San Diego, CA: Academic Press.

—— & Dan Sperber. 1993. "Linguistic form and relevance." *Lingua* 90: 1–25.

——. 2002. "Truthfulness and relevance." *Mind* 111: 583–632.

Wilson, Robert. 2004. *Boundaries of the mind*. Cambridge UP.

Wittgenstein, Ludwig. 1921. *Tractatus logico-philosophicus* (trans. by D. Pears & B. McGuinness). London: Routledge, 1961.

——. 1953. *Philosophical investigations* (trans. by G.E.M. Anscombe). New York: Macmillan.

——. 1958. *The blue and brown books*. New York: Harper & Row.

——. 1967. *Lectures and conversations on aesthetics, psychology and religious belief*. U. of California Press.

Woodfield, Andrew, ed. 1982. *Thought and content*. Oxford UP.

Woods, John. 2003. *Paradox and paraconsistency*. Cambridge UP.

Wright, Crispin. 1993. *Realism, meaning and truth*, 2nd edn. Oxford: Blackwell.

Yablo, Stephen. 1989. Reply to McGee. *Journal of Philosophy* 86: 539–41.

——. 1993. "Paradox without self-reference." *Analysis* 53: 251–2.

Yaqub, Aladdin. 1993. *The liar speaks the truth*. Oxford UP.

Yourgrau, Palle, ed. 1990. *Demonstratives*. Oxford UP.

INDEX

PHILOSOPHICAL STUDIES SERIES

1. Jay F. Rosenberg: *Linguistic Representation.*   1974 ISBN 90-277-0533-X
2. Wilfrid Sellars: *Essays in Philosophy and Its History.*   1974 ISBN 90-277-0526-7
3. Dickinson S. Miller: *Philosophical Analysis and Human Welfare.* Selected Essays and Chapters from Six Decades. Edited with an Introduction by Lloyd D. Easton. 1975
        ISBN 90-277-0566-6
4. Keith Lehrer (ed.): *Analysis and Metaphysics.* Essays in Honor of R. M Chisholm. 1975   ISBN 90-277-0571-2
5. Carl Ginet: *Knowledge, Perception, and Memory.* 1975   ISBN 90-277-0574-7
6. Peter H. Hare and Edward H. Maddern: *Causing. Perceiving and Believing.* An Examination of the Philosophy of C.J. Ducasse. 1975   ISBN 90-277-0563-1
7. Hector-Neri Castañeda: *Thinking and Doing.* The Philosophical Foundations of Institutions. 1975   ISBN 90-277-0610-7
8. John L. Pollock: *Subjunctive Reasoning.* 1976   ISBN 90-277-0701-4
9. Bruce Aune: *Reason and Action.* 1977   ISBN 90-277-0805-3
10. George Schlesinger: *Religion and Scientific Method.* 1977   ISBN 90-277-0815-0
11. Yirmiahu Yovel (ed.): *Philosophy of History and Action.* Papers presented at the First Jerusalem Philosophical Encounter (December 1974). 1978   ISBN 90-277-0890-8
12. Joseph C. Pitt (ed.): *The Philosophy of Wilfrid Sellars: Queries and Extensions.* 1978
         ISBN 90-277-0903-3
13. Alvin I. Goldman and Jaegwon Kim (eds.): *Values and Morals.* Essays in Honor of William Frankena. Charles Stevenson, and Richard Brandt. 1978
         ISBN 90-277-0914-9
14. Michael J. Loux: *Substance and Attribute.* A Study in Ontology. 1978
         ISBN 90-277-0926-2
15. Ernest Sosa (ed.): *The Philosophy of Nicholas Rescher.* Discussion and Replies. 1979
         ISBN 90-277-0962-9
16. Jeffrie G. Murphy: *Retribution, Justice, and Therapy.* Essays in the Philosophy of Law. 1979   ISBN 90-277-0998-X
17. George S. Pappas (ed.): *Justification and Knowledge.* New Studies in Epistemology. 1979   ISBN 90-277-1023-6
18. James W. Cornman: *Skepticism, Justification, and Explanation.* With a Bibliographic Essay by Walter N. Gregory. 1980   ISBN 90-277-1041-4
19. Peter van Inwagen (ed.): *Time and Cause.* Essays presented to Richard Taylor. 1980
         ISBN 90-277-1048-1
20. Donald Nute: *Topics in Conditional Logic.* 1980   ISBN 90-277-1049-X

PHILOSOPHICAL STUDIES SERIES

PHILOSOPHICAL STUDIES SERIES

44. John W. Bender (ed.): *The Current State of the Coherence Theory*. Critical Essays on the Epistemic Theories of Keith Lehrer and Laurence BonJour, with Replies. 1989
ISBN 0-7923-0220-6

45. Roger D. Gallie: *Thomas Reid and 'The Way of Ideas'*. 1989 ISBN 0-7923-0390-3 46

46. J-C. Smith (ed.): *Historical Foundations of Cognitive Science*. 1990
ISBN 0-7923-0451-9

47. John Heil (ed.): *Cause, Mind, and Reality*. Essays Honoring C. B. Martin. 1989
ISBN 0-7923-0462-4

48. Michael D. Roth and Glenn Ross (eds.): *Doubting*. Contemporary Perspectives on Skepticism. 1990 ISBN 0-7923-0576-0

49. Rod Bertolet: *What is Said*. A Theory of Indirect Speech Reports. 1990
ISBN 0-7923-0792-5

50. Bruce Russell (ed.): *Freedom, Rights and Pornography*. A Collection of Papers by Fred R. Berger. 1991 ISBN 0-7923-1034-9

51. Kevin Mulligan (ed.): *Language, Truth and Ontology*. 1992 ISBN 0-7923-1509-X

52. Jesús Ezquerro and Jesús M. Larrazabal (eds.): *Cognition, Semantics and Philosophy*. Proceedings of the First International Colloquium on Cognitive Science. 1992
ISBN 0-7923-1538-3

53. O.H. Green: *The Emotions*. A Philosophical Theory. 1992 ISBN 0-7923-1549-9

54. Jeffrie G. Murphy: *Retribution Reconsidered*. More Essay in the Philosophy of Law. 1992 ISBN 0-7923-1815-3

55. Phillip Montague: *In the Interests of Others*. An Essay in Moral Philosophy. 1992
ISBN 0-7923-1856-0

56. Jacques-Paul Dubucs (ed.): *Philosophy of Probability*. 1993 ISBN 0-7923-2385-8

57. Gary S. Rosenkrantz: *Haecceity*. An Ontological Essay. 1993 ISBN 0-7923-2438-2

58. Charles Landesman: *The Eye and the Mind*. Reflections on Perception and the Problem of Knowledge. 1994 ISBN 0-7923-2586-9

59. Paul Weingartner (ed.): *Scientific and Religious Belief*. 1994 ISBN 0-7923-2595-8

60. Michaelis Michael and John O'Leary-Hawthorne (eds.): *Philosophy in Mind*. The Place of Philosophy in the Study of Mind. 1994 ISBN 0-7923-3143-5

61. William H. Shaw: *Moore on Right and Wrong*. The Normative Ethics of G.E. Moore. 1995 ISBN 0-7923-3223-7

62. T.A. Blackson: *Inquiry, Forms, and Substances*. A Study in Plato's Metaphysics and Epistemology. 1995 ISBN 0-7923-3275-X

63. Debra Nails: *Agora, Academy, and the Conduct of Philosophy*. 1995
ISBN 0-7923-3543-0

64. Warren Shibles: *Emotion in Aesthetics*. 1995 ISBN 0-7923-3618-6

PHILOSOPHICAL STUDIES SERIES

PHILOSOPHICAL STUDIES SERIES

springer.com

Printed in the United States
110866LV00003B/115-129/A